1 Timothy
2 Timothy
Titus

Douglas J. W. Milne

Christian Focus Publications

To Mairi
with thanks for energetic
proofreading and critical comments

© 1996 Douglas J. W. Milne
ISBN 1-85792-169-0

Published by
Christian Focus Publications Ltd
Geanies House, Fearn, Ross-shire,
IV20 1TW, Scotland, Great Britain.
Cover desisgn by Donna Macleod

Printed and bound in Great Britain by
The Guernsey Press Co. Ltd., Guernsey, Channel Islands

Contents

Introduction to the Pastoral Epistles 5

1 TIMOTHY

Introduction 16

Greetings (1:1-2) 21
A Warning About Pseudo Religion (1:3-7) 26
The Law and the Gospel (1:8-11) 29
Paul's Autobiography (1:12-17) 33
Faith and a Good Conscience (1:18-20) 40
Prayers For Everyone (2:1-7) 44
Men and Women (2:8-15) 51
Overseers (3:1-7) 58
Deacons (3:8-13) 64
The Great Mystery (3:14-16) 68
In Later Times (4:1-5) 73
A Good Servant of Jesus Christ (4:6-16) 77
The Church As Family (5:1-2) 88
Widows (5:3-16) 89
Elders (5:17-25) 98
Slaves (6:1-2) 105
Truth and Godliness (6:3-10) 108
The Good Fight of Faith (6:11-16) 113
Well-To-Do Christians (6:17-19) 119
False Knowledge (6:20-21) 121

2 TIMOTHY

Introduction 124

Greetings (1:1-2) 127
Personal Memories (1:3-7) 128
Suffering for the Gospel (1:8-14) 133
False and True Friends (1:15-18) 141
Encouragements in Suffering and Serving (2:1-13) 144
God's Worker (2:14-26) 151
The Last Days (3:1-9) 159
More Personal Counsels (3:10-17) 162
A Final Charge (4:1-5) 172
Paul's Farewell (2 Timothy 4:6-8) 177
Men and Movements (4:9-18) 182
Greetings (4:19-22) 188

TITUS

Introduction 192

Introduction (1:1-4) 195
Overseers (1:5-9) 200
Subversive Talkers (1:10-16) 204
Adorning the Gospel (2:1-10) 210
The Saving Grace of God (2:11-15) 219
Being Good Citizens (3:1-2) 226
The God Who Saves (3:3-7) 228
Necessary Disciplines (3:8-11) 235
Final Counsels (3:12-15) 238

INTRODUCTION TO
THE PASTORAL EPISTLES

Until the modern era of what is called the historical-critical method of studying the Bible (roughly the 19th and 20th centuries), the New Testament letters to Timothy and Titus were accepted universally as having been written by Paul towards the end of his life, during the seventh decade of the first century AD. With the introduction of rationalistic methods of biblical study almost everything that had been accepted about these letters was challenged. Pauline authorship was rejected and the letters were dated in the second century AD.

Even today many scholars question whether Paul could have written all that these letters contain, believing instead that disciples of his patched together extracts from his correspondence, and composed the rest of these letters themselves. Since questions about the authorship, trustworthiness, dating and content of these letters persist among Christian scholars, and in doing so raise doubts in the minds of ordinary Christians, it will be necessary in this introduction to begin by clearing away these doubts about the reliability of these letters.

(1) Who Wrote the Pastoral Letters?

Until recent times the church has always believed that Paul was the author of these letters. This is because letters written in the ancient world always carried the name of the sender at the beginning. In each of these letters Paul's name appears in the opening greeting (1 Tim. 1:1; 2 Tim. 1:1; Tit. 1:1) and there is no reason why modern readers should reject this clear evidence of authorship.

On what grounds then do the critics object to the traditional beliefs about Pauline authorship and the inner trustworthiness of these three letters? They do so on the following grounds:

• The Greek syntax of all three letters is rather different from Paul's usual style, judged by his major letters such as Galatians and Romans.

• A high proportion of Paul's words (vocabulary) is unusual when compared with his other letters.

• The theological teaching contained in these letters does not contain much of the typical Pauline doctrines such as justification.

• The historical and geographical references do not fit into his travels, as recorded in Acts and his other letters.

• The kind of church organisation presented in these letters is more rigid than that of Paul's earlier letters (e.g. 1 Corinthians), and has more in common with the second-century churches with their presbyters and bishops.

When these different arguments are brought together in this way they call for a reasoned defence of Paul's authorship. Without going into all the details of such questions, since this can be done by consulting more scholarly introductions and commentaries on these letters, the following explanations can be offered in reply.

• A person's grammatical style and choice of words can change over the years as studies of great writers and orators have shown. When Paul wrote the Pastorals he had been an active Christian leader and correspondent to the churches of his mission field for at least thirty years.

• There is a strong possibility that Paul himself did not write the Pastorals but didctated to a scribe. Luke was with him when he wrote 2 Timothy (2 Tim. 4:11) and definite similarities exist between Luke's literary style and vocabulary and those of the Pastorals. Since Paul used a scribe in writing Romans (Rom. 16:22), deciding what is usual Pauline style and vocabulary becomes a bit more complex.

• Style of expression and choice of words are largely decided by the topics of conversation. In the Pastorals, Paul is addressing a different set of issues from those in Romans or Galatians. In those letters the issues are largely theological; in the Pastorals the issues are organisational and practical.

• Although the practice of composing documents under the name of some notable religious leader instead of one's own name (what we call pseudepigrapha) was common among the Jews at that time, it raises serious ethical issues for Christians claiming to follow the truth.

• Several of the unmistakable tenets of Paul's gospel, such as salvation by grace through faith in Jesus Christ apart from works, are strongly asserted in these letters (e.g. Tit. 3:4-7).

• The local and personal references, mainly in 2 Timothy, make perfectly good sense on the assumption that Paul was freed from his Roman imprisonment at the end of Acts, and moved around the Mediterranean again for several years. This assumption is supported by early Christian writings (e.g. *1 Clement*).

• The church organisation of these letters, consisting of overseers and deacons in the local congregations, is not peculiar to them, but goes back to Paul's earlier writings (Phil. 1:1) and practice (Acts 14:23).

• No Greek manuscripts exist which do not give Paul's name as the author of these three letters.

• The critics of Pauline authorship disagree among themselves as to which verses and parts of these letters are from Paul, and which have been inserted by his disciples at a later stage.

For all these reasons, as well as others that can be found in more scholarly sources, Paul's authorship of the Pastoral letters can be confidently accepted as being based on sound evidence and reasonable arguments.

But does it really matter who wrote the Pastorals? The answer to that is yes, because by treating these letters as secondary writings of the New Testament (deutero-canonical), their distinctive teachings on such important and current issues as the place of women in the church, faith as propositional belief, Christian ethical standards and normative church order, can be marginalised and explained away. So the question of Pauline authorship is not merely an academic one, rather it is of decisive importance if the churches are to listen to this portion of the Word of Christ in the New Testament canon of writings which is uniquely fitted to guide them through the post-modern era.

(2) When and Where Were These Letters Written?

Attempts have been made to fit the few geographical and historical references contained in these letters into the outline of Paul's life in the book of Acts (chapters 9-28), but this is an impossible assignment. It is much more likely that the biographical information given in the Pastoral letters fits into a later period of Paul's life not covered by Acts. Apart from the evidence in early Christian writing (e.g. *1 Clement*, ch. V) that Paul did visit the western Mediterranean as he had planned (Rom 15:28), it is clear that Paul was only a house-prisoner in Rome (Acts 28:30f.), and that he himself expected to be released (Phil 1:19; 2:23f.).

A period of about five years would be long enough for the movements indicated in the Pastorals to take place, and this is the period of time that must have elapsed between Paul's imprisonment at the end of Acts (c.60-62) and his martyrdom in Rome (c.65-67). It was during the interval between these two Roman imprisonments that his movements (as well as those of Timothy and Titus) recorded in the Pastorals, along with the writing of these letters, took place.

Chronologically, 2 Timothy is the last of the three letters, since in it Paul tells how he had already made his defence before the emperor and was awaiting the death sentence (2 Tim 4:6ff., 16ff.). Because of the similarities in content and interest between 1 Timothy and Titus, it can be conjectured that they were written fairly close to one another, just like Ephesians and Colossians. It is now impossible to say which of the two was written first

A little more information exists about where the letters were written from. Paul was in or near Macedonia when he wrote his first letter to Timothy in Ephesus (1 Tim.1:3), and he was languishing in a dungeon in Rome when he wrote his second letter to Timothy, who was possibly travelling around the eastern Mediterranean (2 Tim 1:16f.; 4:13).

(3) Why Were the Pastoral Letters Written?

Within their own historical context the Pastoral letters were written for two related reasons.

Firstly, Paul is giving instructions to his two young assistants, Timothy and Titus, in the difficult task of reforming the churches at Ephesus and Crete respectively. In particular, there was a need for suitable elders to be appointed in the local congregations if proper leadership and oversight were to be provided for them. This is the reason why a significant part of 1 Timothy and Titus is taken up with lists of qualifications for leaders in the churches.

Secondly, Paul is warning his two assistants against the dangers and errors of certain Jewish-gnostic groups, and telling them how to arrest their infiltration into the churches in their regions. These gnostic tendencies were apparent in such practices as denying (asceticism) or indulging (antinomianism) the needs of the body. Either way there was an underlying belief in the fundamental split between matter and spirit (a traditional division in

Greek philosophy). The Jewish influences in this teaching and way of life were shown up in the obsession of the heretics with the Old Testament law books as well as with Jewish myths and genealogies.

These groups were argumentative, even aggressive, especially in Crete. In Paul's mind only better leadership and sound teaching could remedy and save the situation. As a result he writes with a view to promoting both.

Paul's reasons for writing have decided the contents of these letters, and this in turn has produced their common title - the Pastoral letters. They are about pastors (the overseers) and the problems they face in supervising the churches under their care. This has raised questions about the role of Timothy and Titus, not just in relation to Paul, but whether they represent the introduction of a new kind of office in the organisation of the Christian church.

(4) Who Were Timothy and Titus?

Normally Paul wrote his letters to churches, and this is true of the Pastoral letters as well. Although they bear the names of individuals, and were addressed in the first instance to Timothy and Titus, it is clear that Paul intended that they should be read, or at least that their contents should be communicated, to the churches concerned.

Timothy and Titus were Paul's special representatives to churches in regions where he himself could not be present in person because of commitments elsewhere in his extensive mission-field. This kind of role was not new to either of these men, since their activities in the same kind of service for the apostle are recorded in other parts of the New Testament. Engaged in this way, they were delegated by him to act with his authority and under his personal direction.

It has been argued in the history of church order that Timothy and Titus represent a third type of early church official, above the local overseers and deacons. This idea evolved into the diocesan bishop of the second and third centuries, who claimed apostolic warrant for presiding, like Timothy and Titus, over a number of local churches in a region. But there is no indication whatsoever in these letters or in any others of Paul that he intended through Timothy and Titus to introduce a new, normative order for the churches, or that any such hierarchical officer ever did exist amongst the apostolic churches.

(5) How Do the Pastoral Letters Speak to Us Today?

Above all, the Pastorals make it plain that there is such a thing as right Christian belief and right Christian living, and that there exists between the two an unbreakable bond. These letters constantly appeal to the existence of a body of teaching which has been handed down from the apostles through the churches, called the faith, the truth, the form of sound words, the teaching. This body of doctrine is not just a set of theological affirmations, it carries decidedly ethical and practical implications which the Pastorals affirm equally.

There is little in the Pastorals of the kind of theological discussions that make the letters to the Romans or Galatians so recognisable. This is because they do not address any one belief, but assert the whole body of Christian teaching which was in jeopardy in Paul's day. There are a few memorable summaries of the Christian gospel (1 Tim. 2:5f.; Tit. 2:11-14; 3:4-7), but the faith is never stated for its own sake as though doctrine was its own justification. Rather truth grounds practice, and so the apostolic teaching is recited, asserted and held fast in the interests of Christian morality and godly living in the church itself and in the world.

The theological stance of the Pastorals is *epiphanic*, meaning by this that its teachings and appeals are firmly framed within the two great epiphanies or appearings of Jesus Christ (1 Tim. 3:16; 6:14; 2 Tim. 1:10; 4:1, 8; Tit. 2:11, 13; 3:4). 'Epiphany' and its cognate forms is by far the favourite term for the two advents of Jesus (7 out of 10 references). These two appearances of Jesus are the terminal points of Christian faith, hope and living. So the ethical interests of these letters is eschatologically and redemptively grounded and bounded in typical Pauline and New Testament style. This teaches us the permanent bonding between evangelical doctrine and godly living.

During the final years of Paul's apostleship, he saw that sound teaching resulting in sound behaviour was the pressing need of the churches in that part of the world. The churches were being threatened and infiltrated by sects and new religious groupings which challenged the exclusive claims to truth and salvation teaching that the churches had previously enjoyed. These new movements borrowed from the sacred writings of Christianity, and mingled Jewish and Christian beliefs and practices with foreign elements taken from a medley of philosophical and mythological sources. As a result, the pure word of the gospel of Christ, with its ethical predications, was being blurred and lost sight of while the standards of Christian morality were being challenged and compromised.

Although it is a truism that history never repeats itself because every set of circumstances, and the causal factors that produce them, are always changing (one recalls the Greek philosopher Heraclitus' saying that a person never steps into the same river twice), it is also true that some periods of history resemble each other more than others. Between Paul's time and our own there are certain similarities. Both are times of uncertainty because of the rise of new and alternative spiritualities and religions in the world, with the resulting breakdown and forsaking of Christian social and moral values in practice. Many nominal Christians no longer know what they believe nor how to live in a post-Christian world.

We can go beyond generalities and speak of the particular issues that confronted Paul, Timothy and Titus in the churches around the Mediterranean in the seventh decade of the first century. They have a remarkably modern ring: the role of women in the church, the conduct of worship, the function of the church, qualifications for Christian leadership, forms of ministry, the content of Christian belief, and the nature of Christian morality. This convergence of interests between the middle of the first century and the end of the twentieth makes the Pastoral letters essential reading for modern Christians, churches and their leaders. Hopefully this commentary will go a little way to opening up the treasures of these letters that have often suffered from undeserved neglect.

In an age of religious pluralism and ethical relativism, these letters speak with much needed authority, giving clear directions in today's and tomorrow's world. In a turning time when the cultural and metaphysical paradigms of the last two hundred years (partly Christian) are being increasingly challenged and rejected, Christians need to be reminded of their religious heritage and to rediscover their roots in the apostolic tradition. This is the Word of God which does not change, but challenges each new age of the church to affirm and live by the glorious gospel of the blessed God (1 Tim. 1:11).

1 Timothy

INTRODUCTION

The Circumstances

From the letter itself we learn that Paul had left Timothy in charge at Ephesus while he himself travelled on to Macedonia (1:3). Timothy was instructed by Paul to oppose a group of false teachers who were troubling the Ephesian congregation, and to bring things back to normal. For this reason 1 Timothy could be described as a little book of church order, the first of its kind in Christian history. In Paul's own words he is writing to Timothy so that he may know how to conduct matters in the church of God (3:14f.).

Paul takes into account the kind of person Timothy is, and matches his writing to the man, by words of personal advice and encouragement throughout the letter. In this way Paul the older statesman holds out pastoral oversight to young Timothy, as he faces up to difficult decisions and awkward people.

The letter is addressed in the first place to Timothy, but apparently its contents were meant to be read out to the church as well (6:21, 'you' is plural). With the hindsight of experience Paul saw how important it was for the congregation to respect Timothy by learning what Paul had appointed him to do among them. So 1 Timothy is a letter that combines a great deal of professional advice to a young leader of the church with teaching for the congregation to absorb and practise.

The Destination

1 Timothy is written to the church at Ephesus, the capital city of the Roman province of Asia. It was a natural seaport, a business and entertainment centre famous for its theatres, baths and libraries. Most of all it boasted one of the wonders of the ancient world, the huge temple of Artemis, a fertility goddess whose

image filled the temple and it was claimed had fallen from heaven (perhaps as a meteorite, Acts 19:35).

The church appears to have been founded by Paul during a brief stopover there about 52 AD while he was travelling with Aquila and Priscilla (Acts 18:18f.). He built on this foundation during his third missionary journey, when he made Ephesus the centre for reaching out with the gospel to the whole of Asia (Acts 19:1-20:38). This visit lasted three years, marked a high point in his Gentile work, and established Ephesus along with Antioch as one of the mother churches of the Mediterranean mission field.

The spiritual history of the Ephesian church can be traced through the New Testament. It began zealously in love but degenerated later into formalism (Rev. 2:1-7). It suffered from outside interference by travelling preachers peddling alternative doctrines to the Christian faith, as well as being disturbed by internal disputes due to local faction fighting (Acts 20:29f.). At the time of writing 1 Timothy, Paul has left the Ephesian church in the charge of Timothy who was to contend against the seditious and corrupting influences of gnostic-Jewish groups who were perverting the gospel and the faith of some of the church members and their families.

The Themes
From the point of view of systematic theology, 1 Timothy comes under the topic of the church (ecclesiology), because it has so much to say about the church as the household of God and the pillar of the truth (3:14f.). Its treatment of the church differs, however, from say 1 Corinthians where the church is seen in its members, their group dynamics, problems of discipline, gifts of the Spirit and their control, and misunderstandings of Christian doctrines such as holiness and the resurrection. In 1 Timothy the institutional nature of the church is to the fore, the qualifications for holding office are discussed, the different social groups are addressed, and issues in corporate worship are dealt with. The ap-

proach in 1 Timothy is structural, practical, liturgical and behavioural.

So while a book like 1 Corinthians sees the church dynamically and in a very human way, and Ephesians places the church in the overall plan of God within history, 1 Timothy looks at the church from the standpoint of order and standards of belief and practice. All three approaches are necessary for a balanced understanding and response. In this way 1 Timothy fits into the total perspective of the New Testament concerning the church of Jesus Christ.

Three themes run through the letter, and around them the main message is developed.

• The church needs sound teaching in a period of pluralistic systems of belief, when it is being invaded by new notions of God, salvation and the meaning of spirituality. This teaching is to be found in the apostolic gospel which men like Timothy must faithfully defend and interpret for the people within the churches. The church is the pillar and support of God's truth in the world.

• The church needs sound leaders if it is to survive the culture shock of a pagan world hammering on its doors and subverting its members' faith and morals. Its leaders must be men who have a proven track record in family life and in the workforce, and whose Christian character is visible by example and godly behaviour. They must be gifted in teaching the Word of God and in defending the faith.

• The church needs sound structures and offices if it is to manage its own affairs and present a unified and orderly face to the world. There are to be the right kind of organisational structures, ones that actually promote the gospel and strengthen the faith of those who belong to the church through personal example, public instruction and disciplinary procedures.

Paul's paradigm of the church in 1 Timothy is constructed largely around these three recurring aspects. Like a skeleton they provide the infracture of principles onto which Paul attaches all the practical details of his church doctrine. All three are essential for a working model of the church in the modern world. Without sound teaching the church will lose its saltiness and cease to function in society. Without sound leaders the church will lose its integrity and become like any other social institution. Without sound structures the church will break up into factions and lose its unity and effectiveness. A threefold cord is not easily broken (Eccles. 4:12).

The Modern Message
The religious climate and the social scene at the close of Paul's life in the middle sixties of the first century was one of transition. The Roman empire was beginning to show the first real signs of its eventual collapse due to the personal excesses of its emperors, the restiveness of segments of the population like the slaves, the infiltration of new ideas and religions from the East, and the pressure being exerted inwards by the newly-conquered peoples on its peripheries. Inside this melting pot the Christian movement and the Christian churches were facing the future with uncertainty as they battled against the pluralistic viewpoints in philosophy, popular religion and the immorality of the times.

At the end of the second millenium Christian churches, in the western world most noticeably but globally as well, face an uncertain future in which futurologists have written them out of the score. The pressures being exerted on the Christian faith and the churches are immense, through the rise of a new paganism rooted in secular humanism, hedonistic morality, and the rejection of all absolutes and objective norms in the post-modern movement and mind-set. The temptation to compromise and to accommodate the spirit of the age is great.

But 1 Timothy points us in a different direction. It reminds and assures the modern Christian reader of the certainty of the

Christian faith that has come down to us through the apostolic tradition enshrined in the holy Scriptures. It assures us of the emptiness of much so-called knowledge, particularly in the religious and spiritual realms. It teaches us the right way to live: we are to order our lives corporately in our local churches, and individually in the world, by following the path of godliness, righteousness and good works. It forewarns us of the escalation of wickedness and irreligion in the world in the last days, and forearms us in doing so. It finally reaffirms our faith in the supremacy of God who alone is the Ruler of the world throughout history and controls everything for his eternal glory and the completion of his saving purposes.

As the Christian churches turn the corner into the third millenium of Christian history, 1 Timothy speaks to our situation with remarkable relevance and foresight. As a book written in troubled times, when the first eyewitnesses of the Christian faith were passing away and the apostles were transmitting the gospel for a new generation, 1 Timothy helps the modern churches to navigate the uncharted waters that lie before them. It opens up some safe harbours, clear landmarks and wide horizons for Christian leaders and their people to aim for, and rest in.

1 TIMOTHY: CHAPTER 1

In this opening chapter, after the normal greeting (1-2), Paul immediately addresses the local problems of the Ephesian church (3-7). This in turn leads Paul into two short discussions, one about the Law and the gospel (8-11), the other about his own relationship to the gospel (12-16). This digression ends with the first of two doxologies (verse 17, cf. 6:15f.). Finally Paul comes back to the local situation and Timothy's work in it (18-20). The contents and argument of this chapter are therefore highly diversified, although there is a logical link between each of the sections in sequence.

Greetings (1:1-2)

Letters in the ancient world began with the name of the sender. This letter is from **Paul**, who became the most famous of all Christian missionaries. He was a Jew born in Tarsus, a cosmopolitan city in the Roman province of Cilicia, a fact that made him conscious of pagan culture from birth, and helped him as a missionary to it in later life. He may possibly have been brought up in Jerusalem, the capital city of the Jewish world, and trained there as a rabbi or religious teacher (Acts 22:3; 26:4). Since Paul was a Roman citizen, a status that was his by birth, he possessed three Latin names of which Paul was probably the family one. Paul was sometimes able to use his Roman citizenship in his own defence in the service of the Christian faith (Acts 13:9; 22:25ff.).

He belonged to the strict order of the Pharisees, who tried to live by the laws of Moses in the Old Testament, along with the unwritten sacred traditions that had been handed down in the religious schools for centuries (Acts 21:39; 22:3). All this gave him an intimate acquaintance with the legalist ethos of the Jewish system, which he broke with and wrote against when he became a Christian, as in his letters to the Galatians, the Romans and the Philippians.

In spite of attempts to disprove Paul's authorship of this letter, no Greek manuscript evidence exists to support these efforts. The manuscripts all contain Paul's name in the greeting.

Paul writes as **an apostle of Christ Jesus**, which means that he belonged to a group of men, unique in the Christian church, since each of them had been called in person by Jesus Christ and seen him alive from the dead (Acts 9:4ff.; 1 Cor. 9:1; 15:7f.). Because they were chosen to receive, transmit and explain the message of God's saving plan, which centres in Jesus Christ, his eternal Son, they hold a position that makes them authoritative teachers and pastors of the whole Christian church in history (Eph. 3:2ff.; 4:11ff.). They exercise this authority and teaching office through their inspired writings, which make up the New Testament Scriptures (1 Cor. 2:9ff.; 14:37; Eph. 3:2ff.).

If we think of the whole Christian church as a magnificent temple that is currently being built by the Spirit of God as he adds believers from all nations into its construction, then we can think of the apostles, along with Jesus Christ, the sole Mediator (1 Tim. 2:5), as forming the single foundation of the whole building, once for all laid down (Eph. 2:20; Rev. 21:14).

Paul was entrusted with this position (1 Cor. 4:1f.; 9:16f.; 1 Thess. 2:4) through a divine **command** which had changed his life in an unforgettable way, when he was dramatically and unexpectedly converted from the service of the Law to the service of Jesus Christ (Acts 26:12ff.; Gal. 1:15f.). This command came from **God our Saviour**, who has shown himself to be a Saviour God by intervening personally, and acting savingly, in human history in the person of Jesus Christ. All those throughout the ages, who like Paul have come to place their entire confidence in this God and to serve him alone, can speak of him as **our** God and Saviour, meaning that he is committed to them in love and faithfulness as his own people and possession (1 Pet. 2:9f.).

God has revealed his saving plan, not as a philosophical set of ideas, nor as a system of morality, but essentially as a person – **Christ Jesus**. 'Christ' is a Greek-based word, the equivalent of the Hebrew-based word Messiah which means 'anointed'. In

Israelite practice kings, prophets and priests were anointed with oil as a symbol of their sacred position and of the spiritual gift of the Spirit of the Lord to assist them in their work (Exod. 29:7; 1 Sam. 16:13; 1 Kings 19:15f.). At his baptism Jesus received the anointing of God's Holy Spirit because he was the true and final prophet, priest and king of God's appointing (Acts 2:25-32; 3:22-26; Heb. 7). To carry out such a unique task Christ needed to receive the Holy Spirit without measure (John 3:34; Heb. 9:14). Since his ascension Christ has been given a new access to the Spirit for the sake of his church on earth (Acts 2:33, 36; Rev. 3:1).

'Jesus' was the human, historical name of Christ. He was known as Jesus of Nazareth (Acts 2:22), the town where he grew up and learned the skill of carpentry, and where his family was known (Mark 6:3). He lived during the time of the Roman empire, from the period around the beginning of the first century, when Augustus was emperor, and the years around 30 AD, when Tiberius was emperor (Luke 2:1ff.; 3:1). He died under the governorship of Pontius Pilate in Palestine. He was identical with other men and women in every human trait, with the exception of their innate and actual sinfulness (Heb. 4:15).

By lining up the name of Christ Jesus with that of God our Saviour, Paul is indicating that God and Christ were working together in the plan of salvation, Jesus being the human agent of God's sovereign will. Jesus Christ is **our hope** because the confidence of Christians for the future rests in all that Jesus Christ is personally and has done historically on behalf of sinful men and women who trust in him (Col. 1:27; 1 Pet. 1:20f.). Because of this Christians hope to share in all the glories of the resurrection and the splendours of heavenly existence when Jesus returns. Essentially they hope to see Jesus – as he is, to be like him and to be with him (1 John 3:2f.).

The letter is written in the first place to **Timothy my true son in the faith**. Timothy was already a Christian disciple when Paul first met him (Acts 16:1) and took him to be his helper in the service of the gospel (Acts 19:22). The relationship so deepened that they became like a father and son, full of mutual affection and trust ('my true son', Phil. 2:22; 1 Tim. 1:18). In spite of Timothy's youth and his recurring ill-health (1 Tim. 4:12; 5:23; 2 Tim. 1:6f.), Paul respected and recommended him before all his other helpers because of his selfless motives (Phil. 2:19ff.). As a result Paul sent him on some difficult assignments (1 Thess. 3:2; 1 Cor. 16:10f.). This close working relationship between the two men grew out of their shared faith in the Lord Jesus Christ in spite of their age difference. This shows that there need be no generation gap in the Christian church, and that the one thing needful is a common commitment to the same Lord and his message of truth.

As part of his greeting Paul wishes Timothy **grace, mercy and peace.** 'Grace' and 'mercy' are God's special qualities that he so richly displays and communicates to us in the person of Jesus Christ and his saving work for us. They are a constant reminder to Christians that they have been eternally saved from their sinful and lost existence, not by anything in themselves, but by the free kindness and actions of God alone (Eph. 2:4ff.; 2 Tim. 1:9f.; Tit. 3:4ff.). 'Peace' is the special gift of God's grace and mercy in Jesus Christ, and stands for that total state of well-being that comes to those who are reconciled to God through the blood-sacrifice of Christ's cross (Col. 1:19f.).

These three gifts together point to the favourable, privileged and perfectly secure position that Christians have in the Lord Jesus Christ in relation to God.

All these privileges and blessings come **from God the Father and Christ Jesus our Lord**. Paul frequently singles out the Father as the original source of the plan and gifts of salvation (Eph. 1:3ff.), although he always works through the Son and the Holy Spirit (Gal. 4:4-6). In describing God as Father the apostle is using metaphorical language which is non-literal, but conveys a real truth about him in his relationship to Christians. Like a father he loves, is patient with, forgives, provides for, protects and seeks the very best for believers, who are his spiritual children in Jesus Christ his Son. Having God as our Father is the closest that we can possibly come to him, and is the defining relationship of the kingdom of God according to Jesus (Matt. 6:5-15). God's Fatherhood was already known in the Old Testament (Isa. 63:16) but never on an individual basis as it is in the New Testament.

Some have objected to the name Father on sexist grounds and want to substitute titles for God that are above gender distinctions. But the biblical titles for God are themselves God-given and therefore binding on Christians throughout all ages and cultures. Changing these names changes the truth about him because names are bearers of truth in Scripture (Matt .1:21, 23). To change God's given names is actually to change the truth about him, and to exchange the truth about God for a lie and to end up worshipping the creature rather than the Creator who is to be blessed forever (Rom. 1:25).

Although Paul follows the usual structure of the Greek letter in its general introduction, body and ending, he adapts it freely to his own needs as these two introductory verses show (e.g. 'grace' instead of 'joy', which was the traditional Greek greeting). By adapting it in this and other ways, Paul illustrates the creative freedom that was allowed to the human writers of Scripture, even while being inspired by the Holy Spirit (2 Tim. 3:16).

Study questions

Verse 1: Can there be apostles of Christ Jesus in the churches today? (Mark 3:13-19; 1 Cor. 9:1; 15:7f.; Eph. 2:19f.).

What is the place of hope in the Christian life? (Rom. 5:1-5; 8:22-25; Gal. 5:5; 1 Thess. 1:3; Heb. 11:1; 1 Pet. 1:3f).

Verse 2: What is the relation between the Father and the Son in the work of salvation? (John 5:19-23; Rom. 8: 32ff.; 1 Cor. 15:24-28; Gal. 4:4f.; Eph. 1:3-7; Heb. 1:1-6.; Rev. 1:4-6).

A Warning About Pseudo Religion (1:3-7)

As I urged you when I went into Macedonia, stay there in Ephesus. The letter properly begins here with Paul reminding Timothy of his urgent request to him to stay on in Ephesus, the capital city of the Roman province of Asia, to sort out certain problems that had arisen in the church there. Paul himself had gone on to Macedonia in the north of Greece, perhaps in fulfilment of his promise to the church at Philippi (Phil. 2:24). These movements do not fit in with any of the information of Paul's travels given in Acts. As a result it may be concluded that they belong to a period after Acts (Acts 28:16-31), when Paul was active again in the Mediterranean area (see Introduction).

Paul's commission to Timothy was **that you command certain men not to teach false doctrines any longer**. One of the major concerns of the Pastorals is that of true and false teaching. This is the first of several passages treating this concern. False teachings conceal the truth about God and corrupt people morally. Timothy had the right and authority to confront and correct those individuals who were propagating false teachings. God's revealed Word is the measure of truth and falsehood in doctrine. There are not several ways to truth so that all religious points of view are relatively correct and helpful. There is only one way, and the servant of Christ must defend it jealously (Gal. 1:8f.).

No one can be perfectly clear about who these false teachers were, where they had come from, or what precisely they believed. However, when Paul goes on to say **nor to devote themselves to myths and endless genealogies**, it is fair to say that they were of Jewish background, perhaps in the light of further references to them in the Pastorals, claiming to possess and to offer special and advanced spiritual knowledge. They built their speculative ideas on the basis of their fanciful interpretations of Old Testament genealogies, as for example in Genesis 5 and 11 (2 Tim. 3:8f.; Tit. 1:14; 3:9).

Because their interpretations are not based on a sound understanding of the Scriptures **these promote controversies rather**

than God's work – which is by faith (verse 4). That these
interpretations and teachings lead to argument and controversy
points to the fact that they are alien to God's written Word, and
are rooted instead in the unenlightened human mind. Jesus said
that false prophets are always known by the practical fruits they
produce (Matt. 7:15-20). The real truth produces a reconciling
trust in God, and leads to spiritual healing for men and women.
The apostle will return to this theme of the bankruptcy of false
religious ideas frequently (1 Tim. 4:7; 6:20f.; 2 Tim. 2:16ff., 23;
Tit. 3:9).

Instead of division **the goal of this command is love**, which
is proof of the fact that the ethical teaching of Paul can be traced
back to that of Jesus. Christ taught love as a new command that
in practice would distinguish his disciples (John 13:34f.). Paul
makes the same point in others of his letters (Rom. 13:8ff.; 1
Cor. 13; Gal. 5:13; Col. 3:14) by focusing on love as the supreme
goal of Christian behaviour. This love is an extract of God's own
love, demonstrated so remarkably by Jesus' death for his enemies, and now poured out in the depths of human hearts through
the working of the Holy Spirit (Rom. 5:5ff.). Love is therefore
the measure of our knowledge of God and of the quality of our
Christian service and relationships. Even to do the right thing
without love as the motive is to fail in our actions (1 Cor. 8:1ff.;
13:1-3; 1 John 4:7ff.). Love is also the measure and goal of
Christian preaching as Paul sets it before Timothy here.

But this love is not self-generated, it **comes from a pure
heart and a good conscience and a sincere faith** (verse 5). In
this anatomy of the inner workings of love Paul traces love back
to faith as its source (Gal. 5:6). This is because faith is a personal
trust in the God of salvation which puts us right with God on the
basis of Christ's life and death of obedience for us (Rom. 3:21-
28; Gal. 2:16). At the same time faith in Christ touches the conscience, that inborn moral mechanism which registers favourable and unfavourable verdicts on our conduct in accordance
with the law of God written on our heart (Rom. 2:14f.). The

conscience is released from the burden of guilt through Christ's sacrificial blood and the inner working of the Holy Spirit, and begins to function properly with a new-found vigour (Heb. 9:13f.; 10:19ff.). Finally the heart, the deep centre of the human person, is washed clean by faith in Christ and made a fit place for God the Holy Spirit to live in (Acts 15:8f.; Gal. 4:6). In each case Paul attaches a qualifier ('pure', 'good', 'sincere') to show that he is talking about a genuine work of God which results in definite and permanent changes in character and life. For further on a pure heart, a good conscience and genuine faith, see 1 Timothy 1:19; 3:9 and 2 Timothy 1:3, 5; 2:22.

Paul insists on these traits of Christian character because **some have wandered away from these and turned to meaningless talk** (verse 6). By deliberately rejecting the right path (the same verb is used in 1 Timothy 6:21 and 2 Timothy 2:18), the false teachers have demonstrated that their religious claims to knowledge are spurious. In the same way the apostle John declares that people who forsake the assemblies of God's people make it plain that they have never been true disciples of Christ (1 John 2:19). Apostasy is the proof of terminal unbelief. In the same way these religious gurus at Ephesus preferred the innovations of their own path of enlightenment, and the empty chatter that was part of it.

Apparently they want to be **teachers of the law, but they do not know what they are talking about or what they so confidently affirm** (verse 7). Their ambition is way ahead of their actual ability and knowledge. They covet the teacher's role but they are totally unsuited to the position. Their vain boasting and loud claims are a cover-up for profound ignorance and a total absence of authority. Their public display of spirituality is a balloon, filled with the hot-air of their own vanity and vaulting ambition. They are hollow people lacking all spiritual substance.

Study questions

Verse 3: What is meant by 'false doctrines'? Are all disagreements among Christians due to 'false doctrines'? (Mt. 16:5-12; Rom. 14:1-13; 1 Cor. 10:23-33; Gal. 1:6-9; 2:11-16).

Verse 5: What is the place of love in the Christian life? (Mt. 22:35-40; John 13:34f.; Rom. 13:8-10; 1 Cor. 13; 1 John 4:7-11).

What is a 'good conscience' and how does one get it and preserve it? (Acts 24:14ff.; Rom. 9:1; 1 Cor. 8:10ff.; 10:24-29; Heb. 9:13f.; 10:19-22).

The Law and the Gospel (1:8-11)

Mention of God's law in verse 7 leads Paul into a short discourse about its true character and purpose. *Law* basically means teaching, and includes all the written instructions of the Old Testament which God gave to his ancient people in covenant relationship. The law covers the writings of Moses, the prophets and the wise men of Israel. The ten words or commandments (Exod. 20:1-17; Deut. 5:1-21) formed the core of this body of literature, as the following verses will show.

This law, in the narrower sense, was being mishandled by the religious teachers in Ephesus, with the result that quite wrong ideas were being spread about it. So Paul is engaging in a simple and direct piece of apologetics when he says **we know that the law is good**. The law is good because it reflects the goodness of the God whose Author it is, and because it does people good when they live by it (Psa. 119:68; Mic. 2:7). But the law will only yield its blessing **if a man uses it properly**. This means that people must understand the true intention of the law, and recognise its limitations too. It was never meant to provide a means by which people can justify or ingratiate themselves with God. Its standards are far too high and pure for sinful human beings even to begin to accomplish that (Rom. 3:19f.; Gal. 2:16).

Paul spells out a major function of the law when he says **we also know that law is made not for good men but lawbreakers and rebels** (Verse 9). The NIV translates this reference as being to law generically, including human civil law, but Paul still has in mind the moral law of the ten commandments.

When Paul denies that the law is appointed for good (literally, righteous) people, he is not denying that the law has any positive uses, otherwise his teaching on the law elsewhere would be in conflict with what he says here. He is stating that people have nothing to fear from God's law so long as they live by it. He is focusing attention rather on one particular use the law has, that is, to identify human disobedience and to convince people that they are lawbreakers (Rom. 3:20; 5:20; 7:7; Gal. 3:19). The law has a convicting and restraining function in human life. Yet at other times Paul incorporates the law within his teaching on the Christian life, where it functions as one of the moral authorities that shows the Christian the way to live (Rom. 8:3f.; 13:8ff.; 1 Cor. 7:19; 9:21). But it still operates as a cautionary restraint on the Christian by warning him against sin (Rom. 7:13-25).

When the apostle speaks of 'lawbreakers and rebels' he is using two very general terms which are meant to include all violators of God's law, no matter how they break it. These two categories are meant to introduce his little discourse on the law.

The law is for **the ungodly and sinful, the unholy and irreligious**, those people who sin against the first four commandments of the law, which describe in principle our obligations to God (Exod. 20:1-11; Deut. 5:5-15). Such people sin in a religious way by worshipping gods of their own making in place of the true God, by following their own imagination in religious worship, by blaspheming God's name, and by using the Sabbath day for their own pleasure.

But God's law is also addressed to those who commit social sins in relation to their fellow human beings (Ex. 20:12-17; Deut. 5:16-21):

• It is **for those who kill their fathers or mothers** in violation of the fifth commandment (Honour your father and mother), which demands lifelong respect for one's parents (Eph. 6:1ff.).

• It is **for murderers** who negate the sixth commandment (You shall not murder) by wilfully destroying another person's life even although that other person is an image-bearer of God (Gen. 9:6).

• It is **for adulterers and perverts** (verse 10) who break the seventh commandment (You shall not commit adultery) which is concerned with sexual purity and fidelity. Adulterers break it by acting against the exclusive relationship of marriage (Rom. 7:2f.); perverts break it by acting outside the heterosexual nature of married love (Rom. 1:26f.).

• It is **for slave-traders** who transgress the eighth commandment (You shall not steal) by trading in human beings, thereby taking away their intrinsic dignity and freedom.

• It is **for liars and perjurers** who transgress the ninth commandment (You shall not bear false witness) with its demand for absolute honesty in speech (Eph. 4:25). Liars tell untruths in daily life while perjurers do the same under oath to pervert the course of justice.

Paul leaves out examples of violations of the tenth commandment (You shall not covet) in spite of the fact that it had played a powerful role in his own spiritual pilgrimage (Rom. 7:7f.). His interest here is in public behaviour rather than the hidden sins of the heart.

That this is not meant to be an exhaustive catalogue of the ways people can break God's law becomes clear when Paul adds – **and for whatever else is contrary to the sound doc-**

trine (verse 11) **that conforms to the glorious gospel of the blessed God.** Sound doctrine literally means teaching that brings spiritual health (Mic. 2:7; 2 Tim. 3:16f.). This idea occurs throughout the Pastorals (1 Tim. 6:3; 2 Tim. 1:13; 4:3; Tit. 1:9; 2:1, 8). What Paul says here also indicates that the law and the gospel are not at odds with each other but actually harmonise. They are one in their opposition to all forms of human disobedience and malpractice (Rom. 5:20-6:2; 7:24f.; Gal. 3:21f.).

The gospel is glorious because it is the brilliant shining revelation of the very being of God in the person and work of Jesus Christ (2 Cor 4:3-6). It is also glorious because it has the power to transform believers into the glorious moral and spiritual likeness of Jesus Christ (Rom 8:29f.; 2 Cor 3:18).

God is blessed, or perfectly joyful, because he rejoices in his own being in the delightful knowledge of his own Persons and perfections. Because he is blessed in himself he deserves, and expects, to be blessed or praised by all his creatures, especially by his people redeemed in Jesus Christ (Rom. 9:5; Rev. 5:13; 7:11f.).

Always aware of his stewardship as Christ's missionary (1 Cor. 4:1f.; 1 Thess. 2:4) Paul is quick to refer to the gospel as the God-given message of the truth **which he entrusted to me**. This might sound like egoistical boasting, but Paul's intention is quite different. He wants to assure Timothy and the Ephesian church that he has received a special dispensation in the service of the gospel. This is a personal remark which he now develops in an extended piece of autobiographical recollection which becomes the theme of the next section. Afterwards (verses 18ff.), Paul comes back to his starting-point at verse 3 and the subject of the troublesome teachers at Ephesus.

Study questions

Verse 8: What are the different meanings of the word 'law' in Scripture? (Psa. 19:7; 119:97f.; Luke 24:44; Rom. 7:7; Gal. 4:4f., 21f.).

Verses 10 and 11: What is the relation of the law to the gospel / the Christian's relation to the law? (Rom. 6:14; 7:4-8:4; 10:4-8; 1 Cor. 9:21; Gal. 3:10-12, 17-21; 4:21-26).

What makes the gospel glorious? (Rom. 8:16-21; 2 Cor. 3:7-11; 4:3-6).

Paul's Autobiography (1:12-17)
I thank Christ Jesus our Lord is how Paul begins this section of personal recollections (see further Phil. 3:7ff.). He could never forget all that he owed to the Lord Jesus Christ, because he was the one who died for him and saved him. As a result, Paul's misguided existence had been turned around and changed into something meaningful and useful. Christ is the one **who has given me strength** says Paul, speaking in the first person. His strength enabled Paul to respond favourably to the Lord's commission, and to fulfil his apostolic service and suffering for the sake of Christ's people (2 Tim. 2:10). Paul had learned well the fundamental principle of Christian living and service, that one's own strength is weakness, but that this weakness can become strength in Christ's hands (2 Cor. 12:9). Where the Lord Jesus appoints individual believers for special tasks, he can be relied on to give the strength needed to fulfil them (2 Cor. 3:5f.).

That he considered me faithful is how Paul explains Christ's thinking about him. Just as he had learned the secret of relying on Christ's faithfulness, so Christ had counted on Paul being trustworthy in his service. The Lord had entrusted Paul with a high degree of privilege and suffering (Acts 9:15f.) and he expected Paul to be faithful in all circumstances. The Lord had shown him mercy that he might be trustworthy, not the reverse (1 Cor. 7:25). Divine enabling is always the principal cause of responsible effort in the work of Christ (1 Cor. 15:9f.).

When the risen Christ called Paul he was **appointing** [him] **to his service**. The word Paul uses for service is the most basic term 'diaconia' which in this context expresses Paul's humility. Actual events were to prove it to be a ministry of courageous leadership, public witness and personal suffering for Christ's sake in a variety of settings (Acts 9:6, 15; 26:15ff.). This service was to carry Paul to the borders of the Roman empire and beyond, and through a host of dangers and privations without parallel (2 Cor. 11:23ff.). But through them all the Lord was with him, to sustain, refresh and deliver him as his humble and loyal servant (2 Tim. 4:17f.).

The greatest wonder for Paul was the fact that Jesus Christ had appointed him to his service **even though** [he] **was once a blasphemer and a persecutor and a violent man** (verse 13). When the heavenly Christ called Paul on the Damascus road, Paul was Christ's most bitter enemy. He blasphemed Christ by denying his credentials as the true Messiah and the Son of God; he persecuted Christ by hunting down his people like prey (Acts 26:9ff.; Gal. 1:13ff.); he showed himself a violent man by his rough handling of the first disciples of Jesus, and by handing them over to trial, imprisonment and even death (Acts 26:10f.).

It was while he was engaged in one of these shameful pogroms against the Christians that the Lord confronted Paul by appearing to him in his heavenly glory (Acts 9:3f.). **I was shown mercy** is how Paul sums up this life-changing experience, which transformed the self-righteous Pharisee into a humble and grateful follower of the crucified Saviour and Lord (Phil. 3:8f.). Mercy is undeserved pardon. Paul's conversion was an historic display of the overflowing kindness of the Father of mercies (2 Cor. 1:3). Only such mercy from such a God could rescue proud Paul, locked up in a prison of his own making, the walls of which were his ignorance, hate and unbelief. As a result God's mercy is very prominent in Paul's writing about salvation (Rom. 9:16, 18; 11:30ff.; 12:1f.; 2 Cor. 1:3; Eph. 2:4; Tit. 3:4f.).

The Lord's mercy was shown to Paul **because** [he] **acted in ignorance and unbelief**. In speaking this way Paul does not mean to lessen his guilt, but rather to emphasise the extent of his lost condition and to magnify the saving mercy of Christ to him. Because he did not know God truly, he acted out of ignorance when he reacted against the Lord's disciples and persecuted them (Acts 8:3; 9:1). He lived in unbelief, having convinced himself that Jesus could never be the Christ his followers claimed that he was. Yet Paul's ignorance was one reason for the mercy of Jesus Christ to him. Like others of his nation he genuinely believed that he was rendering service to God by opposing the Christian sect (John 16:2f.), while all the time he was ignorant of the truth. The Lord pitied him in his ignorance, which did not wholly excuse him, but left him amenable to mercy. For the same reason Jesus had prayed for his executioners' pardon (Luke 23:34).

So **the grace of our Lord was poured out on me abundantly** (Verse 14). Paul now uses another word 'grace' which is the undeserved love and favour of God. Grace by definition is rich, a fact Paul was deeply conscious of and loved to mention in his writings (Rom. 5:15, 17, 20f.). Believers are saved by the grace of the Lord Jesus, because, in his amazing grace, he freely chose to come to earth to live and to die for his people. The Lord does not love them in half measures but lavishly, and causes his great love to become known to them in profusion through the generous ministry of the Holy Spirit in their hearts (Rom. 5:5). As a result, Paul saw his ministry vividly as one of proclaiming the unsearchable riches of Jesus Christ (Eph. 3:8).

But Christ's grace did not appear alone for it came **along with the faith and love that are in Christ Jesus**. Christ's intervention in Paul's life not only changed his career, it changed his heart. The controlling passions of prejudice and hate gave way to faith and love. Faith is trust in Jesus Christ as Lord, and love is an attitude of goodwill for all his people (Eph. 1:15; Col. 1:4). Faith and love are the sure evidences that lives have been transformed from within and are not simply passing through a religious phase (2 Tim. 1:13). Out of Christ's fulness Paul, along with all other Christians, received grace to believe and love. Although these fundamental attitudes are expected by God to be present in his people, they are also provided in Christ's grace.

Before he draws out some lessons from his own life story Paul appeals to a piece of early Church tradition. **Here is a trustworthy saying that deserves full acceptance** (verse 15). There are five of these faithful sayings in the Pastoral letters (1 Tim. 1:15; 3:1; 4:9; 2 Tim. 2:11; Tit. 3:4-8). They are pieces of early Christian wisdom, extracted from sayings apparently well-known among the early churches. They vary considerably in their content but each one deserves to be fully accepted.

This one claims that **Christ Jesus came into the world to save sinners** and so announces the very heart of the gospel. It states the purpose of Christ's mission in coming into our world. His very name foretold it (Matt. 1:21), he himself taught it (Mark 10:44f.), and his life on earth bore it out. The words of this saying tell nothing of how Christ was to save, only that he came to save. The rest of the New Testament tells us how – through his unsinning life and sin-bearing death (Rom. 3:24f.; 5:18f.; 2 Cor. 5:18ff.; Gal. 3:13; 1 Tim. 2:5f.; Heb. 9:13f.; 1 Pet. 1:18f.). This wonderfully simple statement of faith carries two strong implications.

First, Christ 'came into the world' thereby implying that he already existed on the other side of time and space. He was the eternal Word of God who was with God, and was God from eternity, and created personally the world of matter into which he came (John 1:1f., 10).

Secondly, Christ came to save sinners, thereby implying that he did not come simply to make them salvable or to help them to save themselves. He came to save them actually and finally by his own presence and actions on their behalf. This is the gospel (Gal. 2:20).

Paul adds to this statement of faith the words – **of whom I am the worst**. This may sound like an exaggerated case of false modesty, but Paul means what he says (1 Cor. 15:9; Eph. 3:8), for the simple reason that he can remember vividly the kind of person he was and the life he once lived. At the same time he includes the person he now is as a Christian ('I am') because he is conscious of his continuing sinfulness and his need of the pardoning and renewing grace of God (Rom. 7:22-25; Phil. 3:12ff.). No doubt there are special provocations in the case of Paul's sin, yet every Christian can identify with his confession because each in their own way has transgressed seriously and persistently against God's law and stands in need of the same grace of Christ as Paul did.

But for that very reason I was shown mercy (verse 16). There was more to Paul's conversion than the dramatic change brought about through the display of God's mercy to a particular individual. Paul's was a test case in the strategy of heaven. His change came about **so that in** [him]**, the worst of sinners, Christ Jesus might display his unlimited patience**. In Paul, Christ deliberately chose the worst case scenario, so as to demonstrate what his patience and grace can do. Paul's conversion is therefore the classic example of the text that says that the Lord is slow to anger and of great patience (Psa. 145:8f.). For years Paul had openly and vigorously persecuted the disciples of the Lord, and in doing so was found to be harassing Jesus Christ himself (Acts 9:4f.). Well might Jesus Christ have been affronted by Paul's behaviour and cut him off. Instead the Lord spared him, even revealing himself to Paul as his personal Lord and Saviour. Clearly Christ's patience is virtually unlimited.

Paul's life-story serves **as an example for those who would believe on him** in all time to come. At the beginning of the Christian era Paul's grand conversion stands out as a sure indicator that the Lord is gracious and will pardon the worst offenders. No one should ever think, in the light of Paul's reception of mercy from Christ, 'I am too bad for Christ to pardon and receive.'

Rather they should reason like this, 'If Christ can receive and pardon Paul then there must be hope for me.' Doubt and discouragement often come with the dawning consciousness of sin in the first stages of conversion. It is then that Paul's acceptance with Christ can act like a powerful reinforcement to persuade the doubting individual to persist in seeking Christ and his mercy. 'Believing on' Christ aptly describes the inner attitude of acquiescence and personal reliance on Christ himself which is the essence of the faith that saves.

People are called to believe on Christ **and receive eternal life**. The connection between reliance on Christ and the gift of eternal life is natural. By his obedience right through his life to the death of the cross (Phil. 2:8), Christ has personally secured the right to give eternal life to all who come to him in genuine trust. Eternal life is the life of the age to come, but those who believe on Christ receive eternal life the moment they believe (John 6:47). The person who has the Son has life, but the one who does not have the Son does not have life, for this life is in God's Son Jesus Christ (1 John 5:11f.).

In the light of these wonders of God's grace Paul closes this section with a doxology, which is a short prayer of praise to God. It consists of four descriptions of the being of God, followed by the desire that God be duly honoured, and then concluded by an Amen.

God is King. **Now to the King eternal** means literally 'Now to the king of the ages', including all the ages of history, past, present and future. God is Lord of all from beginning to end. By contrast the kings and rulers of earth are of a moment's duration (Isa. 40:23f.). The day of Jesus Christ will finally remove every challenge to the Kingship of God (Dan. 2:44; 4:34f.; 1 Cor. 15:24ff.; Rev. 11:17f.).

God is **immortal** which means literally that he is free from the changes death brings. He cannot die, nor ever cease to exist as he is now and always has been. By contrast human beings receive their immortal existence from God as a gift. Only God has life and being in and of himself alone (John 5:26).

God is **invisible** which means that he is not confined to any place or time as we are. He exists outside the limitations of our human existence. He is the eternal Spirit, a pure Being. It is impossible for him to become the fixed object of our scientific investigation. Only in Jesus Christ has God made himself visible, and only then through the medium of a human life. Christ is the image of the invisible God (Col. 1:15).

God is **the only God** who actually exists, although human beings have throughout their fallen history invented many gods and worshipped them. But for Christians there is only one God, the Father, Son and Holy Spirit, the Creator and Sustainer of all things (1 Cor. 8:5f.). Only the only God is worthy of human worship and trust.

To the one, true God **be honour and glory for ever and ever**. This is the express wish of the prayer, that the only God who is immortal, invisible and the eternal King would be duly praised. This will happen when all creation ascribes honour and glory to him in an everlasting liturgy of worship (Rev. 4:9ff.; 5:13f.). Honour and glory are his by right of creation and salvation. **Amen** is a solemn expression of approval at the end of the prayer and is equivalent to 'let it be so' (see also 1 Timothy 6:16).

Study questions

Verse 12: What else does the Bible say about the principles that should guide us in Christian leadership and service? (1 Cor. 8; 9:19-27; 2 Cor. 4:7-15; 11:30-12:10).

Verse 16: What other examples of notorious sinners saved by God's grace do the Scriptures give us? (2 Ch. 33:1-13; Dan. 4; Jonah 3; Luke 15:11-24; 23:39-43; Acts 19:17-20).

Verse 17: What other perfections of God can you think of? (Ex. 34:6f.; Neh. 9:17; Isa. 40:13f., 21ff.; Hab. 1:12f.; Tit. 1:2; Jas. 1:17f.; Rev. 4:8f.).

Faith and a Good Conscience (1:18-20)

Paul returns to the matter of the critical church situation at Ephesus with which he began the letter (verses 3-7). In addressing
Timothy as **my son** he is using the language of fatherhood in a
metaphorical and spiritual way (verse 2). In this way Paul was
able to sublimate the generation gap between himself and Timothy. **I give you this instruction** refers back to the business of
Timothy's staying on in Ephesus to restrain certain people from
teaching false ideas (verse 3f.). Paul says his appeal is **in keeping with the prophecies once made about** Timothy. This must
mean that Timothy's appointment to Christ's service was inspired
by prophets in the local churches, as at Antioch and Corinth (1
Tim. 4:14; Acts 13:1ff.; 1 Cor. 14:29ff.). This reminded Timothy
that his calling to Christian leadership was from God and he could
rely on the same source to carry him through.

During the apostolic age, before the will of God for his church
was finalised in the written and collected documents of the New
Testament, his will was regularly made known through the inspired pronouncements of Christian prophets. After the apostolic
age, when the canon of the New Testament had been completed
and circulated, the need for these prophetic utterances ceased.
Since then, Christians in assembly and in private have relied on a
prayerful and a Spirit-enlightened reading of the Scriptures for
an understanding of the general and particular will of God. By
this means they have also decided who is properly gifted for positions of Christian leadership in the churches (see 1 Timothy 3:1-7)).

Paul reminds Timothy about these prophetic utterances **so
that by following them** [he] **may fight the good fight**. Timothy, who was naturally timid in himself, needed the strengthening
effects of those external prophecies (literally 'by means of them')
to fortify him in the cauldron of Ephesian church politics when
he came under fire. By remembering and being assured by Paul
that he had not chosen himself but that the Lord had chosen him,
he would be helped to continue faithful and effective. In Christian leadership it is essential to have objective criteria, such as

the investigatory approval of the church, or clear instances of guidance from Scripture, or circumstances of the Lord's making to fall back on and appeal to, when opposition arises to one's work for Christ. The Christian leader needs to know also that the good fight is not just against factors such as fatigue and stress, but at a deeper level against the unseen but resilient powers of darkness which make the Christian leader their special target (Eph. 6:10-20; 1 Tim. 6:12; 2 Tim. 2:3f.).

Survival in this spiritual war involves **holding on to faith and a good conscience** (verse 19) which Paul has already brought together (verse 5) and will do so again (1 Tim. 3:9). Faith is the cardinal Christian grace, because it is only by believing in Jesus Christ through the Word of God that fellowship with God can continue. Faith is the bond of the covenant relationship on the Christian's side. But true faith results in works of righteousness of which a good conscience is the indicator. A good conscience is one that witnesses to the sincerity of the Christian's obedience to the will of God (Rom. 9:1; Heb. 13:18). Faith without a good conscience leads to immorality; a good conscience without faith is mere moralism. The true Christian holds on to both faith and a good conscience.

In stating that **some have rejected these**, it is not clear whether Paul is referring to the local group at Ephesus (verses 3 and 4), or whether he is speaking in general terms. Whoever they were, these people were impatient with Christian faith and careless about Christian morals. They had rejected these and **so have shipwrecked their faith**. The Pastorals contain many warnings and examples of people who have drifted away from the apostolic faith into novelties of their own (1 Tim. 6:20f.; 2 Tim. 2:17f.; Tit. 1:10f.). Since the results of this kind of abandonment of the Christian faith are nearly always final and fatal, Paul likens it to a shipwreck in which the whole hull breaks up and the cargo is strewn across the water (see also Hebrews. 6:4ff.; 10:26ff.). King Saul, Judas and Demas are all biblical examples of shipwrecked faith.

Having taught in Ephesus for three years (Acts 20:31) Paul knew the history of the congregation, its individuals and families. So he is able to name two of the ringleaders of the breakaway group – **among them are Hymenaeus and Alexander**. Hymenaeus is mentioned again for denying the bodily resurrection (2 Tim. 2:17f.), and Alexander may very well be the coppersmith who had done Paul so much harm (2 Tim. 4:14). If these two are the same individual, then it may be surmised that the harmful opposition which Alexander rendered to Paul under trial may have been retribution for his earlier discipline at Paul's hands. Such is the cost of faithful Christian leadership and oversight.

Hymenaeus and Alexander were men **whom I have handed over to Satan**. This is an obscure expression which describes some act of church discipline (1 Cor. 5:5). 'Satan' stands for the pagan environment outside the church community, the realm of his moral and spiritual kingdom (2 Cor. 4:3f.; Eph. 2:2f.; 1 John 5:19). 'Handing over to Satan' refers to the judicial act of dismissal from the fellowship of the church. Its purpose was to expose the offender to Satan's power, perhaps in the form of some kind of physical punishment. Under God's supreme command this hopefully would act as a corrective and bring about a change of heart.

Church offenders like this needed **to be taught not to blaspheme**, otherwise they will destroy themselves, and pull down others with them. From this we learn that:

• serious failures of a theological or moral kind need to be confronted by the leaders of the church

• suspension of membership rights and even excommunication are appropriate penalties in such cases

• church discipline should aim ultimately at the good of the offender as well as the church (1 Cor. 5:4f.).

Study questions

Verse 18: Who were the prophets in the early church, and what was their function? Should we expect prophecies in the churches today? (Acts 21:8-14; 1 Cor. 11:4f.; 14:1-33; Eph. 2:19ff.; 3:1-7; 4:7-13; Rev. 22:18f.).

What is the nature of the spiritual war which the Christian and the Church are engaged in, and how best can they wage it? (Mt. 12:22-28; Acts 19:8-20; 2 Cor. 10:3-6; Eph. 6:10-18; Rev. 12:7-11).

Verse 19: Can true believers finally fall away from the faith? (1 Sam. 16:13f.; 2 Sam. 11:26-12:13; Mt. 13:18-23; 26:69-27:5; Luke 22:31-34; Heb. 6:4-9; 10:26-29; 1 Pet. 1:3ff.).

1 TIMOTHY: CHAPTER 2

Paul, at this point, begins to prescribe positively how the church at Ephesus (and elsewhere) should be organised. This section includes the whole of chapters two and three and forms the heart of the letter. The topics covered are public prayer (2:1-7), the activity of men (2:8), the activity of women (2:9-15), qualifications for overseers (3:1-7), qualifications for deacons (3:8-13), and the church's confession (3:14-16).

Prayers For Everyone (2:1-7)

I urge, then, first of all. Paul makes use of his apostolic authority (I urge, cf. verse 3) for building up the church (2 Cor. 13:10). As a matter of priority, he urges that all kinds of prayers should be offered for all kinds of people. This focus on prayer as a priority is typical of New Testament religion (Acts 1:14; 4:23f.; Eph. 6:18; Col. 4:2; 1 Thess. 5:17), being the natural response of God's people to his promise that he will hear and respond to their prayers (Psa. 34:15; Matt. 7:11; Luke 18:7f.; Jas. 1:5).

The apostle uses four different words for prayer, when he urges **that requests, prayers, intercession and thanksgiving** should be offered to God. Each of these terms carries its own shade of meaning:

'requests' are personal prayers made on special occasions for particular needs such as one's own guidance, help or comfort in a given situation.

'prayers' is the most general of the terms and refers to all kinds of requests that believers make, but perhaps mostly for general needs that arise. Both terms occur in Philippians 4:6 and 1 Timothy 5:5.

'intercessions' stands for prayers that are offered on behalf of other people and their known needs; the Holy Spirit and Jesus Christ also make representation on behalf of believers (Romans 8:27, 34).

44

'thanksgivings' are prayers of gratitude to God for his many mercies and particular blessings received from above. These two are to be offered on behalf of all sorts of people. Thanksgiving is always required of God's people (1 Thess. 5:18).

While this accumulation of prayer words shows how varied praying can be, it also emphasises the large place prayer should have in the church's practice. The way in which prayer is expressed and verbalised will depend on the church's situation and needs. The prayers of the Bible, for example those in the Psalms, show this wonderful flexibility and variety of form in coming to God.

The different kinds of prayers are to **be made for everyone**. Throughout these verses Paul repeats the fact that God's interests in the world are widespread and not confined to any one group (see especially verses 1, 2, 4, and 6). The 'everyone' should not therefore be taken literally, but as standing for all classes, groups, nationalities, ages, and so on. The church's prayers should reflect this interest and outlook too. This universal point of view does not conflict with the electing love of God.

A special place in Christians' prayers should be made **for kings and all those in authority** (verse 2). This request holds good whatever form of political system Christians may live under, and whether these civil rulers are Christians or not (few of the Roman rulers were Christians at the time Paul wrote). As rulers they are under God and accountable to him (Rom. 13:1-4; 1 Pet. 2:13f.), and God is able to use them to further his greater purposes in the world (Prov. 21:1), as the examples of such rulers as Cyrus, Nebuchadnezzar and Pilate show.

They are to be prayed for **that we may live peaceful and quiet lives in all godliness and holiness**. Because they hold such positions of influence, civil rulers can affect the whole of society for good or evil. Through their prayers to the only Ruler, the King of kings and the Lord of lords (1 Tim. 6:15), Christians can influence political leaders indirectly so that they adopt policies that make it possible for people to practise religion and morality in a social environment of security and peace. Even non-Christian rulers, because of God's common grace, can oppose violence and crime and protect the rights of decent members of society. Christians therefore have a vested interest in community standards and government legislation.

This is good (verse 3) or morally right. Paul is thinking of his request that prayers and intercessions should be made for all kinds of persons, especially rulers. He also has in mind the ideal of a settled society, where genuine religion and righteousness can flourish. Such a result is a universal good that benefits believers and unbelievers alike.

But Paul has a higher reason in view when he adds **and pleases God our Saviour**. Pleasing God is a higher reason for praying than is pleasing people. God genuinely delights in the wellbeing of human beings whom he desires to save. Although God does not have the same emotional life as human beings, yet he strongly approves the right behaviour of men and women and their responses to his will. Here he is perfectly pleased with the prayers of his people for humanity in general. On God our Saviour see 1 Timothy 1:1. Paul now explains why such prayers please God.

That God is the one **who wants all men to be saved** (verse 4) is the key statement of the whole paragraph from verses 1-7. It explains why Christians should pray for all kinds of people – because God wants all kinds of people to be saved. Since we have established that all sorts and classes of people are under consideration, the obvious fact that not every human being is actually saved should not be a problem in understanding this passage. Every single individual may not be saved, but men and women from all sections of society and from all nations certainly are.

As far as individuals are concerned, we know that God exercises his prerogative in withholding or extending mercy as he chooses (Rom. 9:14-24). The Lord has no pleasure in the death and destruction of those who resist him and perish; he would rather they turned to him and lived again (Ezek. 33:11; 2 Pet. 3:9). God genuinely desires the salvation of the wicked but has chosen not to will it in every case. This is a profound mystery before which we can only be silent (Rom. 9:20). Just as his mercy and love are displayed in the salvation of some, so his justice and patience are displayed in the destruction of others (Rom. 9:22f.). Either way God is blameless.

God's choice of individuals is a matter of his *secret* will to which no one has access. In the practice of evangelism, Christians are to be guided by his *revealed* will in the Scriptures. There we read that the gospel is to be proclaimed to the whole human race in dependence on the sovereign working of God the Holy Spirit. This is the rule which guided Paul in his universal mission to the Gentiles (verse 7), and this is how Christians are always to operate.

God wants all men to be saved **and to come to a knowledge of the truth**. Knowing the truth means more than being intellectually acquainted with the Christian message. Saving knowledge of the truth does have an intellectual content, but it is also strongly experiential, involving a response of repentance and total self-commitment that results in godliness (2 Tim. 2:25; Tit. 1:1). The message is called 'the truth' because it corresponds to the reality of things and is totally reliable. It rests squarely on the revelation of God in Scripture, not on human reason (1 Cor. 2:4f.), and is centred on Jesus Christ (John 1:17; 16:4, 9). People must come to know the truth because they do not naturally know what it is. Only when they come to know it can they know God and so be saved. Knowing the truth is the only way to salvation (Acts 4:12).

For there is one God (verse 5) confirms the fact that all human beings must be saved in the same way, by knowing the same truth. In the ancient world, there was a belief in many gods (1 Cor. 8:5), which led to a smorgasbord of ideas and approaches to salvation. Over against this plurality Paul affirms the Christian view that there is only one God (Gen. 1:1; Deut. 6:4f.; Isa. 45:5f., 21; 1 Cor. 8:5f.). The unity of God underlies the unity of salvation through the one mediator (Rom. 3:30). The apostle may be quoting here from an early church creed.

Paul believes in one God **and one mediator between God and men**. A mediator is someone who acts between two parties to bring them together. Just as Paul has confessed the unity of God, so now he assumes the unity of the human race. The apostle clearly accepted the biblical account of the origin of the human race through a single man Adam, from whom all the nations and ethnic groupings of the human family have come (see Genesis 2:5ff.; Acts 17:26). Since there are only two parties in this dispute between God and Man they can be represented by a single mediator. Later, Gnostic theology taught a series of divine or semi-divine emanations between God and humanity. Paul's statement excludes every idea of this kind because there is no need for any third-party other than Jesus Christ.

In the words **the man Christ Jesus** Paul identifies the one mediator between God and Man. He is ideally qualified to represent God to humanity, and humanity to God, since he himself is both God and a human being. For historical reasons Paul's accent here falls on the manhood of Christ. The apostle will later (3:16) expand on this central Christian mystery of the Person of Jesus Christ, but here he is content simply to assume it. Only someone who was fully human could legally and sympathetically act on behalf of other human beings. This is the logic behind the birth of Jesus when God took a human form of existence and made himself the second and last Adam (John 1:1f., 14; Rom. 8:3; 1 Cor. 15:45; Phil. 2:5ff.; Heb. 2:10f., 14f.; 4:15). This strong declaration of the full humanity of Jesus Christ stands over against every form of docetic teaching which denies that God became fully human (1 John 4:2f.).

As the one **who gave himself as a ransom for all men** (verse 6) Christ Jesus has shown his complete efficiency as a mediator. A ransom was the price paid in ancient cultures for the release of slaves or prisoners of war. Paul lifts this type of transaction to the higher plain of God-Man relations in arguing that Christ has paid a ransom price for the rescue of human beings from the enslaving powers of the world, Satan, sin and death. He did this when 'he gave himself' – a clear reference to the self-giving and sacrificial action of Jesus on the cross when he handed himself over to death as a liberating act for sinful men and women. His life was exchanged for theirs (the Greek indicates a substitution of one in the place of another), that his life might become theirs (2 Cor. 5:21).

The ransom price was Jesus giving himself in his own Person as God and Man in the most astonishing disclosure, and acting out of God's love for us (Mark 10:45; Eph. 5:2; 5:25f.). In giving himself a ransom for all men, Jesus died in the place of all kinds of people, a fact that is borne out by the spectrum of human beings who come to faith in him. Because he is God, his ransom is effective for the salvation of the whole of creation (Col. 1:19f.). Because he is a man, his ransom is effective for men and women from every culture throughout history (Col. 3:10f.). This is the basis of the gospel message of salvation.

The assertion that Christ died for all sorts of people does not contradict the belief that he also died with the intention of only actually saving some. If he had died for every single individual, then every single individual would be saved, which is obviously not true. Human freedom is curtailed by its own fallenness, so that the unbeliever cannot escape from the closed circuit of his unbelief. By his ransom-death Christ actually redeemed all those whom the Father gave him to be saved, and secured the faith by which they would be united to him (John 10:11-15; 17:9-12; Acts 20:28; Eph. 5:25ff.).

The concluding expression **the testimony given in its proper time** probably means that through the death of the man Christ Jesus, God gave his final and supreme witness to his desire to save men and women of all kinds. This took place at 'the proper time', the time most conducive to the universal proclamation of the gospel message. With regard to the choice of the particular time of Jesus' birth, we can only guess that this may have been due to such factors as the collapse of the great world empires of the middle east such as Assyria and Babylonia, the failure of

Greek and Roman philosophy to provide answers to life's problems, and the moral bankruptcy of the ancient world order (Rom. 5:6; Gal. 4:4).

The words could also be predictive, pointing forward to the public testimony that will be given throughout history by Christian witnesses to the substitutionary ransom of Jesus Christ. They would then read – 'the testimony which will be given in its proper time'. There is no verb in the Greek to tie the time down to the past or future.

And for this purpose I was appointed a herald and an apostle ... and a teacher of the true faith (verse 7). Just as in chapter one (1:11ff.), discussion of the gospel leads Paul to reflect on his own part in God's universal purpose of salvation. Paul gives himself three titles in describing his role. Firstly, as a *herald* he was authorised by Christ to proclaim the message of the one true Ruler (1 Tim. 6:15). Secondly, as an *apostle* he was commissioned to establish Christ's church throughout the world (Gal. 1:15f.). Thirdly, as a *teacher* he was entrusted with the task of transmitting the truth of God's Word to future generations (Eph. 3:3ff.).

Paul's apostolic ministry of preaching and teaching was directed **to the Gentiles** as further proof of the universal love and plan of God. It further justifies the prayers of the church for people of all kinds (verses 1f.). Although he was a Jew, Paul was not at all ashamed of his mission to the Gentiles. He could see in this the outworking of God's purpose of mercy for all humanity (Rom. 11:13f., 30ff.).

He protests his sincerity in the strongest possible terms – **I am telling the truth, I am not lying** – since people frequently challenged his apostolic authority or objected to his work among Gentile peoples. But Paul had learned, like Christ, to make himself the servant of all so that he might by all means save some of them (1 Cor. 9:19-24). His work among the Gentiles was living proof of the universal love of God in its missionary expression.

Study questions

Verses 1-2: Are there other classes of people that Christians should pray for? (Jer. 29:7; John 17:20f.; Acts 12:5; Eph. 6:18ff.; Heb. 13:3; Jas. 5:13ff.)

Verses 3-4: What other verses can you think of that teach the universal love of God? (Gen. 12:3; John 3:16)

Verse 5: What else does the unity of God teach us? (Deut. 4f.; Mark 12:29f.; Rom. 3:29f.; 10:11f.; Jas. 2:19)

Men and Women (2:8-15)

The fact that Paul now addresses gender issues means that there must have been some confusion about this subject within the church at Ephesus. **I want men everywhere to lift up holy hands in prayer**. The apostle begins by addressing the men, as distinct from the women, whom he addresses from verse nine onwards. 'I want' is a variant of 'I urge' in verse one, but is no less a carrier of Paul's apostolic authority. That men are called *everywhere* to life up holy hands in prayer shows that Paul is prescribing here universally for the churches, not only for the local Ephesian situation. Clearly the male members of the churches are intended to give the lead in praying in the assemblies of worship.

Lifting up the hands (Psa. 28:2; 63:4; 134:2) or the eyes to heaven (John 17:1) in prayer was body language that expressed the inner attitude of trust and submission towards God. In the matter of prayer and worship the physical position is less important than the actual life of the worshipper. Holy hands stand for a life in which the bodily members themselves have been presented to God as instruments of righteousness and in which sinful desires are being denied the mastery.

The moral principle here is that sin in the heart blocks the interchange of prayer (Psa. 66:18). This principle is dictated by the fact that God is holy and requires his people to be like him in holiness if the dialogue of prayer is to be meaningful (1 Pet. 1:14ff.).

At the same time this praying must be **without anger and disputing**. While holiness takes into account the moral life of the man who prays, these two requirements look into his relations with fellow members in the family of God. Nothing hinders effective praying so much as friction between Christians. Unresolved conflicts between Christians, particularly when they occur within the same assembly, deny outright the unity and peace of the body of Christ and do great damage. Anger and disputing hinder, and destroy, that united form of praying which our Lord promised in a special way to honour and to respond to (Matt. 18:19f.).

I also want women to dress modestly, with decency and propriety (verse 9). Since the apostle has just instructed the men in what they are to do in the life of the congregation, he now turns to the women. For their direction he introduces the question of their attire and public appearance. God's church is holy (1 Cor. 3:16f), consequently the apostle wants to avoid anything that would awaken unholy sexual desires or promote immoral behaviour between men and women. Although men are as responsible as women in this matter, Paul is aware of the powerful effects that women can have on men by the way they dress and present themselves. As a result he calls for modesty and thoughtfulness on their part, as their way of contributing to the spiritual health of the congregation.

Negatively this means dressing **not with braided hair or gold or pearls or expensive clothes**. We know from Greek and Roman sources that among the upper classes of society, female hairdressing in a variety of styles was popular. Paul calls the Christian women to follow a different set of social standards which mirror the less obtrusive, yet more refined inner values of the Christian gospel. Not that Paul is opposed to a simple pride in one's appearance. But women who habitually dress in demonstrative ways are open to the charge of dressing for effect, of prostituting themselves to cultural mores, and of showing that their values are largely cosmetic (!) and self-centred. In every culture there will be special occasions, normally connected with rites of passage such as weddings, when social custom requires a certain conformity to established practice. But then also, Christian women are to be conscientious and consistent in practising the gospel ethic of modesty in dress and appearance.

Positively, this means that Christian women ought not to beautify themselves extravagantly in visual ways, **but with good deeds, appropriate for women who profess to worship God** (verse 10). Christianity is primarily concerned about the beauty of personal character, expressed in a life devoted to good works (Eph. 2:10; Tit. 2:11-14). Human beings look on the outward appearance but God looks into the heart and its attitudes (1 Sam. 16:7). This is particularly appropriate for Christian women who profess godliness and want to cultivate the authentic and lasting beauty of the inner person (1 Pet. 3:3f.). This true beauty of femininity can be a potent instrument in God's hands for awakening and blessing others (1 Sam. 25:1-35; Rom. 16:1-15; 1 Pet. 3:1f.). Women such as Hannah, Abigail, Mary the mother of Jesus, Mary Magdalene, and Lydia are outstanding examples of this biblical understanding of true feminine beauty.

A woman should learn in quietness and full submission (verse 11). Paul draws out the full implications of what he has already said about the place of women in the church. Although some of the women at Ephesus may have forced Paul to address this issue more urgently, he uses the opportunity to address Christian women generically. In spite of local factors, the apostle's pronouncements about women are based on non-cultural grounds, not on local and first-century criteria. Paul is fully consistent, since what he lays down here is in harmony with his other pronouncements on the subject (1 Cor. 11:7ff.; 14:34f.). That this is a distinctively Christian and religious position is further shown by the fact that women, in certain cultures of the Graeco-Roman world, enjoyed a large degree of social status and freedom (Acts 13:50; 17:4, 12).

By commanding quietness and submission, Paul is not demanding a vow of absolute silence from the female members of
the congregation, as though the women were not to speak under
any circumstances. Nor is he merely commending the grace of
inner tranquillity. He is prescribing for their conduct in the public
assemblies, in relation to the ruling-teaching function of the elders
(verse 12). Their position and function required the overseers to
address the congregation as a whole and in an authoritative way.
It is from this sort of official speaking and teaching that the apostle debars the women and commands silence. But it is silence
which he requires as a sign of their submission to the God-given
authority of their male overseers (1 Cor. 11:10).

At the same time Paul is keen that the women should learn as
genuine disciples in the school of Christ. While setting certain
limits to the speaking and leadership role of women in the church,
for reasons that are creation-based and historical (verse 12), Paul
recognises everywhere the intrinsic worth of women (1 Cor. 7:2ff.;
11:11f.; Gal. 4:4), their equal status with men in the common
salvation in Christ (Gal. 3:28), and praises their supportive ministries (e.g. Rom. 16:1-16; Phil. 4:3).

When Paul says **I do not permit** (verse 12), he is drawing upon
his apostolic authority to speak in Christ's name, so as to give
sound teaching to the churches. Before explaining the historical
and theological grounds for his restriction on women, Paul states
the nature of the prohibition itself. In substance it is twofold. It
forbids **a woman to teach or to have authority over a man; she
must be silent**. Since teaching and having authority (or ruling)
over others are the twin functions of the elders in the Pastorals (1
Tim. 3:2, 4f.; 5:17; Tit. 1:5f., 9), Paul is excluding women from
the ruling-teaching office of overseers. Apart from these two
functions, Paul sets no limitations on the ministry of women in
the church. In other contexts they are encouraged to exercise
authority and to teach, for example in the home and in relation to
other women (1 Tim. 5:14; Tit. 2:3ff.). It follows that the requirement of silence must have definite reference to the public speak-

ing that the pastoral leaders are involved in when addressing the
congregation in preaching and ruling.

Arguments have been used to say that the action word 'to
have authority over' should be translated 'to domineer'. This would
have the effect of reducing the scope of Paul's teaching about
women. But this rendering of the Greek term has negative connotations whereas the normal use of this word in Greek usage is
positive. Where it appears, as it does here, along with another
verb that is positive (to teach), then it is always positive in its
meaning. On these linguistic and grammatical grounds the only accurate translation is the one provided, for example, in the NIV
text. The authority under consideration is perfectly legitimate,
but not when exercised by a woman.

The apostle's reasoning is not based on male chauvinism,
personal prejudice, or cultural factors from his day, but it is based
squarely on historical and factual evidence provided in the Word
of God. He appeals to the biblical account of creation and the
fall (Gen. 2 and 3). **For Adam was formed first, then Eve**
(verse 13). The order (and the way, 1 Cor. 11:8f.), in which the
man and the woman were created by God (Gen. 2:18-25), carries a theological message and establishes a paradigm for understanding gender relationships and roles. The man was created
before the woman to establish his headship or leadership in the
relationship of the two. The woman was then formed *from* the
man to achieve a unique intimacy, and *for* the man to create a
certain kind of dependency. But nowhere does Scripture deduce
from these facts about the origin of the woman that she is inferior, less valuable or less gifted than the man. Yet a finely nuanced
difference between them exists from the order of creation, one
in which the man is meant to lead and the woman is meant to
follow and support.

Paul's second argument runs along the same lines. **And Adam
was not the one deceived** (verse 14) recalls the fact that the
tempter first of all confronted the woman with his invitation to
disobey God (Gen. 3:1ff.). The result was that the man was not

the first in time, or order, to be deceived by the temptation and so to partake of the forbidden fruit (Gen. 3:6). The personal circumstances of Adam's original sin were different from those of the woman. Unlike the woman who listened to the voice of the tempter directly, the man heard the voice of the tempter through the voice of his wife, who invited him to partake of the forbidden fruit with her (Gen. 3:17). Having first become entangled in the temptation herself, Eve then solicited Adam to become a party with her in that first act of human disobedience (Gen. 3:17). Paul does not deny the fact that the man became a sinner like the woman, only that he was not the one who initiated the course of sinning.

So **it was the woman who was deceived and became a sinner** when she yielded to the seductive arguments and promises of the tempter (Gen. 3:6). Because of his covenant headship as representative of the whole human family, only Adam the man could decide the future destiny of humanity, including that of the woman (Rom. 5:12); yet it was the woman who fell into the temptation and was first to be deceived by the lies of the evil one. This fatal involvement of the woman in the first transgression is another reason (see verse 13) why the apostle forbids women to teach and rule in the church. She is to exercise her gifts and ministries in co-operation with men, and under their overall supervision.

Just as Adam's action has affected all those who have come after him in history (Rom. 5:12), so Eve's action has affected all women in an adverse way (Gen. 3:16). She was a representative or prototype woman, with the result that her action has helped to settle the place and role of women ever since. Her part in the fall of humanity does not, however, jeopardise her place in salvation as a full member in the family of God through Jesus Christ (Gal. 3:28).

But women will be kept safe through childbirth (verse 15) is a gracious concession given to women by God the Judge and Saviour (see Genesis 3:15). These words promise Christian women that God will reverse the judgement pronounced on the woman (Gen. 3:16) by overcoming the pains of childbirth experienced as a penalty for sin. Instead, she will be kept safe (literally 'saved', see 4:10 for a similar use of the word), in the sense that the Lord will watch over her in childbirthing. The child-bearing role of the woman (1 Tim. 5:14; Tit. 2:4f.) was hallowed by God when he promised that one day a child would be born of a woman (Gal. 4:4f.). This child of the woman would fatally strike the serpent who had deceived the woman (Gen. 3:15). In this way the woman would be revenged and she herself would be saved.

The promise of safety through childbirth is only valid **if they continue in faith, love and holiness with propriety**. These four virtues describe a few of the essential qualities of the Christian, believing woman. The promises of God never stand alone, they always work in association with his commands and the responsibilities of believers. Christian women will only be finally secure if they continue in the faith and persevere in their obedience to the end (Matt. 24:13; Col. 1:23). Mary the mother of Jesus would be a good example of the type of woman Paul has in mind. Paul's teaching assumes that the child-bearing and maternal role is normal for the woman, especially as she has come to faith in Jesus Christ as her Saviour.

Study questions

Verse 8: What other attitudes and moral qualities are necessary in praying? (Psa. 66:18; Matt. 18:19f.; Mark 11:23ff.; Eph. 6:18)

Does our posture in prayer really matter? (Psa. 51:17; Mark 14:35; Acts 7:59f.; 20:36; Rev. 5:14)

Verse 12: Granting the restrictions on women teaching and ruling the congregation, what other forms of ministry are open to women? (Acts 1:14; 16:14ff.; Phil. 4:3; 1 Tim. 3:11; 5:9f., 14, Tit. 2:3f.)

Verses 13-14: What other, related truths about men and women come out of the narrative of the creation and the fall in Genesis 1-3? (Matt. 19:3-6; 1 Cor. 11:7-12; 2 Cor. 11:2f.)

1 TIMOTHY: CHAPTER 3

In this chapter Paul continues to address organisational matters in the church at Ephesus. Having already prescribed for public worship, including the respective functions of men and women (2:1-15), he now states the qualifications for overseers (3:1-7) and deacons (3:8-13), after which Paul confesses the mystery of the church's faith (3:14-16).

Overseers (3:1-7)

Here is a trustworthy saying introduces the second of those Christian sayings scattered through the Pastorals in five places (1 Tim. 1:15; 3:1; 4:9; 2 Tim. 2:11; Tit. 3:8). They are semi-confessional in form and trustworthy in what they say, because they popularise different kinds of evangelical truth. This one is about church order and the authoritative position of the pastoral overseer.

If anyone sets his heart on being an overseer. The **overseer** or supervisor appears to have been the fundamental church functionary in the apostolic age. The position of overseer or presbyter or elder (since the terms are interchangeable, see Acts 20:17, 28; Titus 1:5, 7; 1 Peter 5:1f.), was, as the name suggests, one of responsibility for the spiritual welfare of the congregation. Its origins are in the Old Testament, where the elders of Israel were representatives of the people in local and national councils. Following the growth of the Jewish state in the inter-testamental period, the elders of the people became an influential part of the high court called the Sanhedrin in Jerusalem (see Exodus 19:7f.; 24:9; Numbers 11:16f.; 1 Kings 12:6ff.; 2 Chronicles 34:29; Ezra 6:14; Matthew 26:57; 27:1; Acts 4:5f., 21). Because it was so much a part of the theocratic government of Israel, the eldership passed over in a very natural way into the organisation of the Christian churches (Acts 14:23; 15:6, 22f.; Phil. 1:1; Tit. 1:5). The prominence that Paul gives it suggests that it was intended to be the standard type of leadership in the post-apostolic church (1 Tim. 3:15). According to the New Testament, a body of elders supervising the local congregation is the appropriate form of church order.

Becoming a local overseer is not about promoting one's own interests or seeking power, it is about an individual wanting to serve the congregation by using those particular gifts and qualities which the Lord has given him. Peter elsewhere warns against selfish and materialistic motives in carrying out the elder's tasks (1 Pet. 5:2f.). Behind the desire to be an overseer should lie a divine awakening and leading. But this desire on the part of an individual must be confirmed by the church on the visible evidence of certain qualities which the apostle is about to describe.

Where the right motive is present, a candidate for the eldership can be sure that **he desires a noble task**. The elder's task is literally a 'work' which involves commitment and labour in the Lord's service (1 Tim. 5:17f.; 2 Tim. 2:15). It is not therefore a position for the lazy or self-indulgent. Yet it is a noble work which carries its own inherent dignity and attractiveness, because it is performed in the name of the Lord Jesus Christ and brings about the welfare of the whole church (Acts 20:28; 1 Pet. 5:2ff.).

Now the overseer must be above reproach (verse 2) which means that he must be free from scandalous sins and any offensive habits that would lay him open to public criticism (Tit. 1:6). He cannot be sinless, but he must commend the Christian way of life by his own mature qualities and exemplary behaviour under all circumstances. The sentences that follow unfold in a number of specific ways the actual meaning of being *above reproach*.

First of all he must be **the husband of but one wife.** This is a notoriously difficult phrase (also in 1 Tim. 3:12; Tit. 1:6) which could mean that:

• the pastoral leader must not have been married more than once under any circumstances. But Paul does not forbid second marriages so long as they are to fellow Christians (Rom. 7:3; 1 Cor. 7:8f., 39).

• the overseer must not be a bigamist or polygamist, that is, he must be married to only one wife at a time. This is the most natural way to read the phrase, and was so understood by the earliest commentators who stood nearer to the original cultural context than we do.

• the overseer must be sexually faithful to his wife and avoid any extra-marital affairs. This interpretation takes the words in a metaphorical, non-literal way. It includes the second view since marital faithfulness automatically cuts off multiple marriage partners.

Each of these three interpretations has its own difficulties but on balance the third makes the best sense, and has the advantage of including the second in it. It is also in line with general New Testament teaching about the purity of marriage (Heb. 13:4). The overseer must mirror for the congregation the highest standards of marital-sexual behaviour. At the same time there is nothing said or implied that would exclude from church office a divorcee or remarried man, provided his divorce and remarriage were conducted in accordance with biblical teaching (Matt. 5:31f.; 19:8f.; Rom. 7:2f.; 1 Cor. 7:8-15). The nature of the overseer's work, and the qualities required for it, make it clear that the overseer should normally be married and a family man (see verses 4 and 5).

Temperate, self-controlled, respectable are three closely related qualities which it is impossible to differentiate sharply. 'Temperate' is about being mentally alert, 'self-controlled' is about having the mastery of one's natural reactions, and 'respectable' is about living a life that bears up under public scrutiny. Being **hospitable** is a requirement of all Christians (Rom. 12:13), but the congregational leaders were to give the lead in meeting the social and travelling needs of fellow-Christians in the early communities (Heb. 13:2; 1 Pet. 4:9). This meant offering bed and board to Christians travelling around the empire (Acts 16:14f.;

21:7f.; 28:13f.). Hospitality can also be a means of evangelism.

Finally, the overseer must be **able to teach** as part of his role as congregational leader. While some of the elders spent their whole time in teaching and preaching, and were remunerated for their labour (1 Tim. 5:17f.), all the elders had to be able to defend and commend their faith publicly (2 Tim. 2:24; Tit. 1:9). This was because sound teaching is indispensable for the well-being and growth of the congregation as the church of the living God (1 Tim. 3:15).

Not given to much wine (verse 3) is not a demand for total abstinence (1 Tim. 5:23), but means that the overseer must be free from any addiction to alcohol. In the modern context this should include drugs and other addictive stimulants. Drunkenness was no less common in the ancient world than in the modern, and could affect Christians as well as others (1 Cor. 11:21). It is a work of the flesh which results in a loss of self-control, whereas the Christian ought to show that control of his words and actions which is given by the Holy Spirit (Eph. 5:18).

Not violent but gentle is an absolute requirement for one called to follow the example of Christ, the gentle Shepherd (1 Pet. 5:3f.) who was himself meek and lowly in heart, and invited the weary and burdened to come to him for rest (Matt. 11:28; 2 Cor. 10:1). Gentleness, rather than physical force, will always elicit the desired response of trust, respect and affection from the congregational members. This quality of gentleness, and the renunciation of violence that it implies, applies first of all to the home-life of the overseer in his treatment of his wife and children.

The next quality, **not quarrelsome,** differs from the last qualification by focusing on the overseer's habits of speaking as distinct from his way of behaving. The quarrelsome overseer is a contradiction in terms, since he offends wherever he goes, and so destroys the very work that he is supposed to be building up. Instead of being quarrelsome, the overseer must be kind and patient in the way he speaks to everyone, gently instructing those who oppose God's Word (2 Tim. 2:24f.).

Finally, the overseer must be **not a lover of money,** which includes both a craving for money itself, and the lavish kind of lifestyle that money can buy (Heb. 13:5). The overseer must show himself to be a responsible steward, both of his own and of the church's monies, by investing and using them wisely (Luke 19:12-26). At the same time he must show by his personal attitudes and public record that his own trust and hope are in God, who continually sets him free from the sort of materialistic cravings and schemes that corrupt and destroy others (1 Tim. 6:9f.).

He must manage his own family well (verse 4). The reason for this requirement becomes clear in the next verse. The overseer is a manager first of his own family, then of the family of God. The same description appears in 1 Timothy 5:17 and Romans 12:8, and highlights the aspect of total leadership involved in this role. But it is not the manager of a company that the overseer is called to be, rather the manager of people, with the goal, not of larger company profit margins, but of spiritual growth in the life and faith of the congregation.

The further explanation – **and see that his children obey him with proper respect** – is literally 'having his children in submission with all reverence'. The father is responsible for the submission and obedience of his children. The attitude and behaviour of the children is therefore a good test, though not infallible, of the parental competence of the man. But if children are to obey and be in submission, then they must be taught to recognise in their father a God-given authority which they are bound to respect (Eph. 6:1-3; Col. 3:20). In a well-run family their submission and obedience will be willing, relatively free from rebellion and self-will. The spiritual reasoning behind this qualification now follows.

(If anyone does not know how to manage his own family, how can he take care of God's church?) (verse 5) is a question that contains its own answer. The family is a microcosm of the local congregation, just as the congregation can be considered as an extended or larger family of God (Eph. 2:19). The same sorts of skills of supervision and leadership are required for both. Family life is the natural training-ground for church leaders, so that if a man appears to lack competence, sensitivity or wisdom in the lesser sphere of his own family, it should send a clear signal to the congregation that he will not likely succeed in the larger and more prestigious household of God's church.

He must not be a recent convert (verse 6) is a sensible requirement, though the length of time before a person should be entrusted with official oversight is not stated. That this period could not always have been lengthy appears from the apostle's practice of appointing elders in all the churches which he had founded, sometimes after what could only have been months after the church was founded (Acts 14:21ff.). A recent convert is like a seedling (literally 'neophyte', a horticultural word), just planted out, and needing to grow and to receive constant attention and nurture (1 Cor. 3:6).

But the regulation is wise, **or he may become conceited and fall under the same judgement as the devil**. The Bible frequently uses classic cases of good and evil as a comparison for later times. Here Paul alludes to the fall of Satan when he came under the judgement of God (Luke 10:18; Rev. 12:9f.). In a similar way, the young convert may fall from a position of trust and responsibility within the congregation. The root cause in both cases is the same: the sin of pride and vanity, involving the inflation of the ego ('conceited' means being puffed up and becoming blinded as a result, Rom. 12:3; 1 Tim. 6:4; 2 Tim. 3:4).

He must also have a good reputation with outsiders (verse 7) because the opinion of unbelievers, based possibly on long and close observation, is an important guide to a man's real worth and his suitability for church office. Also worth considering is the fact that the world forms its opinions of the church largely by the conduct and character of its leaders. Thus the candidate for eldership must prove himself trustworthy in the two related spheres of the home and the community.

This precaution is **so that he will not fall into disgrace,**

and into the devil's trap. If he falls into scandalous sin, or turns out to be defective in some serious way for a position of trust, then he will fall into public disgrace, and the church with him. As well as falling into disgrace, he will fall into the trap set by the devil (2 Tim. 2:26), who is like a hungry lion prowling around for prey (1 Pet. 5:8), and who loves nothing better than to pull down church leaders (Luke 22:31f.).

Study questions

Verse 1: What is the relationship between gifts and offices in the New Testament? (Acts 6:2-6; 13:1ff.; 14:21ff.; Rom. 12:3-8; 1 Cor. 12:4-11, 28ff.; 14:6, 26; 1 Tim. 4:14; Heb. 13:7, 17).

Verses 2-7: What other qualities, not mentioned in this passage, do you think are desirable in church leaders? (Jos. 1:6-9; Isa. 6:5-8; Dan. 3:16ff.; Matt. 13:52; Acts 11:22ff.; 20:28ff.; Phil. 2:19ff.; Col. 4:12f.).

Verses 4-5: How does the Bible define the family, and what does it say about its importance and role? (Gen. 1:27f.; 2:18, 21-24; Lev. 20:13; Matt. 1:18-21, 24f.; Acts 2:38f.; 1 Cor. 7:14; Eph. 5:22-6:4; 1 Tim. 5:1f., 4, 14, 16).

Deacons (3:8-13)

The word 'deacon' is used in a variety of settings in the New Testament. The role of the deacon involves service of a practical kind, such as serving tables or washing feet. Since Christianity is based on the servant example of Jesus Christ, deacon is the standard term for every kind of Christian worker (Rom. 16:1; 1 Cor. 3:5; Col. 4:7; 2 Tim. 4:5, 11). Paul frequently uses it to describe his own ministry as an apostle (2 Cor. 3:6; Col. 1:23). But it does also get used, in a specialised sense, to refer to a group of people who were set apart for a particular role as servants of the local church visiting and distributing the material goods of the church. This is the sense in which it appears here in 1 Timothy.

The work of the **deacons** appears to have been supplementary to that of the overseers, so that the overseers are bracketed with the deacons (Phil. 1:1). The deacons **likewise** require certain qualities which presumably are particularly relevant to the nature of their work. They are **to be men worthy of respect**, a description already used about Christians in general (2:2) and about the presbyters in particular (3:4).

Three qualities are noted using a negative format, the first of which is **sincere**, (literally 'not double-tongued'). This shows that deacons have to be absolutely trustworthy and consistent in their speech, not giving out conflicting information to different people as they move around the homes of the members. It is also necessary that deacons be **not indulging in much wine**, a qualification also required of the overseers (verse 3). Since Paul advises Timothy (1 Tim. 5:23) to drink wine, albeit for medicinal reasons, it is clear that Paul is opposed to the level of consumption that results in loss of self-control so that a deacon's reputation is damaged.

Finally, deacons should **not** be **pursuing dishonest gain**. Perhaps we may conclude from this that the deacons were responsible for holding and distributing the church's finances, and were to resist temptations to misappropriate the funds entrusted to their management. Whereas the presbyters were not to love the money paid to them (verse 3), the deacons were not to steal the money entrusted to them.

Although the work of the deacons was more humanitarian in nature, **they must keep hold of the deep truths of the faith with a clear conscience** (verse 9). While the overseers must be ready to teach (1 Tim. 3:2; Tit. 1:9), especially those labouring in the word and teaching (1 Tim. 5:17), it is enough for the deacons simply to hold the truth faithfully in their own lives. This ensures that their practical service springs out of their faith in the gospel, and not from merely humanitarian motives.

The *deep things* of the faith is literally 'the mystery' of the faith, a favourite Pauline term (Rom. 16:25f.; 1 Cor. 2:7; Eph. 3:4f.; Col. 2:2f.). It stands for those truths of the gospel which would have forever remained unknown, had God not revealed them openly in and through the life and teaching of Jesus Christ, who is the heart of the divine mystery. Once again a good conscience is the real test of a Christian profession (1:4f., 19).

To safeguard the church's work and witness the deacons **must first be tested** (verse 10). The Greek text reads 'let them also first be tested', an order and choice of words which imply that the presbyters, as well as the deacons, were subjected to some kind of screening procedure. Common sense itself would dictate this, but the New Testament advocates the use of stringent tests before the churches make appointments (Acts 6:3; 1 Cor. 16:3; 1 Tim. 3:7). The nature and length of this probationary procedure is left to the decision of the individual churches. It follows that **then if there is nothing against them, let them serve as deacons**. No indication is given how long their tenure of office would normally last, but presumably this would continue for several years or until they resigned.

Up to this point the deacons have been men, however Paul now associates women with them in their diaconal activities. **In the same way, their wives are to be women worthy of respect** (verse 11). The word translated 'wives' may well be translated 'women', since there is no possessive adjective ('their') or definite article ('the') in the Greek. This suggests that the best translation is 'women' rather than 'wives', and that this verse is referring to those women, wives of the deacons or not, who were associated with the deacons as helpers in their work. Undoubtedly the work of the deacons would involve situations where the presence of women would be an advantage.

However, since Paul does not actually call these women 'deacons', and in verse twelve reverts to calling the men 'deacons', it is strictly more correct to regard these women not as deaconesses (particularly since this term carries connotations from a later period of the church) but women helpers, auxiliaries to the male deacons.

The close involvement of these women in the diaconal ministries of the church means that they must possess certain qualities **in the same way** as the deacons. They too must be **worthy of respect**, responsible (verse 8), **not malicious talkers** in their contacts with the members and families of the congregation, **but temperate**, self-controlled in their personal habits, **and trustworthy in everything**, which is a general qualification highlighting the large element of trust extended to the deacons and their female assistants by the congregation.

When Paul states that **the deacon must be the husband of but one wife** (verse 12), he is linking up again with what he had said in verses eight to ten, before his aside about the women in verse 11. Being the husband of but one wife (apart from inferring that the deacons like the overseers were normally married men, verse 2), points to the high value placed on the life of the home in general, and on marital integrity in particular, by the early Christians. This is underlined by the next requirement.

The deacon must manage his children and his household well, which, just like the overseers (verse 4), shows the need for parental and leadership skills in the home, before being entrusted with the special responsibilities involved in looking after the wider family of God (verse 5). Since the ancient household could include servants, as well as other family members such as grandparents, Paul is prescribing here for more than the modern nuclear family (1 Tim. 5:4, 8, 16).

Paul concludes this section about deacons by pointing out two of the principal rewards that follow faithful service. **Those who have served well** (verse 13) is Paul's way of encouraging and giving recognition to excellence among the servant-leaders of the churches (1 Tim. 3:4, 12; 4:17). Such individuals **gain an excellent standing** in the eyes of the congregation because of their loyal and loving service over many years. As a direct result they may be entrusted with greater responsibilities. The other advantage for faithful deacons is **great assurance in their faith in Christ Jesus**, which is an additional benefit to their own faith (Eph. 3:12). This results from putting faith into practice in the service of the congregation, and finding Christ faithful in giving strength to those who humbly depend on him (Phil. 4:13).

Study questions

Verses 8-13: From the qualifications listed what do you think are the practical tasks of the deacons?

Verse 8: Do you think Acts 6:1-6 records the installation of the first deacons?

Verse 11: What other activities in the full life of the church may women participate in and effectively support? (Acts 1:14; Rom. 16:1-16; Phil. 4:3; Tit. 2:3ff.; 1 Pet. 3:1f.).

The Great Mystery (3:14-16)

Paul here fills in a little of the background and purpose of the letter, but gives no clues as to his whereabouts when writing it. **Although I hope to come to you soon** expresses his usual aim to visit his congregations whenever and wherever possible so as to confirm them in their new-found faith (1 Thess. 2:17-3:10). Paul knew well the special value of being present in person to address his churches. Because this was not always possible, he developed a correspondence with many of his churches as a substitute presence. So he says **I am writing you these instructions.** In this way his letters became, both for his churches and for the churches throughout history, an extension of his apostolic authority and counsel (see 1 Corinthians 5:1-5).

When Paul adds, **so that, if I am delayed, you will know how people ought to conduct themselves in God's household** (verse 15), he is outlining the major purpose of 1 Timothy. The letter is a statement of those principles and practices which should guide God's people in their worship and behaviour as members of the family of God on earth. 1 Timothy is a reminder that Christians have not been left to make pragmatic decisions about such issues as worship, church order, Christian beliefs and morality, but have been given definite guidelines and rules to follow, both for their own welfare and for the glory of God.

The reason for these instructions lies in the nature of the church as the household (or family) of God. In this letter (3:4f.) the church finds a natural analogy in the human family. Just as every biological family has leaders, house-rules and civilities, so too does the church as the spiritual family of God.

Paul provides a fuller description of God's household when he says that it is **the church of the living God**. This language is borrowed from the Old Testament, and demonstrates the real continuity that exists between Israel in the Old Testament and the Christian church in the New Testament. The word 'church' means 'assembly', and it was used in referring to Israel as the people of God gathered together into covenant relationship with him (Acts 7:38). In a similar way, though without ethnic limits, the Christian church, through its various local assemblies, constitutes the new covenant people of God (1 Cor. 11:17ff., 33f.; 1 Pet. 2:9f.).

The God of Israel was the living God in contrast to the idols of the pagan nations, whose gods were nonentities incapable of responding to their devotees or ever rescuing them from their sin and suffering. As the living God he is the Giver of life as well as the Lord of history and of the nations. Under the new covenant era of the gospel, he makes himself known still further as the God and Father of our Lord Jesus Christ (2 Cor. 3:3; 6:16; 1 Thess. 1:9; 1 Tim. 4:10), through whom he gives eternal life to all those who trust in him (John 6:57).

Finally, an engineering metaphor is used for the church, as in Paul's other letters (1 Cor. 3:9, 16f.; Eph. 2:20ff.). As **the pillar and foundation of the truth** the church receives its true calling and identity, that is, to be the witness and upholder of God's word of truth in the world (Eph. 1:13). The truth is to be found in God's special communication of himself and his purposes in the history of Israel and in the personal history of Jesus Christ and his church, now and forever inscribed in the sacred writings of the Bible (Luke 24:27, 44; 1 Cor. 3:11; Eph. 2:20; 3:1-11). Far from the church authorising and producing the truth, it is the truth of God's revelation in Christ and Scripture that creates and authenticates the church. God's truth defines and empowers the church, never the reverse.

This leads Paul to an actual confession of the gospel but before he does so he bursts out in wonder – **beyond all question, the mystery of godliness is great**. He has already used the technical term 'mystery' for the body of revealed truths that make up the gospel message (verse 9). There he called it 'the mystery of the faith' ('the deep truths of the faith', NIV). Now he calls it the mystery of godliness because it is the gospel mystery or divine revelation which generates godliness in those who accept its message and live in obedience to it. Paul's interest in the Pastorals is in the practical and existential power of the gospel in human lives. He is no armchair theologian.

The greatness of the Christian mystery is now expressed through what is almost certainly the metred lines of an early hymn (see also Eph. 5:14; 2 Tim. 2:11-13). It consists of six lines which form three contrasting couplets. The subject of the verse of the hymn is Jesus Christ, and the lines follow roughly the saving events of his personal history as recorded in the Gospels, from incarnation to glorification.

He appeared in a body, a statement which affirms that he became truly and fully human. It recalls John's similar statement about the eternal Word (John 1:1, 14). Only as God became fully human could he truly represent us in relation to the demands of his own law (Gal. 4:4f.). Yet his becoming human did not mean that he shared personally in our sinfulness, for then he could never have saved us from our sin (Rom. 1:3; 8:3; Heb. 4:15).

Christ **was vindicated** (literally 'justified') **by the Spirit** when he rose from the dead. His death had been a miscarriage of justice, but one brought about by the sovereign plan of God (Acts 2:23). As a result he had died as a criminal at law, in the company of other criminals (Mark 15:27). The real truth of his personal innocence came to light in his resurrection, when it became clear that death could make no just claims against him (Acts 2:24). Now he was seen to be what he claimed to be – the righteous servant of God, who knew no sin of his own, but had chosen to submit himself freely to the death of the cross for the sake of his people (Acts 2:23f.; 2 Cor. 5:21; 1 Pet. 3:18). The Holy Spirit was the personal agent of the resurrection (Rom. 8:11; 1 Pet. 3:18).

Christ **was seen by angels** both before and after his resurrection, as the Gospels and Acts make clear (Mark 1:13; Luke 24:23; Acts 1:10f.). Angels are no part of a pre-scientific mythology but belong to the world of solid reality as part of God's created universe. Because of this, Christ's saving life and death affected the fortunes of angels, and the historical outworkings of his salvation continue to be the object of their intense interest (1 Tim. 5:21; 1 Pet. 1:12).

The crucified and risen Jesus **was preached among the nations,** after he ascended and the Holy Spirit descended at Pentecost, when many from the nations of the Jewish diaspora were present in Jerusalem and heard, through Peter's preaching, of Jesus' life, death, resurrection and enthronement (Acts 2:5-11, 22-36). In obedience to Christ's great commission the disciples of Jesus went everywhere preaching his word, and so did their followers (Acts 8:4; 11:19ff.). Since then Jesus Christ has continued to be preached among the nations, resulting in Christianity becoming a world religion.

Not only was Christ preached among the nations, he **was believed on in the world**. Since Pentecost there have always been those who have received him by trusting in his name. The order here is only loosely chronological.

Finally Christ **was taken up in glory**. The ascension of Jesus was the point at which he exchanged his lowly, earthly condition for a heavenly and exalted one (Luke 9:51; 24:51; Acts 1:1f., 9). The glory refers to the absolute splendour of God's presence which he inherited as the reward for his earthly obedience (John 17:5). Now he waits in heaven until the moment of his glorious reappearance as the universal Lord, the worthy recipient of all creation's praise (Phil. 2:9ff.; 1 Thess. 4:16f.; 2 Thess. 1:6-10).

Study questions

Verse 14: What uses do the New Testament writings have? (Luke 1:1-4; John 20:30f.; Eph. 3:1-7; 2 Tim. 3:15ff.; 2 Pet. 3:15f.; Rev. 1:3).

Verse 15: What images does the New Testament use for the church, and what does each one teach us? (Matt. 16:18; 18:15ff.; Acts 20:28f.; 1 Cor. 12:12-27; Eph. 2:19-22; 5:22-33; Heb. 3:16-4:10; Rev. 21:9-27).

Verse 16: What are the facts and truths of the gospel that make it great? (Matt. 1:21ff.; John 1:1-5, 14-18; Rom. 8:31-39; 1 Cor. 15:51-57; 2 Cor. 5:18-21; Eph. 1:3-14; 1 Pet. 1:3ff.; Rev. 21:1-7).

1 TIMOTHY: CHAPTER 4

Having laid down ground rules for the conduct of worship and the organisation of the leadership of the church, Paul now predicts the fortunes of the church in this age (4:1-5), and then addresses Timothy as a representative of the church's leadership in his work of pastoral oversight (4:6-16).

In Later Times (4:1-5)

Paul returns to the subject of the false teachers who were active in the city of Ephesus (see chapter 1), but now sets them within the framework of Christian prophecy. **The Spirit clearly says that** may refer to a private revelation given to Paul himself (cf. 2 Thess. 2:3-11) or to pronouncements made by Christian prophets, which had become common knowledge around the churches. Acts 11:27f.; 13:1-4; 21:10-14; and 1 Corinthians 14:1-19 illustrate the way in which the Spirit could convey such inspired messages for the guidance and upbuilding of the first assemblies of believers.

What the Spirit says concerns a 'falling away' that will take place **in later times** due to evil spirits working through religious teachers. These later times includes Paul's own day, since he is writing about these things in explanation of the false teachers at work in Ephesus. The phrase 'later times' must refer to the whole of the final period of human history (otherwise called 'the last days' or 'times', Acts 2:17f.), beginning with Christ's first advent and concluding with his second. Already in the first century those ideological, moral and spiritual tendencies were appearing that will climax in the great rejection of Christianity and in the acceptance of falsehood and wickedness at the close of the age (2 Thess. 2:1-12; 2 Tim. 3:1-5). This is consistent with the prophetic teaching of Jesus and the other apostles (Matt. 24; Mark 13; Luke 21:5ff.; 2 Tim. 3:1-5; 2 Pet. 2:1-3; 3:3-9; Rev. 13). Being forewarned in these ways by the Holy Spirit, Christians ought never to be surprised by bold, and ever new, forms of error and evil.

The Spirit's prophecy is that **some will abandon the faith**, which presupposes that the Christian faith has previously been widely propagated. The Greek verb used here gives us the English word 'apostasy' and means to fall away from a Christian way of life. Christians themselves must be constantly on their guard against apostasy by mutually encouraging each other and holding fellowship (Heb. 3:12f.; 10:23ff.). Jesus himself foretold that there will always be some people who fall away from their first acceptance of the gospel of the kingdom of God (Matt. 24:11f.; Mark 13:5f., 21f.).

These people will fall away because they will **follow deceiving spirits and things taught by demons**. Evil spirits belong to the invisible side of creation, which makes up a significant part of total reality (Mark 5:1-20; Eph. 6:11f.; Rev. 12). These demonic powers generate false systems of belief and behaviour in the human world so as to ensnare people. Some people fall unsuspecting victims to the demonic authorities because the powers of darkness operate indirectly through the plausible personalities and propaganda skills of human spokespersons who are only front-people. These representatives of diabolical error have already wilfully surrendered themselves to the lies that they peddle (2 Cor. 11:13ff.; 2 Thess. 2:9-12; 1 John 4:1-6; Rev. 13). True to their nature these evil spirits are only capable of teaching deceptions and lies, which they circulate under the guise of truth. We learn from this that behind all anti-Christian systems demonic forces are actively engaged (2 Cor. 10:3ff.; Eph. 6:10ff.).

Paul is far from laying all the blame for these teachings on the evil spirits, for **such teachings come through hypocritical liars** (verse 2). The evil spirits that are active in the propagation of false teachings and evil practices could gain nothing without the willing co-operation of human agents. The human teachers are *hypocrites* because they proclaim one message and live another, and *liars* because they propagate teachings that they know to be untrue.

They are people **whose consciences have been seared as**

with a hot iron. Conscience figures prominently in the Pastorals (1 Tim. 1:5, 19; 3:9; 4:2; 2 Tim. 1:3; Tit. 1:15). See further on 1 Timothy 1:5. Because conscience functions along with the moral law, it has a restraining effect on human behaviour under normal circumstances. But through repeated and wilful acts of sinning, conscience can become seared or deadened to such an extent that it virtually ceases to function.

Paul now gives examples of the teachings of these agents of the devil. **They forbid people to marry and order them to abstain from certain foods** (verse 3). These sorts of negative and legalistic rules have all the signs of the beginnings of the Gnostic movement of the second century. In movements of that type, the Greek dualism between the body and the spirit was married to a Christian framework of ideas. The root cause of evil and suffering was traced to the material body, its natural functions and appetites. Salvation came through the denial of such bodily functions as sex and eating. In this way the higher world of the spirit was entered and freedom enjoyed. Since the Ephesian errorists were syncretists, drawing their doctrines from a variety of sources, the prohibition about foods may have had something to do with the dietary regulations of the Mosaic law (Lev. 11).

Paul refutes these ascetic practices with the biblical doctrine of creation since foods **which God created to be received with thanksgiving** are part of the Creator's good gifts to the human race. He has provided a vegetable and meat diet for men and women since creation and the flood (Gen. 1:29f.; 9:3f.). Natural foods are therefore to be received and enjoyed with heartfelt gratitude to the divine Giver. The rejection of his natural gifts, especially for religious reasons, is a fundamental misunderstanding of the purpose of God, and an attitude of extreme ingratitude.

Thanksgiving is certainly to be expected from **those who believe and know the truth**, which is a common way in the Pastorals of referring to genuine Christians (1 Tim. 2:4; 2 Tim. 2:25). By coming to know the truth about God and his will for the whole world, Christians above all people are in a position to praise their Maker for all those natural things that he has given them so richly to enjoy (1 Tim. 6:17).

Paul reinforces his argument with a clear declaration of the goodness of God's material creation, **for everything God created is good** (verse 4). When God completed his work of creation he considered it all and pronounced it very good (Gen. 1:31). This included the very things objected to by these hypocritical liars – human sexuality and food (Gen. 1:29f.). The goodness of created things consists in the way in which they demonstrate the goodness of the Creator by meeting the needs of men and women and giving them pleasure. They further illustrate the special care God has for men and women as his image-bearers (Gen. 1:26f.; Matt. 5:45; Acts 14:17).

The deduction is obvious – **and nothing is to be rejected**. Jesus declared all foods clean in his lifetime (Mark 7:18f.), and Peter was taught the same lesson in a dramatic way (Acts 10:9-16). We learn from this that natural, material things are not the cause of moral evil or human unhappiness. Ascetic rules and practices approach the problem of human evil from the wrong direction and are based on wrong assumptions – 'Get rid of the material object and you will save the human subject'. Rather they should say – 'Change the human subject and you will correct the use of the material object' (Rom. 14:14).

Paul adds the proviso, **if it is received with thanksgiving**, which repeats the need for thanks to be expressed to God, the heavenly Giver. Here is a warrant for saying grace before meals, a habit practised by both Jesus (Mark 6:41; 8:6; 14:22f.; Luke 24:30) and Paul (Acts 27:35; 1 Cor. 10:30).

The reason why natural food should be received with thanksgiving is **because it is consecrated by the word of God and prayer** (verse 5). A prayer of thanks, like other prayers, should normally make use of the word of God in Scripture and the gospel. In so doing it should set the Christian's mind free from unreasonable fears, traditional taboos and moralistic scruples. The everyday acts of eating and drinking should then become for the believer religious acts of an enlightened faith, free from anxiety, and enjoyed in freedom (1 Cor. 10:31).

Study Questions

Verse 1: What are some of the reasons for people falling away from the Christian way of life, and what are some of the preventative measures Christians may take against this happening? (Matt. 13:18-23; 24:10-13; Gal. 6:7-10; Heb. 10:19-25; Jude 17-21).

Verse 3: What does the Bible teach about the single life? Is it right to hold up singleness as a sign of greater spirituality or as an inferior lifestyle? (Judges 11:29-40; Matt. 19:10ff.; 1 Cor. 7:1-7, 25-35; Rev. 14:1-5).

Verse 4: What else does Scripture teach us about the Creator and his creation? (Isa. 40:12-26; Acts 14:15ff.; 17:24-29; Rev. 4:9ff.).

A Good Servant of Jesus Christ (4:6-16)

The words of verse six ('a good minister of Christ Jesus') form a fitting caption for the section that follows. We should know that:

* Paul begins to address Timothy directly in the second person singular ('you'). This section is for Timothy as a teaching elder. Paul inserts another section like this in chapter six, verses eleven to sixteen.

* Paul writes to Timothy in the command form of address. This expresses the urgency of the matters being discussed and that Timothy must be insistent about them.

If you point out these things to the brothers (verse 6) is the way Timothy must proceed in the service of Christ. 'Pointing out' these things means teaching them in such a way that people can grasp them clearly for themselves and feel confident about implementing them in their own lives. 'These things' refers both to the matters discussed in the previous paragraph (verses 1-5) and to the whole teaching of the letter up to this point. 'Brothers' is a description of fellow Christians, which goes back to Jesus himself (Matt. 23:8) and the first Christians (Acts 2:44f.; 6:3; 9:17). Spiritual ties in Christ create a new family circle of relationships that transcends earthly ones (1 Tim. 6:2; 2 Tim. 4:21; 1 Pet. 5:9).

In so doing, Paul tells Timothy, **you will be a good minister of Christ Jesus**. 'Good' includes such qualities as being true to one's calling and purpose, morally excellent, praiseworthy, pleasing to God and useful. The word used for minister means 'deacon', which could be used in a technical sense (3:8-13), or, as here, generically of all who serve in Christ's name, whatever their status or Christian service may be (Rom. 12:6f.; 1 Tim. 1:12; 1 Pet. 4:10f.). It is applied to all believers (Matt. 23:11), because they are followers of Jesus who came to serve others (Mark 10:45; John 13:3-15). See further on 1 Timothy 3:8. In all his activity and service for others, the Christian minister must remember that he is serving Jesus Christ first of all and that his primary aim must be to be pleasing to him (2 Cor. 5:9).

Paul continues: **brought up in the truths of the faith and of the good teaching that you have followed**. Timothy had been nourished ('brought up') in the truths of the Scriptures from his childhood (2 Tim. 3:15) due to the godly upbringing of his mother and grandmother (2 Tim. 1:5). He had also learned to follow these truths by putting them into practice in his life. This sound teaching would now be useful to him in the demanding task of reforming the church at Ephesus. 'The words of the faith' means that the Christian faith is an objective, propositional message that can be formulated in truth statements (see also 1 Timothy 1:19; 3:9; 4:1; 5:8; 6:10, 20f.). The Scriptures, which are the source of these teachings and statements, are the Christian minister's great resource as he seeks to serve others in Christ's name.

The Christian leader must be a follower of the teaching which he has learned and teaches to others. He is always a disciple whose great aim is to transmit the received teaching of his instructor and to follow the pattern of it in his own life. Jesus Christ is the example for all his followers to copy (John 13:12-17). In this way he is the perfect teacher and they are true disciples.

Paul's first imperative is negative as he reaches back to the speculative notions of the local false teachers (1 Tim. 1:4). **Have nothing to do with godless myths and old wives' tales** (verse 7). These notions are godless or profane because they are the very opposite of everything that is sacred and useful, and are only fit to be believed by the senile and superstitious. There is only one wise and safe response to them – complete rejection. Paul distinguishes sharply between the deep religious truths taught in the Bible and the incredible stories of the gods in ancient literature.

Rather, train yourself to be godly. Instead of being sidetracked by these fantastic speculations, the Christian teacher must aim at godliness in his own life. Again the apostle contrasts the theosophical speculations of the false teachers with genuine godliness. For Paul godliness is *Godlikeness* and sums up the kind of life that God approves. Godliness is the goal of the Christian revelation, and consists in a solid moral character that is fed from the living springs of a settled faith in the living God (1 Tim. 2:2; 3:15; 6:3, 11; Tit. 1:1). With the word 'train' (English 'gymnastics') Paul introduces an athletic metaphor (1 Cor. 9:24-27) which carries over into the next verse. In contrast to the religious exercises of the groups in Ephesus, which relied on outward techniques in their programmes of personal growth, godliness is the goal of the moral disciplines of the gospel (1 Tim. 6:11f.).

The apostle does not discount physical exercise entirely, **for**

physical training is of some value (verse 8). As someone
who was more dependent than most on a strong physical consti-
tution for carrying out his missionary work, Paul must have come
to recognise the value of physical fitness (2 Cor. 11:23-28). **But
godliness has value for all things**, in comparison with physical fitness. The more enduring value of godliness consists in its
holding promise for both the present life and the life to come.
A doctrine of the two ages (Eph. 1:21) structures this statement.
According to this frame of reference the present age is domi-
nated by Satan's evil kingdom (Gal. 1:4; Eph. 2:1f.), while the
age to come is the age of the kingdom of God (2 Tim. 4:1).
Godliness holds promise for both ages because the kingdom of
God has already penetrated this present evil age and is secretly
present in its midst. This is the mystery of the kingdom of heaven
that Jesus proclaimed in many of his parables (Matt. 13:3-52;
18:23-35; 25:14-46; Mark 1:14f.). Consequently, godliness, which
is a sure sign of the kingdom's presence in a person's life, brings
its own rewards and hopes for the believer in both ages (Mark
10:29f.). Godliness gives believers the best of both worlds. By
contrast the benefits of physical exercise belong exclusively to
this age.

This is a trustworthy saying that deserves full acceptance
(verse 9) is the third of the faithful sayings of the Pastorals (1
Tim. 1:15; 3:1; 2 Tim. 2:11; Tit. 3:8). It is uncertain whether this
saying should go with verse 8, in which case it closes that paragraph, or (as in the NIV) with verse 10, in which case it opens a
new paragraph.

Paul's athletic imagery resurfaces here when he affirms **(and
for this we labour and strive)**. The subject of this parenthetical
statement is godliness, and the promise of life that goes with it
(verse 8). Paul speaks in the first person plural for all true disciples of Christ, who give clear evidence of the sincerity of their
faith throughout their lives by relentlessly pressing toward the
goal (for it is not easily achieved) of their heavenly calling in
Christ Jesus (Phil. 3:12-15).

The content of the faithful saying is **that we have put our hope in the living God**. The tense of the Greek verb conveys the thought that Christian hope in God is an attitude that needs to be constantly renewed, as new trials emerge to test the Christian's stamina (Psa. 42:11; 2 Cor. 1:9f.; Heb. 10:23). Hope is well-placed in God, since he is the living or true God (1 Tim. 3:15; 6:17; Acts 14:15; 1 Thess. 1:9), who is well able to give life and strength to those who wait for him (Isa 40:30f.). Because of this he himself is the God of hope who encourages his people to be filled with hope in him (Rom. 15:13). Jesus Christ is the object and mediator of this hope (Col. 1:27; 1 Tim. 1:1).

This God of hope is at the same time the one **who is the Saviour of all men, and especially of those who believe**. 'Saviour' and 'salvation' are words that can sometimes denote physical safety and the preservation of life (Luke 6:9; Acts 27:31). In the same way the verb 'to save' is often used for the healing miracles of Jesus and the apostles (Luke 18:42; Acts 14:9). Because of the comparison ('especially') here with those who believe, 'Saviour' here must refer to something other than eternal salvation since there are no degrees of such salvation, a person is either saved or not. God as the Saviour must mean that he is rich in mercy to all sorts of people (see 1 Tim. 2:1, 4, 6), preserving their lives and blessing them with food and gladness (Acts 14:17). Believers are the special recipients of this fatherly attention and protection.

This confession of God's care for the whole human family is an example of what has been called God's common or general grace. He does not give the gifts of salvation to everyone, but he does show to everyone some measure of his kindness in the course of everyday life. Men and women are totally undeserving of this kindness because of their sin, which is why it must be called grace. Unlike God's saving grace, his general grace falls short of actually bestowing on people the gift of eternal life (Acts 14:17; 17:24-28). Yet it is such a definite and clear witness to his existence, sovereignty and goodness (Matt. 5:44-48) that it is inexcusable for anyone to fail to be thankful to him, or to fail to worship and serve him (Rom. 1:21).

God's providential care is true **especially of those who believe**, because their relationship to God rests on an entirely different footing to that of unbelievers. Unbelievers are under God's law, believers are under his grace; unbelievers are without Christ and without hope, believers are united to Christ and abound in hope. Believers are children of the covenant and members of the family of God in Christ. For them he works everything together for good in his loving and eternal purpose (Rom. 8:28ff.). God is their Father, Christ is their Brother, the Holy Spirit is their Sanctifier, and God's infallible providence surrounds and keeps them. No-one is nor could be more secure or cared for than believers.

Timothy must **command and teach these things** (verse 11). This is the same word ('command') as in 1 Timothy 1:3, and sounds the same high note of pastoral authority. The reason for this firm charge to Timothy appears in the next verse. Commanding and teaching are different parts of the pastoral leader's role, but they are inseparable because they have the same referent, the Word of God. *Commanding* means enforcing the duties of the Christian faith, *teaching* means explaining them and the religious foundation on which they rest. Commanding comes first here perhaps because the Ephesian situation had greater need of it; likewise the pastoral leader must be able to respond to situations that may need more exhortation or instruction as the case may be. But in the normal course of things commanding will involve teaching, and teaching will involve commanding. Christian theology and ethics are one.

Don't let anyone look down on you because you are young (verse 12) is another very personal word of advice to Timothy. Since youth in the ancient world could include anyone up to forty years of age, we may suppose that Timothy was in his early or middle thirties. Ancient culture generally admired age before youth. The problem of relative inexperience was compounded for Timothy because of his sensitive personality which naturally made him withdraw from stressful situations (1 Cor. 16:10f.). The generation gap can prove a real hurdle for a younger minister, particularly in his first congregation, where individuals among the elders or from the congregation may use it to devalue his teaching and undermine his authority.

The best answer is for the young pastor to take the initiative – **but set an example for the believers in speech, in life, in love, in faith and in purity.** Timothy is to lead by example. This way he will stand the best chance of silencing his critics and the sceptics. Paul constantly aimed to model the gospel for his converts and churches, and never tired of exhorting others in leadership positions to do the same (Phil. 3:17; 2 Thess. 3:9; Tit. 2:7). Seeing the gospel lived out in practice is a powerful stimulant to imitation, and a dissuasion to criticism. Christian leaders must practise what they preach if they are to see what they preach practised.

Paul highlights five areas where Christian example is called for in a special way. The first two touch on Timothy's public life, the other three on his inner life:

• *Speech* and *life* refer to Timothy's audible and visible social presence in everyday situations. The preacher's words and actions must match his preaching.

• *Love* is the crowning Christian grace (Col. 3:14) because it is an extension of God's own love for his people. It is always owed (Rom. 13:8) and is nearly always successful (1 Cor. 13:4-7, 13).

• *Faith* could stand for faithfulness (Gal. 5:22), in which case it refers to the trust and dependability that should be shown in all of life's relationships and responsibilities.

• *Purity* includes the sexual purity that is always expected from the Christian leader (1 Tim. 5:1f.), but it also refers to his moral integrity in general (2 Cor. 6:6).

By cultivating these kinds of personal qualities, Timothy (and any young pastor) will offset the disadvantages of age.

Again the apostle mentions his hope of returning to Ephesus, and how his letter is meant as an interim statement to Timothy (1 Tim. 3:14f.). **Until I come, devote yourself to the public reading of Scripture, to preaching and to teaching** (verse 13). Here Timothy is given a set of practical priorities to which he needs to devote himself entirely. These terms describe some of the central activities of Christian worship. The fact that each one carries its own definite article ('the') in the Greek text (cf. Acts 2:42) indicates that they were already clearly defined.

• The *public reading* of Scripture was taken from the Jewish synagogue service (Luke 4:16-20; Acts 13:14f.). In time, readings from the Gospels and Epistles began to be added to those from the Law, the Prophets and the Writings of the Old Testament (Col. 4:16; 1 Thess. 5:27). A special blessing for reader and hearer alike was attached to this public reading of Christ's Word (Rev. 1:3).

• *Preaching* is here 'exhortation', a term that was widely used for sermonising. It was based on a passage of Scripture, which could be the one read out in the service (Acts 13:15; 15:21). Hebrews may be a good example of this kind of exhortatory preaching, since it speaks of itself as a word of exhortation (Heb. 13:22). Consequently it may be made up of a series of sermons based on Old Testament passages pointing to Christ and his people. It is certainly full of pastoral exhortations.

• *Teaching* was closely connected with preaching in congregational worship (Rom. 12:7f.). The Christian teacher is responsible for faithfully transmitting the inspired Word of God and the traditional teaching connected with it. The teacher is not expected to add anything to it, but only to explain its meaning and the applications it might have in new life situations.

Among other things this responsibility includes the pastoral teacher looking out for trustworthy men to whom he can entrust the apostolic teachings, so that they will be able to teach others after them (2 Tim. 2:2).

Paul continues to motivate Timothy by telling him, **Do not neglect your gift** (verse 14). This is presumably the *charisma* or gift of leadership in teaching. Timothy is in danger of neglecting to develop and use his gift through timidity, or undue deference to those who were older or more experienced. The leadership gifts of the Spirit must be continually stirred up by a deliberate effort on the part of those who have received them (2 Tim. 1:6). Only through constant use will they develop fully and be effective.

This is the only mention of *charisma* in the letter, a fact which is in striking contrast to Paul's first letter to the Corinthians. The relative absence of any mention of or interest in the miraculous gifts of the Spirit in the Pastorals has been taken to mean that they were already beginning to disappear from the churches with the passing of the apostles. Instead Paul outlines the grace-gifts of Christian character which all leaders of the church must possess and show (1 Tim. 3:1-13).

Timothy's special gift is one **which was given you through a prophetic message**. This is another reminder to Timothy of the divine approval that was placed on his future ministry in the gospel (1 Tim. 1:18). At the time of his being set apart for his ministry, a prophetically inspired utterance was given about him in confirmation of his calling by God to the work (Acts 13:1ff.).

The fact that this happened **when the body of elders laid their hands on you** shows that symbolical forms of appointment to special ministries were used from the beginning of the apostolic age. This rite goes back to Old Testament times, when individuals were set apart for the special service of the Lord in this way. It seems to have signified three things:

• Consecration to the service of God (Acts 6:5f.; 13:2f.).

• The promise of the Holy Spirit for service (Deut. 34:9).

• The transfer of divine authority (Num. 27:18-23).

Paul claims to have participated in this act of ordination (2 Tim. 1:6), perhaps playing a leading role because he was an apostle as well as a father figure in Timothy's life and work. There is no conflict between Paul's participation and that of a number of representative elders from the churches.

'The body of elders' is a singular, collective word in the Greek, and shows that the local elders acted together in a body of authoritative leadership. This follows the practice in Israel. See comments above on 1 Timothy 3:1. This council of elders may have belonged to a single congregation, or it may have included elders from a number of congregations gathered for the special occasion of Timothy's setting apart. The council of Jerusalem illustrates the way in which elders and teachers from local churches in different regions could confer and reach decisions on matters of mutual concern, which were binding on all the local churches represented (Acts 15:1-16:4).

Be diligent in these matters; give yourself wholly to them (verse 15) is another call to Timothy to be totally committed to the task before him. Nothing less than complete consecration will bring about the sorts of results that the Christian leader is committed to see. Paul's intention is clear – **so that everyone may see your progress.** Commitment in the Lord's service should and will always show, though it should never be showy. There is a law of return here. Persistent commitment in practice will produce personal growth and greater confidence in doing the Lord's work. As God's people see the spiritual progress of their young pastor they will be spurred on to persevere themselves and to grow in grace as well. Paul applies the same law of return to the deacons (1 Tim. 3:13).

The final words of caution are, **Watch your life and doctrine closely** (verse 16). In order of priority Timothy's concern should be first for his own life, then for his public teaching. Only as his own life is spiritually correct will his doctrine be effective. This is not selfishness but sanity, because it is only as the Christian leader keeps his own faith and morals in order that he can possibly help to save and build up others. Doctrine alone is not enough, for it must be powered by a blameless life (1 Tim. 3:2).

The Lord's servant must **persevere in them**. This is a reference to all those pastoral instructions given by Paul in this section (1 Tim. 4:6-16), **because, if you do, you will save both yourself and your hearers**. Adhering strictly to Paul's apostolic principles will bring about Timothy's own salvation, as well as the salvation of those entrusted to his oversight. Unless he preaches to himself as well as his people he may prove to be disqualified (1 Cor. 9:27) for real usefulness in the Lord's service even while retaining the outward trappings of leadership. Godly ministers and their faithful preaching are the Lord's appointed means used to save his people. These same principles and norms have been written down in this letter for the instruction and comfort of all God's servants in the hope that they too will choose to follow Paul's faith and example.

Study Questions

Verse 10: In what ways does God show himself to be the Saviour of his creation? (Psalm 145; Matt. 5:44f.; Acts 14:17; 17:25-28).

Verse 12: What does the New Testament say about Christ being the supreme example for believers? (John 13:12-15.; 1 Cor. 11:1.; Eph. 5:1f.; Phil. 2:3-8; 1 Pet. 2:21ff.).

Verse 16: Why is sound doctrine essential for salvation? (Matt. 16:6-12; Acts 4:10ff.; Rom. 6:17f.; 1 Cor. 1:17-24; Gal. 1:6f.).

Paul addresses a series of pastoral problems connected with groups within the congregation.

The Church As Family (5:1-2)

To help Timothy with his pastoral relationships Paul uses the analogy of a human family, where there is a father, a mother, brothers and sisters. If Timothy relates to the congregational members in the way he would treat his own family members, then he will be greatly helped to know how to approach each of them in appropriate ways and without awkwardness to himself or to them. This comparison of the local church to a human family is a helpful one, because it takes into account differences in gender and age and is able to cater for these in practice. It has the added advantage that it is easy to put into practice.

Do not rebuke an older man harshly (verse 1). As a younger man Timothy needed advice about how to deal with both his elders and his peers within the congregation. Older men presented a special difficulty since they had age and experience on their side. The temptation was for Timothy to become abrupt with them, or even violent, because of their possible hesitation in responding to his leadership. Paul's word 'rebuke' could be misunderstood as allowing for stand-over tactics, but he has already ruled out physical and authoritarian methods from the professional baggage of the congregational pastor (1 Tim. 3:3).

Paul's pastoral advice is, **but exhort him as if he were your father**. There may be times when the pastor must confront an erring or troublemaking older man in the Christian fellowship. In a case of that kind he must be dealt with respectfully on the basis of his seniority. Respect for the aged was a standing principle and practice in God's law (Lev. 19:32). 'Exhort' is less harsh than 'rebuke', and carries the special meaning of actually aiming to win someone over from their mistakes by means of sympathetic appeals.

So **treat younger men as brothers, older women as moth-**

ers, and younger women as sisters. Paul bore in mind that Timothy was a young man and unmarried, so he adds to his words about the last group **with absolute purity** (2 Tim. 2:22). The high incidence of cases of immorality between pastors and female members of congregations in modern times, often growing out of too intimate counselling sessions, only underlines the necessity and wisdom of this cautionary advice.

These two verses are full of excellent advice which should be of particular value to a young minister working in his first congregation. A combination of youthful idealism and impatience can too easily lead, under the impulse of a genuine spiritual enthusiasm, to the alienation of the members of his congregation. This can do irreparable damage to his own reputation and future prospects of usefulness in the service of Christ, as well as bringing the cause of Christ into disrepute.

Study Question

Verses 1 and 2: In what ways does the New Testament use the family as a model for the church? (Mark 3:31-35; Acts 16:30-34; Eph. 2:19; 1 Tim. 3:4f.)

Widows (5:3-16)
From the early chapters of Acts it is clear that from the beginning of the church there were many widows among the Christians. It may be that they chose to move to the urban centres to finish their days because the larger city churches could do more for their support. This would explain the sizeable widow groups in Jerusalem and Ephesus. The amount of space given here to the widows shows that they were not only a large group within the church, but that they presented practical problems that needed to be addressed.

Paul's advice, **give proper recognition to those widows who are really in need** (verse 3), is a call for some kind of screening process to be put in place whereby the most needy cases among the widows could be recognised and dealt with. This implies that there were counterfeit widows willing to exploit the good will of the churches for their own selfish ends. 'Giving proper recognition' literally means 'honour' and recalls the fifth commandment of the Law (Exod. 20:12). This kind of recognition is one way of keeping that commandment. It involves more than mental respect, it entails practical help, as in Acts 6:1 and 9:39.

The church could give material support, **but if a widow has children or grandchildren, these should learn first of all to put their religion into practice by caring for their own family** (verse 4). It was not thought right that the church should be forced to care for widows who could be well provided for by their own families (see further verse 16). In addition it was good for the younger generation to put their faith into practice by providing for the needs of their older relatives. The family is the original social unit created by God (Gen. 2:24), and is appointed by him for the training of all its members through mutual caring and sharing. Paul is prescribing here for Christian children, but in verse 8 he makes it clear that this kind of duty also belongs to the natural instincts of human beings in accordance with God's moral law written on their hearts (Rom. 2:14f.).

For 'to put their religion into practice' Paul uses his favourite word for summing up the Christian life in practice – godliness (1 Tim. 3:16; 4:7f.; 6:3, 5f., 11). So godliness should not be restricted to the more private domain of prayer and personal spirituality, but should appear in such concrete ways as the thoughtful and unselfish service towards the other members of one's family who are older, traumatised or dependent.

By acting in this way towards a widowed mother the family members will be discharging a lifelong obligation – **and so repaying their parents and grandparents**. When the children are dependent on the parents, it is right that the parents should provide for the children, but the roles are reversed in later years when the parents become dependent on their children. The death of one of the parents can be a special opportunity for the children to repay, in loving and practical ways, some of the care bestowed on them in earlier years. Grandparents are mentioned with parents because the ancient world knew little of the modern nuclear family. Three generations often lived together in the same house, so that grandparents took an active share in the upbringing of the children (Timothy's own case in 2 Timothy 1:5).

But the greatest incentive for this kind of extended family care was a religious one, **for this is pleasing to God**. One of the criteria for helping the Christian to decide what is morally good is the consideration of what will please God (Rom. 12:1f.; Eph. 5:17). This is a general principle, but the Lord has made it perfectly plain in his written Word that he commends needy members of society, like widows, to the special care of his people. This is because he himself is a God who has a special kind of compassion for those who are destitute, marginalised and vulnerable (Exod. 22:22; Deut. 10:18; 24:17, 19ff.; Psa. 68:5).

The genuine widow, who deserves the church's patrimony, is **the widow who is really in need and left all alone** (verse 5), without supportive relatives or friends. As a result **she puts her hope in God and continues night and day to pray and to ask God for help**, just as Anna did (Luke 2:36f.). The God-fearing widow will accept the loss of her earthly and human supporter as an opportunity to make the Lord her refuge in a new way, and to grow in her faith. She will devote the rest of her life to the private and public ministry of prayer, not only for her own needs, but for the needs of other members of her own family and the family of God. Her changed circumstances call for such a response of faith and hope.

But, in contrast, **the widow who lives for pleasure is dead even while she lives** (verse 6), a description found elsewhere of a church (Rev. 3:1). Instead of treating widowhood as an opportunity for a new kind of Christian service, this kind of widow seized on it as an opportunity for indulging a sensual life-style (Jas. 5:5). 'Living for pleasure' is a strong term which suggests a

wasteful and extravagant way of life, including immoral relationships. Obviously this kind of person did not warrant the church's
support.

Repeating his advice in other parts of this letter (1 Tim. 4:6,
11) Paul again urges Timothy to **give the people these instructions, too** (verse 7). Families and individuals need to be taught
their respective responsibilities. These problem areas provide
positive openings for ministry to the pastor who is alert and eager
to train his people in godliness. Paul's aim is **so that no one may
be open to blame**, which could refer either: (1) to the widows
themselves, who by being informed of the church's standards
might be discouraged from making unreasonable demands on
the church's limited resources; or (2) to well-meaning members
of the congregation who otherwise might be eager to help unsuitable women candidates. This way all parties would be informed,
and so unable to plead ignorance of the church's requirements.
From this advice the overseers of the congregation were made
aware of the practical wisdom of making known their policies
and standards by communicating them clearly to the whole church.
Paul encouraged the practice of an open, though firm, administration in the churches.

Paul concludes the first part of this discussion about widows
in the form of a moral and religious principle. **If anyone does
not provide for his relatives, and especially for his immediate
family, he has denied the faith and is worse than an unbeliever** (verse 8). The obligation to care for one's own family members when they are in genuine hardship is a double one for church
members. Christianity preaches love as the apex of religious behaviour (Matt. 22:37-40). Since this love is for fellow human
beings in general, including even enemies (Matt. 5:43f.; Luke
10:25-37), it most certainly includes the members of a person's
own family. Jesus set the pattern of this for all time when in
circumstances of the greatest personal discomfort he made direct arrangements for his widowed mother before he died (John
19:25ff.). If even unbelievers out of natural affection care for

their own kind, how much more ought Christians, who claim to know the God of compassion! The failure to make proper provisions for ailing and aging family members is a practical denial of the faith, and exposes a person to the criticisms even of non-Christians (1 Cor. 5:1).

The way Christians treat their family members should differ markedly from that of non-Christians. In many cases aged or dependent parents are abandoned in nursing/old people's homes (granny-dumping), where they do not receive the attention and affection that they need and deserve. Christians who have had abusive or neglectful parents will find it particularly difficult to respond to Paul's ethic here. But the healing mercies of God's grace in Jesus Christ can enable even traumatised children to extend forgiveness and to show honour to unworthy parents in their later years.

Here follows a list of qualifications that widows need to have if they are to be put on the list of those eligible for the church's support. **No widow may be put on the list of widows unless she is over sixty** (verse 9). This has been taken as evidence that Paul is creating an order of widows for specific ministries within the congregation, even instituting another office within the church. But:

• an order of widows post-dates the apostolic age and has to be read back into this biblical passage.

• the role of these widows here and elsewhere is passive, not active. They are recipients of the church's aid, not workers, in the church's service.

• the action words describing the qualifications of these widows (verse 10) all belong to the past tense, whereas they would be in the present tense if Paul was calling for candidates for a new office.

• if widows were a new office in the church, Paul would have listed them with the elders and deacons in chapter 3.

Paul is proposing a number of criteria for identifying those women who would be worthy candidates for the patrimony of the church. By setting an age limit of sixty, Paul was preventing younger widows from making use of the church's generosity for a time, before opting out and marrying again.

It is further required that she **has been faithful to her husband**. This is the NIV interpretation of the phrase 'wife of one husband'. The similar expression 'husband of one wife' has been explained at 1 Timothy 3:2 and 12 where it was understood to be referring essentially, as here, to marital faithfulness. This qualification was important in showing that she was likely to be the kind of person who would take seriously any vows not to remarry.

The widow eligible for church aid **is well-known for her good deeds, such as bringing up children, showing hospitality, washing the feet of the saints, helping those in trouble and devoting herself to all kinds of good deeds** (verse 10). These qualifications illustrate the sorts of caring and practical ministries expected of Christian women. Good deeds are enjoined on all Christians (Eph. 2:10; Tit. 2:14), but widows seeking the endorsement of the church needed to have a record of good works as godly women and mothers. These good works are now itemised. 'Bringing up children' suggests that they have successfully managed to work through the rigourous demands of being a mother and homemaker. 'Hospitality' and 'washing the feet of the saints' point to an open house where visitors and travellers were always welcome in the Lord's name (Rom. 12:13; Phil. 22). The feet-washing could be literal or metaphorical: Jesus encouraged both by his own example (John 13:3-17). Finally the worthy widow would have helped all kinds of people troubled in mind and body, and generally have been known for her devotion to good works.

So the account closes as it began with an emphasis on good works, since Christianity is nothing if it is not practical. These works are considered to be the visible proof of the widow's living faith in God (Tit. 2:4f.), and evidence of her worthiness to receive the church's support. Having served others throughout her life, the time has now come for her to receive in turn from others.

As for younger widows, do not put them on such a list (verse 11). Paul warns against including younger widows on the list of those eligible for church support, for biological and religious reasons. **For when their sensual desires overcome their dedication to Christ, they want to marry.** The natural urge to marry will return to these younger women, with the very real danger (a reality in some cases, see verse 15) that their natural desires will overrule their religious ones. This happened when these younger women were so bent on marriage that they were willing to marry even unbelievers. As a result their new marriages would actually lead them away from Christ.

Thus, that is, by wanting to remarry or actually remarrying, **they bring judgement on themselves, because they have broken their first pledge** (verse 12). The judgement that these younger women bring on themselves is God's active response to their wilful disobedience in marrying unbelievers. In doing so they have broken their first pledge, literally their first 'faith'. This must refer to their original faith-commitment to Christ as Lord of their lives, including their married lives.

But there are other dangers involved in enlisting younger widows. **Besides they get into the habit of being idle and going about from house to house** (verse 13). This results from their extra free time and undisciplined energies. Their desires and circumstances make them restless, and they are unable to resist the social temptations that confront them in home-visiting. **And not only do they become idlers, but also gossips and busybodies, saying things they ought not to**. As they visit around the congregation they fall into the temptation to gossip and to interfere in other people's business. They make provocative statements or pass on confidential information. As a result the whole congregation may be destabilised.

So I counsel younger widows to marry (verse 14) is Paul's realistic advice in these circumstances, and proves his own commitment to marriage as an institution of God. In 1 Corinthians 7 (especially verses 7-9) he also commends the single life, but recognises that sexual self-control is God's gift to some Christians and not to all.

Nor does he advise them only to marry but also **to have children**. When God created men and women he also commanded them to be fruitful and multiply (Gen. 1:26-28). This creation mandate has never been withdrawn, and Christian women can honour it in practice with greater reason than non-Christians because of their personal knowledge of God the Creator in Christ. Child-bearing is not the only, or even the primary, purpose of marriage (Gen. 2:18), but it is certainly a natural and significant part of it.

Again, they are **to manage their homes**, which translates a Greek verb that points to authoritative rule within the home. This ruling function of the Christian wife does not infringe on the supreme authority of the husband (Tit. 2:4f.), but it indicates that she has been given a large sphere of influence and freedom in the area of home-making and child-rearing.

And to give the enemy no opportunity for slander is a frequent refrain of Paul's in his genuine concern for the public image of the gospel and the church (1 Tim. 6:1; Tit. 2:5, 8). The enemy is the devil (Eph. 6:11f.; 1 Pet. 5:8; Rev. 12:13-17), but he uses men and women as his agents to raise trouble for the church (Acts 8:1; 12:1ff.; Tit. 2:8). Christians and churches ought to be concerned for a scrupulously clean image in the eyes of the world, based on consistent Christian practice in all departments of their corporate and individual life and work. This applies to all groups within the congregation, especially those who are married.

Paul's cautionary words are based on local knowledge, since **some have in fact already turned away to follow Satan** (verse 15) . 'Turning away' (1:6) suggests that some widows have done more than just remarry, in their haste to do so they have been willing to marry non-believers, contrary to Christian standards (1 Cor. 7:39), and so to stray back into Satan's kingdom in the world (1 Cor. 5:4f.; 2 Cor. 6:14f.; 1 Tim. 1:19f.).

The apostle concludes his discussion of widows by repeating his opening advice (verse 4). **If any woman who is a believer has widows in her family, she should help them and not let the church be burdened with them** (verse 16) . The onus is on the Christian woman to show practical care by making proper arrangements for widows within their own family circle. Paul singles out the believing woman because:

• Paul is writing here on behalf of women who have lost their life partners.

• she may be herself unmarried and so in a better position to give time and effort to a destitute relative.

• she may be well-to-do (Acts 16:14f.; 17:4) and so able to provide the needed resources.

• she may be married and the one responsible for making domestic arrangements (1 Tim. 5:14; Tit. 2:4f.).

• it would not be appropriate for a man to host a widow in his home particularly if they were not closely related.

This is **so that the church can help those widows who are really in need**. If the church tried to cater for all widows, irrespective of their personal and family circumstances, then it would soon exhaust its limited resources, and widows in extreme need might miss out. For this reason Paul has proposed a system of grading based on age, family support, and individual means.

This whole passage (5:3-16) makes it clear that the early churches did not only cater for the spiritual needs of their members, but were also engaged in providing for their social and personal needs (Acts 6:1), where these could be shown to be genuine and press-

ing. In those days there were few govermental or privately funded
agencies for the relief of the poor and needy.

In the spirit of the same gospel the passage prescribes for
Christian families and local churches today, by encouraging them
to organise practical support for their most needy and dependent
members. In some parts of the world Paul's proposals may apply
directly, but even in richer countries where government services
for the poor or aged exist, the churches and their families should
do what they can to support, in material and caring ways, their
needy members. The passage in the first place is about widows,
but it can be applied quite effectively and in some of its details to
other groups within the Christian community such as the unem-
ployed, those with disabilities, the homeless and the terminally ill.

Study Questions

Verses 4, 8, 16: What social responsibilities towards the aged,
the terminally ill, those with learning difficulties, and similarly needy
members are suggested here for Christian families? (Jas. 1:27).

Verses 3, 16: What social responsibilities does the local congregation have towards the needy among its members, and how can
it meet these obligations? (Acts 6:1-4; Gal. 6:10; Phil. 4: 10-18;
Jas. 5:14f.).

Verse 14: What are some of the purposes of marriage? (Gen.
1:26ff.; 2:18, 21-24; Song 2-4; 1 Tim. 3:4f.).

Verse 14: What roles does the woman have within marriage?
(Ruth 4:13; Prov. 6:20; 31:10-31; Eph. 5:22f., 33; 1 Pet. 3:1-6).

Elders (5:17-25)
The next group that Paul prescribes for is the elders. The biblical
background of this function was discussed at 1 Timothy 3:1.
Having there described the qualifications for this position, Paul

here says something about the functions, remuneration, discipline and appointment of elders.

The elders who direct the affairs of the church well (verse 17) is a reminder that the primary function of the elders was to rule over the affairs of the congregation. The elders are essentially overseers or pastors of the local assemblies of the Lord's people. The word for 'direct the affairs of' occurs again at Romans 12:8, 1 Thessalonians 5:12, and 1 Timothy 3:4f. Paul's special interest is in those elders who excel in their work by ruling well. From these other passages we learn what this means – that the elders rule with diligence (Rom. 12:8), that they work hard and counsel the people (1 Thess. 5:12), and that they rule their own households well by having their children in reverent submission (1 Tim. 3:4f).

It is implied that the elders share the rule together as equals, since there is no mention of any one elder being above the others in status. Their authority for ruling comes from Jesus Christ as the source of all church authority because he is the sole Saviour and Head of the church. This authority is conveyed by other elders acting together, as a body or presbytery, with the laying on of hands in the appointment of new elders (1 Tim. 4:14).

Those who rule well (1 Tim. 3:13) **are worthy of double honour**. They deserve respect firstly for the position they hold (1 Thess. 5:13), but in addition for their special diligence in performing it (Phil. 2:29f.). Verse 18 suggests that this honour should take a material form of some kind. **Especially those whose work is preaching and teaching** indicates that some of the elders, in addition to directing the affairs of the congregation, also spent their time and energies labouring in the service of the Word of God and teaching, just as Paul has taught Timothy to do (1 Tim. 4:11, 13). 1 Timothy 3:2 and Titus 1:9 require all the elders to have some aptitude for teaching and defending the faith, but those who spent their whole time preaching and teaching would presumably be able to show an above average ability for this demanding and specialised work.

For the Scripture says, 'Do not muzzle the ox while it is treading out the corn' (verse 18), which is a quotation from Deuteronomy 25:4 and is quoted by Paul in 1 Corinthians 9:9f. for a similar purpose. This Mosaic law about the proper care of labouring animals enshrined a principle which applies even more to human beings. The principle is that honest labour deserves proper remuneration. In terms of church leadership this means that elders, who expend their time and energy on serving the church in public teaching and preaching, should be rewarded in the form of the church's material support. Although Paul did not always claim this right himself, it was one that he defended vigorously (1 Cor. 9:3-18).

In addition to quoting Old Testament Scripture, Paul quotes from one of the sayings of Jesus: and 'The worker deserves his wages' that makes the same point (Matt. 10:10; Luke 10:7). Here the worker deserves his bed and board in exchange for his faithful service in the work of the kingdom of God (Luke 10:8, 9). Local churches are therefore obligated to provide a living for those it appoints as pastoral leaders.

Incidentally, the fact that Paul can quote the words of Jesus alongside those from an Old Testament passage illustrates the way in which the New Testament was, already in Paul's lifetime, beginning to form a second collection of sacred and authoritative writings (canon) in addition to the Old Testament. See also Colossians 4:16; Revelation 1:3; 22:18f. Although Paul rarely quotes from Jesus' sayings, these few occasions where he does show that he was acquainted with this primary source in formulating the Christian faith. See also Acts 20:35; 1 Corinthians 7:10 (Matthew 5:32).

Do not entertain an accusation against an elder unless it is brought by two or three witnesses (verse 19). In God's covenant community of the local church, one member cannot go about slandering another individual, especially if this other member happens to be a leader of the church. The Mosaic legislation to which Paul appeals here guarded against this possibility by instituting the law of double evidence. By this law a charge against another member of the community would only be considered if two independent witnesses came forward (Deut. 17:6; 19:15). Paul applies the same standard to Christian church life, so as to prevent individuals or groups acting out of prejudice, jealousy or animosity against a church leader who might have acted justly in the discharge of his responsibilities.

The fact that Paul refers back in these two verses to the Old Testament laws for direction and support in making judicial and organisational decisions for the churches, proves that the civil laws of Israel contain principles that have ongoing validity for the Christian church (2 Cor. 13:1). Jesus followed the same practice in teaching the same principles for church discipline in controversial cases (Matt. 18:16).

If the charges are brought by more than a single witness and proven to be true then **those who sin are to be rebuked publicly** (verse 20). 'Publicly' could mean with the whole congregation present or only in the council of the elders. The gravity of the charges, and the strength of the evidence, could dictate that the whole congregation be involved in the disciplinary process as at Corinth (1 Cor. 5:1-5). Lesser offences could be better dealt with in the confidentiality of the elders' council, with the final decision either being kept within the council or communicated to the congregation.

The benefit of acting publicly is **so that the others may take warning**. Publicly confronting and penalising sin in the behaviour of church leaders acts like a deterrent on the others (Deut.13:11). The 'others' could be the other congregational members or the other elders, depending on which procedure is adopted and followed by the pastoral team. Others may be tempted to sin in the same way, and need to be restrained and forewarned of the consequences of their actions (1 Cor. 10:11f.; Gal. 6:1). Another reason for public discipline is given in 1 Timothy 1:19f.

I charge you in the sight of God and Christ Jesus and the elect angels (verse 21) is a solemn way of calling Timothy to treat his pastoral duties as a matter of conscience before God (1 Tim. 6:13f.; 2 Tim. 4:1). The church leader will be answerable in the day when Jesus Christ comes to judge the enduring quality of his servants' work (1 Cor. 3:10-15; 4:1-5; 2 Cor. 5:9f.; 1 Thess. 2:4ff.).

This is the only mention of 'elect angels' in Scripture and they are included by Paul to give added solemnity to his appeal to Timothy. God's choice of some of the angels differs from our election (Eph. 1:3f.), in that they were chosen to be prevented from participating in Satan's rebellion against God, whereas we were chosen to be saved out of our sinning, after we had joined in Satan's rebellion (Jude 6; Rev. 12:7ff.).

This solemn charge is all the more necessary because Timothy is **to keep these instructions without partiality, and to do nothing out of favouritism**. Nothing is more sacred in judicial proceedings than impartiality (Deut. 16:18ff..). Where the parties under discipline are already known to those who are making the decisions, as will normally be the case in church life, then the pressures to become either too lenient or too severe can be very great. Personal friendships or dislikes can so easily and subtlly influence a person's final judgement. Remembering and meditating on the fact that God himself is a righteous Judge who always judges justly, and that all our earthly judgements will be reviewed in the great day of judgement, should help the Christian leader to form and adhere to only honest decisions in his pastoral oversight.

Do not be hasty in the laying on of hands (verse 22) is a timely warning against rushing into choosing and appointing a man to church leadership before he has been properly tested and approved from experience. Men may be voted into leadership simply because there is no one else available, or because they have status or influence. Instead, prospective candidates should be carefully selected on the basis of their personal qualities and gifts (Acts 6:3, 5f.). Laying on hands was the usual method in the early church for transferring the authority of leadership and marking the occasion of new leadership (Acts 6:6; 13:3; 1 Tim. 4:14).

The second part of this statement really explains the thinking behind Paul's warning – **and do not share in the sins of others.** Those who lay hands on unsuitable candidates for church leadership must share, to some extent, in the blame and guilt of any scandalous sins into which these men subsequently fall. The only way to avoid this outcome is by taking the utmost care in screening candidates (1 Tim. 3:10), and by not appointing novices (1 Tim. 3:6).

On a personal note Paul advises Timothy to **keep yourself pure**, which, in the context, should be read as a call to all-round godliness, including but not confined to, sexual morality (1 Tim. 5:2). If the pastoral leader is to form sound judgements about the lives of others, then he must keep his own in good working condition through attention to sound teaching and personal godlines (1 Tim. 4:16). This is a constant refrain in the Pastoral letters.

Stop drinking only water, and use a little wine because of your stomach and your frequent illnesses (verse 23) comes as something of a surprise in the middle of a passage about elders. But these words are not so strange when we read them along with Paul's last advice to Timothy to keep himself pure. Perhaps the young missionary, in his zeal for personal holiness, was neglecting his health. The drinking water in middle eastern and Mediterranean countries can be harmful to health, so Paul advises him to avoid too strict a diet by using the wine of those areas to supplement his liquid intake. This word is a wise, middle way between total abstinence on the one hand and over-indulgence on the other (Eph. 5:18; 1 Tim. 3:8). The Lord God has created and given many natural gifts for our enjoyment and profitable use (1 Tim. 4:3f.; 6:17), but moderation, self-control and the consideration of other's welfare are the Christian rules in using them (1 Cor. 6:12; 10:23f.).

It may be that the two last verses of the chapter refer, in

general terms, to pastoral oversight of the congregational members, but they make very good sense if they are read as a concluding observation about the appointment of elders. In verse 22 Paul warned against appointing men hastily to the eldership, now he explains why. The main point is that time is the great revealer of someone's suitability or otherwise for a position of leadership. On the negative side **the sins of some men are obvious, reaching the place of judgement ahead of them; the sins of others trail behind them** (verse 24). Some men exclude themselves immediately because of their sinful lives, with the result that a judgement about them can be reached quickly. Other men may be just as unsuitable, but their sins are not immediately obvious and time is needed for them to appear.

In the same way, good deeds are obvious, and even those that are not cannot be hidden (verse 25). On the positive side the good lives of men suitable for leadership will stand out. At the same time other men may be just as suitable, but their good works are more hidden, so that time is needed to get a complete picture of them. Strong, demonstrative persons do not always make the best pastoral leaders; sensitivity and developed character are essential for leaders in whom other people will confide and follow.

Study-Guide Questions

Verse 17: Is the distinction between ruling and teaching/preaching elders a valid one, and, if so, how far should it extend? (Acts 14:21-23; 15:2ff., 22; 20:17, 28; Rom. 12:6ff.; Tit.1:9; 1 Pet. 5:1-4).

Verse 18: What weight did the scriptures have in the thinking and teaching of Jesus? (Matt. 5:17ff.; 12:3-8; 13:14f.; 19:4-9; 22:23-46; 26: 51-56; 27:46).

Verse 23: What does the Bible teach about drinking alcohol? (Gen. 9:20-23; Psa. 104:14f.; Luke 22:14-20; John 19:28-30; Eph. 5:18).

1 TIMOTHY:CHAPTER 6

Since the beginning of chapter 5 Paul has addressed various group needs within the congregation. These have consisted of different age and gender groups, the widows and the elders. Now, lastly, he considers the special needs of slaves within the church (6:1-2). Paul then reverts for the last time to the false teachers, their motives and their messsage (6:3-10), before addressing Timothy as a man of God (6:11-16). Paul recommends how to instruct the well-to-do members (6:17-19), then signs himself off with a passionate appeal for Timothy's personal loyalty to the one true gospel (6:20f.).

Slaves (6:1-2)

Paul describes this group as **all who are under the yoke of slavery** (verse 1). By calling slavery a yoke Paul recognises that the slaves' existence is a burdensome and negative one which is not theirs by choice. But he does not recommend rebellion as the way out of their condition (in 1 Corinthians 7:21 he encourages them to take their freedom if it is made available). Instead he advocates a positive attitude of respect towards their human masters, based on Christian beliefs and values. See also Ephesians 6:5-9, Colossians 3:22-25 and Titus 2:9f.

Slaves formed a large part of the population of the Roman empire (on some estimates one in every three persons or more was a slave), and were obviously well represented in the membership of the Christian communities. Clearly the gospel had a special appeal to those without rights and with only the basics of existence (1 Cor. 1:26-29).

Unlike marriage and parenting which are creational institutions, such practices as divorce and slavery belong to a fallen world in which men and women can exploit one another mercilessly. The Christian faith addresses people where they are to be found, without excusing their mutual wrongdoing. Paul did not recommend political action for the slaves, since such uprisings had been tried without success and with great loss of life. Instead he knew that the gospel was the power of God to change people in their deepest values and attitudes (Rom. 1:16; 12:1f.). The letter to Philemon is an actual example of how this change would take place, as Christian masters began by treating Christian slaves as brothers and human equals, and by implication choosing to set them free. As a result of the gospel working in people's hearts, the quality of their relationships would be changed, and a new society of justice emerge. This is what in fact happened in the first centuries of the Roman empire.

Christian slaves **should consider their masters worthy of full respect**, whether they were fellow-Christians or not. The master's position of authority demanded respect in itself, since the Christian is called to respect human institutions (1 Pet. 2:13-17). There was the further reason that the master was a human being, an image-bearer of God, and worthy for that reason of respect, however he behaved towards his slaves.

Christianity has the moral resources (Rom. 6:14) to create a new society, one founded on justice and love, because it can regenerate people within themselves and so produce a new set of social attitudes and goals. Paul's little letter to Philemon illustrates how this radical new attitude in human relationships might work itself out between a Christian master and a Christian slave. In that case the onus was on the Christian master to initiate changes for a better working relationship.

Paul's instruction was **so that God's name and our teaching may not be slandered**. In Titus 2:9f., Paul offers the same advice and for the same reason – the good name of the Christian faith. The gospel could be irreparably damaged by the bad behaviour of those representing it in the work-force, whether slaves or freedmen (Tit. 2:5).

Although employees and workers in modern democracies differ from slaves in the ancient world (mainly in having rights and freedom), Paul's principles can apply today. Respect for the boss, the company or the product is an important ingredient in loyal and honest service. Above all, Christians ought still to be motivated and guided in their public service by a concern to protect and to commend the good name of God and the Christian faith.

Those who have believing masters are not to show less respect for them because they are brothers (verse 2). The revolutionary powers of the Christian gospel meant that people from different classes were brought together and reconciled as brothers and sisters in the new human family of God in Jesus Christ (Eph. 2:14ff.). Believers from all walks of life had to treat one another as equals in Christ, in whom there were no races, classes or genders (Gal. 3:28). At the same time the forms and institutions of this world have not yet passed away. The Christian slave remains a slave in everyday life, and the Christian master still owns his slaves, even although they may in fact be fellow believers. The Christian slave must not exploit the working relationship to his master on the basis of their shared Christian faith. The contrary is the case.

Instead, they are to serve them even better, because those who benefit from their service are believers, and dear to them. Instead of allowing the common brotherhood between master and slave to breed an undue familiarity, Christian slaves should serve their Christian masters with greater zeal. They can render their service not only to God but to a dear brother in Christ (Phlm. 15f.).

These are the things you should teach and preach closes the present paragraph, but these words could just as well open the next paragraph (see also 1 Timothy 4:11). In which case they would set up a contrast between a faithful teacher of the truth like Timothy and those false teachers who peddle their falsehoods as truth (verses 3-10).

Study Questions

Verse 1: How does the Old Testament attitude to slavery differ from that in the New Testament? (Ex. 21:1-6; Deut. 15:12-18; Jer. 34:8-16; 1 Cor. 7:20ff.; Eph. 6:5-8; Col. 3:22-25; 1 Pet. 2:18-23).

Verse 2: What difference should it make to inter-personal relations that people are fellow-believers? (Matt. 23:8; Rom. 14:10-13; 1 Cor. 6:4-8; 8:8-13; Eph. 4:25; 1 Thess. 4:3-7).

Truth and Godliness (6:3-10)
For the last time in this letter Paul takes up the subject of the false teachers. This time he examines and exposes their real character and aims.

If anyone teaches false doctrines and does not agree to the sound instruction of our Lord Jesus Christ (verse 3). In the New Testament there is such a thing as heresy or false teaching. The postmodern idea of relative truth is unknown to the biblical writers. The words of Christ and his teaching are the measure of truth and error in religion and ethics. Whatever seriously departs from his standards of truth and right is fatally flawed and ranks as error. His instruction is said to be sound (literally 'healthy') because it alone has the intrinsic power to restore genuine moral and spiritual health to those who accept it into their lives. He is the great healer, who has come into the world to make humans well through his message of repentance towards God and his kingdom (Mark 2:17).

When Paul adds **and to godly teaching** he may be thinking of the later apostolic teaching (such as in his own writings) which derives from that of Jesus and accords with it. Together the recorded teachings of Jesus in the Gospels and those of his apostles in the remainder of the New Testament form the final deposit of God-given truth. Its hallmark is that it produces godliness in the heart and life (2 Tim. 3:16; Tit. 1:1). By contrast the false systems promise personal fulfilment and happiness but never godliness.

As he had analysed the anatomy of faith (1 Tim. 1:5), Paul now analyses the anatomy of error and unbelief. By his reaction to Christ's truth the false teacher shows that **he is conceited and understands nothing** (verse 4). He is not impartial and certainly not excusable for his negative response to the Word of God. He already knows the truth about God but suppresses it (Rom. 1:18ff.). Being conceited means literally being puffed up – with pride (1 Tim. 3:6; 2 Tim. 3:4). This is the real cause of the false teacher's reaction to godly teaching. Heresy is not so much an intellectual problem rooted in the mind as a moral one rooted in the heart.

Pride is an inborn prejudice against the truth and has a blinding effect on the person's spiritual powers. Under the claim to superior and extensive knowledge the heretical teacher is actually taken captive by a subtle form of ignorance. The devil also participates in the blinding of the minds of unbelievers as a penalty for their wilful disobedience (2 Cor. 4:3f.).

He has an unhealthy interest in controversies and arguments, just as Paul has noted previously (1 Tim. 1:3f.). He carries on this medical reference by claiming that such an individual is spiritually sick. The symptoms are an argumentative and a critical spirit. If these disputes were about the truth and in defence of it they might be justified, since believers are to contend earnestly for the faith entrusted to them (Jude 3f.). But this person loves controversy for its own sake, regarding it as a mark of the truly religious. This type of controversy is normally based on ignorance and leads nowhere (2 Tim. 2:23; Tit. 3:9). It is a fruitless battle over technical religious terms (2 Tim. 2:14).

His controversial arguments are those **that result in envy, quarrelling, malicious talk, evil suspicions**. The destructive and divisive results of these controversies point to the evil root from which they spring. The picture portrayed here is one of a total breakdown of group trust and respect, of conflict, hostility and mutual vilification as an accepted way of life. The evil root of pride produces a bitter harvest of broken relationships, or like a terminal cancer it spreads until every organ is destroyed.

These controversies and arguments produce bitter fruits **and constant friction between men of corrupt mind** (verse 5). There is no end to the conflict generated by these disputatious attitudes once they have taken control. They attract men of like mind, **who have been robbed of the truth** (Rom. 1:28; 2 Cor. 4:4; Eph. 4:17f.) as a just punishment for their wilful unbelief (2 Thess. 2:10ff.) **and who think that godliness is a means to financial gain**. It is a measure of how far such people may depart from the true intention of the gospel that they are able, without shame, to measure godliness by its monetary rewards. They turn their training and position as religious teachers into a lucrative business. The world of religion has become for them a marketplace for personal gain (John 2:14ff.; Tit. 1:11). This is the sin of Balaam, the false prophet who hired himself out for a fee (Num. 22:7). He has his counterparts in this age of Christianity (2 Pet. 2:15; Jude 11). Paul, by comparison, liked to preach free of charge (2 Cor. 11:7).

Paul meets them on their own ground by agreeing that godliness is gainful, but he redefines the term 'gain' in doing so. **But godliness with contentment is great gain** (verse 6). For the Christian, godliness is its own reward, and when joined with contentment is productive of great and lasting good (1 Tim. 4:8). Contentment was taught by the Stoics as a virtue, a sort of mental and emotional self-mastery that created detachment from the harsher experiences of life. Paul also teaches contentment, but he traces it back to Christ who dwells in the Christian through the Holy Spirit. Secretly and sovereignly Christ strengthens the Christian in adversity by enabling him to rise above his lesser self and to submit to his circumstances with trust and composure (Phil. 4:11ff.).

For we brought nothing into the world, and we can take nothing out of it (verse 7). This is Paul's way of further arguing against the false teachers and their love of money. Wealth, and all it stands for, belongs to this passing world (1 Cor. 7:29ff.). People owned nothing when they entered life and they will leave life in the same condition (Job 1:21; Psa. 49:16-20; Eccles. 5:15). This proves that only the bare necessities of life, such as food and clothing, are essential to human existence and that we should guard against greed (Luke 12:15). What Christians possess and enjoy over and above these few necessities is given in the generosity of God (Mark 10:29ff.). Satisfying and lasting wealth belongs with the kingdom of heaven, as Jesus taught (Matt. 6:19f.).

But if we have food and clothing, we will be content with that (verse 8) is the Christian perspective on wealth and possessions. Jesus assured his disciples that a heavenly Father would provide the basic necessities of life and that they should never therefore be anxious about their material needs (Matt. 6:25-32). Instead they should put God and his kingdom first (Matt. 6:33). Through Christ strengthening him Paul had learned the secret of being content whether he had more than he needed or whether he had less (Phil. 4:11ff.). Not only Christians in wealthy countries and with high incomes, but Christians throughout the modern world, need to guard against greed and to discover the Christian art of contentment with the simple things of life.

On the contrary, **people who want to get rich fall into temptation and a trap and into many foolish and harmful desires** (verse 9). Paul is generalising now, he has moved beyond the false teachers and their quick gain philosophy. Greed is endemic to fallen human nature and affects nearly everyone in different degrees. It is one of the desires of the heart that produces moral corruption in the world (2 Pet. 1:4). But it deceives people by leading them into many more destructive attitudes and practices than they can hope to escape from. For example, gambling is a popular way out of poverty into greater wealth and a grand lifestyle, but it can become an addiction which ruins family life, leading to dishonesty in business practice and even into crime. These cravings are foolish because they are irrational, and harmful because they destroy personal and social happiness. Mention of a trap recalls the snare of the devil (1 Tim. 3:7; 2 Tim. 2:26). This suggests that the devil is the one who is actively at work, through the alluring voice of greed, in drawing people to their own destruction.

Greed generates desires **that plunge men into ruin and**

destruction. Paul uses the words 'ruin and destruction' else-where to describe the final state of those who disobey God and do not believe the gospel (2 Thess. 1:9; Phil. 3:19). Unless the possessive love of money is checked by repentance and new obedience of faith in Jesus Christ, it will lead straight on to eternal death. Even in this life, those who live for material possessions will begin to experience a condition of spiritual emptiness and sorrow. The power of greed is so strong that it can act like deep water that drowns those who cannot swim in it.

For the love of money is a root of all kinds of evil (verse 10). Paul repeats his solemn warning that greed is a craving that will always prove deadly, unless it is cut off by the regenerating power of God. By saying that greed is *a* root of all evil rather than *the* root of all evil, he is making room for the fact that there are other root evils that spawn wickedness in human nature. Nor does Paul condemn wealth outright as an evil in itself. His focus is on the individual's attitude to wealth, the place that he gives it in his affections. He likens the craving for wealth to a persistent root that produces numerous off-shoots, like lying, jealousy, self-love, arrogance, and even murder. The Bible records actual examples of most of these products of greed (1 Kings 21:1-16; Matt. 26:14ff.; Luke 12:15-21; 16:19-25).

Some people, eager for money, have wandered from the faith and pierced themselves with many griefs. Most tragically of all, greed can ruin people's religious life by drawing them away from the practice of their faith and into the costly world of wilful sin. Paul is speaking here from his knowledge of the church at Ephesus, where some members had seriously compromised their Christian profession through the love of money and who had paid the inevitable price in the form of personal sorrows. Paul may not therefore be writing about people who had only appeared to be Christians and who had then disproved their claim by returning to the world and its ways (see Matthew 13:20ff., Hebrews 6:4-8 and 1 John 2:19f.). Greed is a cruel and destructive master whoever chooses to serve it.

Study Questions

Verse 6: How should Christians cultivate true contentment? (Job 1:20ff.; Psa. 73:23-26; Matt. 6:25-34; Phil. 4:10-13).

Verse 9: What does Scripture say about sinful desires? (Rom. 6:12ff.; 1 Cor. 10:6-11; Gal.5:24; Eph. 2:1ff.; Jas. 1:13ff.; 2 Pet. 1:3f.).

Verse 10: What other root sins are there which lead to all kinds of evil? (2 Sam. 11; 1 Kings 21:1-16; Acts 5:1-11; 1 Tim. 3:6; Heb. 12:15ff.).

The Good Fight of Faith (6:11-16)

With the exception of verses 17-19 the remainder of the letter is personally and feelingly addressed to Timothy.

But you, man of God. The conjunction 'but' along with the emphatic 'you' draws a sharp contrast between Timothy and the self-serving false teachers. 'Man of God' is a title from the Old Testament for the Lord's servants (Deut. 33:1; 1 Sam. 9:6f.; 1 Kings 13:1, 4ff., 7f.; 2 Kings 4:9, 16, 21f., 25ff.; 5:8; Neh. 12:24). It indicates that this person is entirely at God's service in proclaiming his word and living in obedience to his will. Timothy, as a minister of Christ under the new covenant, belongs to this noble line of faithful servants of God (Phil. 2:19f.; 2 Tim. 3:17).

Just because he is a man of God Timothy must **flee all this**. The sins of materialism, self-indulgence, deception and pretence that control the false teachers can have no place in the heart and life of the man of God. He must not even think about them, and he must run away from them when they propose themselves in his mind because this is the only strategy that succeeds against them (1 Cor. 6:18; 10:14; 2 Tim. 2:22).

But Christ's servant must have positive goals to aim for, as well as knowing what to avoid. He should **pursue righteous-ness, godliness, faith, love, endurance and gentleness**. The placing of the two verbs (flee, pursue) next to each other in the Greek text highlights very sharply the two-sided nature of the Christian life. The Lord's servant must run *away* from some qualities, he must run *after* others. Some of the most basic Christian virtues are included in this list of positive goals (2 Tim. 2:22):

• Righteousness comes first because, in contrast to the greedy teachers of Ephesus, it means doing what is morally right and pleasing to God. Although right is defined by the commands of God's moral law (1 Tim. 1:9ff.), righteousness is a Christian quality because the gospel incorporates it. Through Christ's sin-destroying death and the life-giving Spirit the believer is enabled to fulfil the law's righteousness (Rom. 8:2ff.).

• Godliness is a deep, inner attitude of reverence for God that inspires righteousness, and penetrates the whole heart and behaviour of the Christian. Righteousness and godliness appear together again in Titus 2:12 as outstanding qualities of the Christian who is living an unworldly life.

• Faith is both a personal confidence in God through Jesus Christ and a mental acceptance of the truth of the gospel message and Scripture. Faith is the radical grace of the Christian life, but Paul is not following a logical order here (2 Pet 1:5.ff.).

• Love in Paul's writings is always the outworking of faith (Gal. 5:6). Basically, love is an attitude as well as an emotion, which makes its presence felt by words and actions. Paul uses the same word here as is used elsewhere for God's sacrificial, self-giving love in Jesus Christ (1 John 4:7-11). This means that the Lord's servant must aim at reproducing the same quality of love in his own life and relationships.

• Endurance is the strength to continue in the faith in the face of opposition (Col. 1:11). This opposition can come from inside the church or from the world outside. Either way the Lord's servant will only survive through endurance, which is the Lord's own strength tested and proved in his endurance to the end (Heb. 12:2).

• Gentleness is the ability to respond without anger to human criticism just as Jesus did (2 Cor. 10:1; Gal. 5:22). His meekness and gentleness were the basis of his appeal to his followers (Matt. 11:29). Without gentleness the Lord's servant will soon damage the work and alienate people from himself and the gospel.

Paul encourages Timothy to **fight the good fight of faith** (verse 12). The Greek suggests any kind of contest that involves strenuous effort, whether it be athletic or military. Paul often highlights the tough demands made on the Lord's servants in rendering faithful Christian ministry (1 Cor. 9:24ff.; Phil. 2:16; 3:12ff.; 1 Tim. 4:7; 2 Tim. 4:7). What makes the contest so difficult is the fact that it is not just against people, but against the unseen forces of moral and spiritual darkness (Eph. 6:10ff.). Paul tells Timothy that he must go on engaging in this contest (the verb 'fight' is in the present continuous tense). Although this contest is an intense one, it is also good because of the God in whose name Timothy serves, and because of the eternal results that come from it. Paul describes it as a contest of faith because it is by faith that the Christian grasps the promises of God and draws on the strength that God gives to those who trust in him.

At the same time Timothy is told to **take hold of the eternal life to which you were called when you made your good confession in the presence of many witnesses**. As Timothy engages in the contest of faith, he must lay hold of the eternal life which the Lord gives to all true believers as their reward and inheritance. It is experienced now in part because the age to come is already here in principle (1 Tim. 4:8), but eternal life will be possessed and enjoyed fully and forever on the day of Christ's return (John 6:40, 47). Like all Christians Timothy was called by God to receive the gift of eternal life when he heard the gospel (1 Cor. 1:9; 1 Thess. 2:12).

To strengthen Timothy's resolve, Paul recalls the time when the young man publicly confessed his faith in the presence of many witnesses who will one day testify to the fact of his public confession. This happened when Timothy stood before the assembled congregation and was received into the official membership of Christ's church. Paul's other letters give examples of this practice of public confession which was essentially a personal statement about Jesus Christ as Lord and Saviour through his death and resurrection (Rom. 10:9f.; 1 Cor. 12:3; 15:3ff.). Since Timothy's call to eternal life was fundamental to his service of Christ, Paul's reference is to Timothy's public profession of the Christian faith (church membership) rather than to his public appointment to its service (ordination).

Paul reminds Timothy that he lives his life and fulfils his service **in the sight of God, who gives life to everything** (verse 13). The conviction that he stands and speaks in the presence of God imparts a special authority and engenders a deep sincerity in every true servant of God (1 Kings 17:1; 18:15; 2 Cor. 4:2; 2 Tim. 4:1). This conviction is an essential part of the servant's equipment for effective and persevering service. The thought of God as the one who continuously animates all living things is a reminder of his all-encompassing kingdom and power (Acts 17:24f.).

Paul commands these things in the sight of God **and of Christ Jesus, who while testifying before Pontius Pilate made the good confession**. The thought of God as the source of all life is an awesome one, the thought of Jesus Christ as the faithful witness is an inspiring one (Rev. 1:4f.; 3:14). Timothy is being asked to follow in the steps of his Lord, who by his own fearless witness has set the example and shown his servants that it can be done (Heb. 12:1). Since 'before' could also be translated 'in the days of' (as in Mark 2:26), the confession made by Jesus could include his whole public witness by words and deeds (Acts 10:36-43). But because Pontius Pilate is mentioned by name, the reference is probably to the moment of Jesus' trial when he confessed to the Roman governor his heavenly kingship (John 18:33-38). Jesus' confession was 'good' because it corresponded to the truth of God. He was to seal it with his death the very same day.

I charge you is the same strong expression used at earlier points in the letter (1 Tim. 1:3; 5:21). There is a note of urgency and authority about the word 'charge'. The Lord's servant must not be afraid or ashamed to make use of that authority and commission that the Lord himself has bestowed on him.

This verse states the charge, it is **to keep this commandment without spot or blame** (verse 14). Since Paul is drawing his letter to a close the 'commandment' probably refers to the whole mandate Paul has given Timothy from the beginning of the letter. In a word it is the command to put the Ephesian church in order following the lines laid down by Paul within this letter. Timothy must aim to keep his record clear and blameless. To help him to achieve this aim, Paul has charged him in the presence of God and Jesus Christ, to whom he must render an account one day.

Paul sets Timothy's Christian ministry within the horizon of Christ's return – **until the appearing of our Lord Jesus Christ.** The appearing (literally 'epiphany') of Jesus Christ as a real event in the future sets a limit to the strenuous effort of Christian service. When he appears he will reward his saints and servants for their sacrifical work for him on earth (Rom. 14:10ff.; 1 Cor. 3:10-15, 2 Cor. 5:9f.). Paul does not make any prediction about when the Lord will appear, he simply notes the fact as a certainty. His attitude is based on that of Jesus himself (Mark 13:32). This clear reference to the second appearing of Jesus Christ refutes the argument that in the Pastorals the church has settled down in this world and abandoned its original hope of Christ's return.

The appearing of Christ is an event **which God will bring about in his own time** (verse 15). Even Jesus as the Son of God did not claim to know the time of the end of the age and his coming again in glory (Mark 13:32). God here is the Father, the one who initiated and who will finish the work of salvation in this world. Just like the first coming of Jesus (Rom. 5:6ff.; Gal. 4:4f.), the second will be in the Father's own time. His right and ability to do this is shown in the doxology which now follows.

This God is further described as **God, the blessed and only Ruler, the King of kings, and Lord of lords**. Paul is beginning a doxology here that compares with the one that appears in 1:17. Certain elements are the same (for example, God's immortality) but this doxology is more developed and has more to say about the absolute supremacy of God:

• God is *blessed* because he is perfectly contented and happy in himself alone. He is self-blessed, not depending on anything outside himself for his eternal well-being. The blessed God is worthy of being blessed (Rom. 1:25; Eph. 1:3; 1 Pet. 1:3).

• God is the *only Ruler*, not because other powers and authorities do not exist (Col. 1:16), but because they all receive their right to rule from his originating source of power (Dan. 4:34f.; 7:13f.; Matt. 25:31f.; Rev. 15:3f.).

• God is *King of kings and Lord of lords*. These titles are taken from the Old Testament (Deut. 10:17; Psa. 136:3; Dan. 2:47) and are applied freely to God and Jesus Christ in the New Testament (Rev. 17:14; 19:16). The political leaders of this world are all subject to the eternal King.

The Christian God is further the one **who alone is immortal** (verse 16), that is, free from the possibility of death and dying, along with the corruption that they bring (1 Tim. 1:17). Only God possesses intrinsic immortality, human immortality is God's gift (Gen. 1:27; 2:17).

God alone is the one who is immortal **and who lives in unapproachable light, whom no-one has seen or can see**. Because of human sinfulness, and because of the infinite distance between God and human beings, God can never be seen as he is. No one can see God and live (Exod. 33:17-23). But Christ is the image of the invisible God (Col. 1:15) who succeeds in mediating the knowledge of God to redeemed humans (John 1:18; 2 Cor. 4:6). Even in the new creation redeemed men and women will 'see' God only through Christ as mediator, the Lamb that was slain (Rev. 21:23; 22:3ff.).

To him be honour and might forever. Amen. As is customary with doxologies, the recital of God's attributes is followed by a prayer for certain qualities to be his forever. Because the focus of this doxology is on the supremacy of God, Paul uses 'might' rather than 'glory' as in the first doxology (1:17).

Well-To-Do Christians (6:17-19)

Command those who are rich in this present world singles out another and the last group within the church, the wealthy. Just as there were numerous slaves in the early church so there were a few well-to-do believers. Once again Paul grounds his Christian ethics in the theology of the two ages (1 Tim. 4:8). There is the present age to which believers belong by birth, there is the age to come to which they also belong by supernatural rebirth (1 Tim. 6:19; Tit. 2:12). Christians must learn to live within the present age by the standards and powers of the age to come.

For the wealthy this means that they are **not to be arrogant nor to put their hope in wealth, which is so uncertain**. These are natural temptations for the rich, who must constantly remind themselves that their opulent lifestyle is already passing away (1 Cor. 7:29ff.). Wealth can breed a highmindedness that looks down on the less fortunate, and makes the wealthy indifferent to them

(Prov. 21:13; 28:11; Luke 16:19ff.). Riches may become a substitute for God, an object of trust and confidence for the future,
in spite of the fact that the unreliability of wealth is proverbial
(Prov 18:11; 23:4ff.; Luke 12:16-21).

They are not to trust in riches **but to put their hope in God**,
like the widows who do so out of their poverty (1 Tim. 5:5). God
is the one **who richly provides us with everything for our
enjoyment**. In his generosity the Creator has endowed this world
with many useful and enjoyable things for the delight and benefit of human beings. But he does not mean us to make a god of
the creation in place of the Creator, as fallen men and women
are inclined to do (Rom. 1:25). Clearly the gifts of reason and the
senses have come from God who approves their use in the exploration and enjoyment of his created universe (1 Tim. 4:3ff.). The
Creator is no kill-joy, but a generous and thoughtful Giver to
men and women.

**Command them to do good, to be rich in deeds, and to be
generous and willing to share** (verse 18). Paul nowhere states
that riches are an evil in themselves, or that Christians should
not be rich, rather he catalogues the definite goals and priorities
rich believers ought to adopt. They are to lay out their wealth to
relieve the needs of others, to be rich in personal character and
kind actions, and to be generous in sharing what they have for
the benefit of others, following the example of God the Father
(Matt. 5:43-48). In other words wealthy Christians are to practise, within the context of their privileged circumstances, the
golden rule of self-denial in the service of others, out of love for
God and neighbour (Luke 23:50ff.).

**In this way they will lay up treasures for themselves as a
firm foundation for the coming age** (verse 19) is reminiscent
of Paul's promise to the deacons in 1 Timothy 3:13. Sacrificial
giving of oneself and one's possessions for Christ's cause never
goes unrewarded in the affairs of the kingdom of Christ, either
in this age or the one to come (Prov. 11:24f.; Matt. 10:40ff.;
Mark 10:29f.; Luke 12:33f.; 16:9ff.;18:22; Col. 3:23f.). Well-to-

do Christians should act in this way **so that they may take hold of the life that is truly life.** Wealth is touted as the key to life and happiness (see Luke 12:16-21 and 18:18-23), but it is faith and hope in the living God that brings the reality of eternal life (John 17:3). Rich believers are therefore to take firm hold of that better, fuller life that God has mercifully offered them in Christ, and to be thankful (Jas. 1:9ff.).

False Knowledge (6:20-21)

The letter closes with a passionate appeal in which Paul makes a final plea to **Timothy** to be faithful to the gospel. **Guard what has been entrusted to your care** (verse 20) refers to the gospel message which is like a legal deposit solemnly placed in another person's care (2 Tim. 1:12, 14). God has entrusted his Word to his saints on earth (Jude 3) for its perpetual propagation in the world (Matt. 28:19f.; Mark 13:10; 1 Thess. 2:4). This deposit of saving truths, which is a special revelation from God through his apostles and prophets (Eph. 3:1-7), needs to be guarded against the attacks of the unbelieving and disobedient (2 Pet. 2:1ff.; 3:15f).

In order to guard the gospel Timothy must **turn away from godless chatter and the opposing ideas of what is falsely called knowledge.** Paul is unrestrained in his invective as he contemplates the eclectic religious system of so-called knowledge at Ephesus. He brands it empty, contradictory and false. Because Paul uses the word *gnosis* (knowledge) to describe it, some writers have claimed that this local false teaching was an early form of the second-century movement called Gnosticism which infiltrated Christian circles and threatened the very existence of the gospel. But this may be reading too much into what is after all a common term for any type of human wisdom.

Tragically, it is one **which some have professed and in so doing have wandered from the faith** (verse 21). This concoction of speculative and erroneous notions is a heady brew, as certain members of the community have proven (1 Tim. 1:19f.; 2 Tim. 2:17f.). Having experimented with this cocktail of theosophical ideas they found that they had lost the way to religious truth.

Grace be with. The 'you' is plural, showing that Paul is no longer addressing Timothy alone but is including the whole church. This suggests that the letter was intended to have a dual audience all along, Paul speaking to the congregation through Timothy. Paul's simple greeting appears in other letters (Col. 4:18; 2 Tim. 4:22; Tit. 3:15). Grace was the note with which he began, and with it he closes. This is a typical ending for Paul, the apostle of the gospel of the unlimited and unmerited love of God (Rom. 5:20f.; Eph. 2:8f.).

Study Questions

Verse 15: How should the supremacy of God as King affect believers? (Psa. 93; Dan. 3:16ff.; John 10:27ff.; Rom. 9:14-24; Rev. 11:15-18).

Verse 16: If God dwells in unapproachable light, how can human beings ever approach him? (John 1:14, 18; 14:6-9; 1 Tim. 2:5f.; Heb. 1:1ff.; Rev. 21:22ff.).

2 Timothy

INTRODUCTION

The Writer

This is Paul's last letter before his martyrdom in Rome about AD 66. His personal circumstances give the letter a special pathos, which is quite strongly communicated to the reader through what the aged and dying Paul shares with Timothy, his young colleague and successor in Christ's work. As a result, we could call this letter Paul's last will and testament, in which he bids farewell, confesses his faith for the last time, and gives directions for the future management of the church's life and witness.

The Bible is interested in and frequently records the last words of dying saints for the encouragement and instruction of believers in all ages. So we have the dying testimony of Jacob (Gen. 49), David (2 Sam. 23:1-7) and Simeon (Luke 2:25-35). The last words of Jesus from the cross have also been preserved and have ministered light and comfort to many of his disciples through the ages. To this list can be added the letter of Second Timothy which is an extended valedictory address. What makes its contents so moving and memorable are its style (open-hearted), the personal circumstances of the writer (in prison and facing martyrdom), the identity of the writer (Paul) and the historic moment (the death of an apostle).

The Addressee

When Timothy received this letter he had been working with Paul for about fifteen years from the time that the apostle first chose and trained him for missionary service (Acts 16:1-3). In spite of certain personal frailties Timothy was Paul's most valued helper because of his self-denying and Christ-regarding spirit (Phil. 2:19-24). Naturally Paul used Timothy extensively by taking him with him (Rom. 16:21; Phil. 1:1; Col. 1:1), or sending him alone on some of the most sensitive missions among the Gentile churches (Acts 20:4-6; Phil. 2:19). As Timothy worked with Paul, he learned from his example by observing first-hand his methods and motives as well as his message in the complex situations of the mission field (2 Tim. 3:10ff.). The relationship between the two men was like a father-son partnership (1 Cor. 4:17; Phil. 2:22; 1 Tim. 1:2), full of affection, mutual respect and trust (2 Tim. 1:3f.).

Because of Timothy's physical and temperamental difficulties (1 Cor. 16:10f.; 1 Tim. 5:23), Paul found it necessary to support him throughout by private correspondence containing words of counsel and encouragement. He does this with this final letter between them. It overflows with the sharing of personal memories, and the giving of confidences and appeals. Conscious of his imminent death, Paul's primary intention in this letter is to strengthen Timothy this one last time and to set before him the nature and goals of church ministry and leadership.

The Issues

The certain prospect of Paul's death was a moment fraught with peril for the Gentile churches. For thirty years the rugged apostle had put the marks of his unique style of leadership on the churches of the Greek-speaking world. His death meant the changing of the guard, a moment of transition in which the leadership of those churches would pass to a new generation of leaders who would have the solemn responsibility of establishing the Christian churches in the post-apostolic period. Prominent among these future leaders was Timothy, who because he had trained under Paul, knew his vision for the future of Christianity.

In this letter Paul summons him for one last meeting and act of fellowship, in which final goodbyes can be made. But the primary aim of the letter, barring Timothy's arrival in Rome, is to steel Timothy's resolve for the future of the gospel ministry by strongly urging him to hold fast the faith against all its opponents. This appeal to Timothy is reinforced by Paul's referring to his own example in suffering, preaching and leadership, and by his confessing his faith in the face of death.

The Modern Message

The lasting message of 2 Timothy can be summed up as *Hold fast the pattern of sound words* (2 Tim. 1:13). This is a reference to the apostolic teaching which had been built up around the life and teaching of Jesus, and preserved conscientiously within the churches. It was a finished product of divine teaching, which has been finally transmitted in the sacred writings of the New Testament (Luke 1:1-4; Eph. 3:1-7). This is the deposit of truth that Timothy must guard and transmit for teaching to the next generation of teaching elders (2 Tim. 2:2). The turbulence and uncertainty of the times made the safe transmission of the gospel a matter of deep concern to the dying apostle.

Although the apostolic teaching has now been handed on to each new generation through two millenia of Christian church history to the present day, the fundamental shift in cultural values that is underway in major centres and institutions in the modern world raises again a genuine concern for the safe transmission of the gospel for the future. Although Paul's generation was a unique one in laying the foundation of Christian revelation (Eph. 2:20), the movement away from Christian beliefs and morals throughout the world today signals an intense conflict for those churches and leaders who want to be true to the apostolic faith and standards. For them the letter of Second Timothy comes as a sure guide and strengthener. It sounds a clear call to Christian trust, courage and faithfulness in times that are out of joint, and in so doing imparts the very strength, courage and endurance that are necessary for such times. This is because it is a precious and integral part of the living and abiding Word of God (1 Pet. 1:23ff.).

SECOND TIMOTHY: CHAPTER ONE

After the customary greetings (1:1-2), Paul recalls his last meeting with Timothy, his family faith and the need Timothy has to stir up God's gift within him (1:3-7). This is followed by a clarion call to Timothy to stand up for the gospel which has accomplished such great things (1:8-14). Paul then brings Timothy up to date about those who have forsaken Paul, and about Onesiphorus who proved so loyal (1:15-18).

Greetings (1:1-2)

The letter starts in the customary way with **Paul, an apostle of Christ Jesus by the will of God**. On Paul's apostleship see 1 Timothy 1:1. To offset every charge that he was promoting himself and advancing his own interests, Paul did not lose any opportunity to reaffirm the fact that he was an apostle, not by self-appointment, but by divine appointment. Christ had called him in person when he set him apart for his special service (Acts 9:1-9; Gal. 1:1, 15). This was in accordance with the sovereign will of God the Father (1 Tim. 1:1).

Paul's divine calling to be an apostle was **according to the promise of life that is in Christ Jesus**. The gospel or Christian faith is about God's promise of eternal life in Jesus Christ his Son. This life comes to people as they receive Jesus Christ personally by trusting in him alone for salvation. This promise of life was given by God from eternal ages so that Jesus Christ came into the world to fulfil it on the basis of his sacrificial death (John 6:51; 2 Tim. 1:9). Paul's part in all this was to be Christ's witness, throughout the Gentile world, to the fact that God had kept his promise, not only for the Jews, but also for the Gentiles (Eph. 3:1-7).

The letter is written **to Timothy, my dear son** (verse 2). On Timothy and Paul's relationship see 1 Timothy 1:2. In writing this final testament of his faith and work to Timothy, Paul is passing the mantle of responsibility for Christian leadership and oversight of the churches to him as his immediate successor. There is

no indication, however, that Paul is transferring to Timothy his
own unique apostolic authority and inspiration in office. These
are transferred to Paul's writings in the New Testament, not to
any individual coming after him in the history of the church.

**Grace, mercy and peace from God the Father and Christ
Jesus our Lord.** For this identical greeting see 1 Timothy 1:2.

Study Questions

Verse 1: What are some of the characteristics of life in Christ?
(John 10:10; Rom. 6:23; 8:2; 1 Cor. 15:53f.; Eph. 2:4-7; 1 Thess.
5:9f.)

Verse 2: Discuss the special qualities of grace, mercy and peace.

Personal Memories (1:3-7)
I thank God is typical of Paul's greetings in his letters (1 Cor.
1:4ff.; Phil. 1:3ff.; Col .1:3ff.; Philem. 4f.). This follows the
usual Hellenistic letter style, but with a definitely Christian slant.
What Paul gives thanks for appears in the sentences that follow.
Paul's God is the one **whom I serve, as my forefathers did,
with a clear conscience**. Paul's service as an apostle is a form
of worship in which he is totally devoted to God in body and spirit
(Rom. 1:9). Paul is also keen to point out the continuous link
between his Christian apostleship and the historical tradition of
faith within his family and nation. The Jews of Paul's day alleged
that his message about Jesus as Christ was a heretical departure
from the faith of Israel. Paul claimed that Jesus Christ was the
goal of the law, and that all God's promises to Israel came to
fulfilment in him (Rom. 9:3ff.; 10:4; 2 Cor. 1:19f.; Gal. 3:6-9).
This is a major tenet in Paul's belief system, as he reflects for the
last time on his life of apostleship (2 Tim. 2:8). It is still an important part of the Christian witness to Israel that Jesus is the Christ

who lived, died and rose again in accordance with the Jewish Scriptures (1 Cor. 15:3-5).

Throughout the Pastoral Letters Paul insists on the need for a godly life in general, and a good or clear conscience in particular, in serving God (1 Tim. 1:5, 19; 3:9). This is because God is a holy God who demands moral righteousness from those who serve him (1 Pet. 1:15f.). Living by a good conscience means that we are living in accordance with God's commandments, and that we are finding forgiveness for our failures in the blood-sacrifice of Jesus Christ (1 John 1:7ff.). Living morally is not the same as legalism, because the Christian keeps God's commandments out of gratitude in the outworking of his faith in Jesus Christ as Saviour and Lord. This is no light matter since the neglect of a Christian conscience can shipwreck a person's faith and life (1 Tim. 1:19; Tit. 1:15).

Paul thanks God **as night and day I constantly remember you in my prayers**. Paul's prayer-life is legendary for its breadth of interest and for its regularity. This is all the more remarkable when it is remembered how active and pressured Paul normally was in Christ's work (2 Cor. 11:24-28). Admittedly in prison Paul had time to pray at any hour of the day or night, yet all his letters tell the same story of persistent and intimate praying for individuals and churches (Rom. 1:8ff.; Eph. 1:17ff.; 3:14ff.; Col. 1:3f.; 1 Thess. 1:2f.; 2 Thess. 1:2). That Paul could assure individuals like Timothy that he constantly remembered them in prayer is a tribute to his personal spirituality and his pastoral care. Paul did not rely on organisational skills but on spiritual methods in his work for the kingdom of Christ.

Recalling your tears, I long to see you, so that I may be filled with joy (verse 4). No words could illustrate more finely the strength and depth of the ties of fellowship among the Christians of the New Testament. They were not afraid to express their emotions in actions or words. The outcome of this open and rich fellowship was a shared joy that welled up within them. No wonder these believers longed to renew their contacts with one another in the service of Christ. As a prime example of this quality of fellowship in practice, Paul often expresses his hope for reunion with other Christians (Rom. 1:11; Phil. 1:8; 1 Thess. 2:17f.). Remembering Timothy's tears when the two men last parted makes Paul long for one last meeting with Timothy, so that Paul himself may be filled with heavenly joy before he faces the loneliness of death by execution.

I have been reminded of your sincere faith, which first lived in your grandmother Lois and in your mother Eunice and, I am persuaded, now lives in you also (verse 5). Timothy's faith was sincere (free from pretence) because it really lived in his heart, the fruits of it being evident in his life and work for all to see. For this reason Paul was persuaded about it. Just like the period in which Paul lived, our age has a proliferation of movements for spiritual enlightenment, all inviting a kind of religious faith. The church itself is mixed and confused. Therefore, how imperative it is to distinguish the qualities of genuine faith in God. Timothy's was known because it was accompanied by a pure heart, a good conscience and a fervent love (1 Tim. 1:5).

Timothy's genuine faith had been passed on from his grandmother to his mother, and so to him. Timothy's father was a Greek who apparently did not share the faith of his Jewish wife (Acts 16:1). We know nothing about the marital circumstances of Lois the grandmother. It was the women in Timothy's family who preserved and passed on the true faith of Israel to him. Here is another example of the very positive role of Christian women in the home and in the church. Even in the unfavourable circumstances of a mixed marriage, Eunice was able to communicate her faith in God successfully to her son, who was to become an eminent Christian leader. This same maternal influence is needed in the modern church, and can be successfully exercised even in the absence, literally or spiritually, of a father.

In each generation of Timothy's family there was a gracious visitation of God, bringing at least one member to a saving faith. This was in keeping with the covenant promise of God to Abraham that he would be the God and Father of his descendants throughout their generations (Gen. 17:7; Gal. 3:16, 26-29). As spiritual members of the family of Abraham this promise continues to hold true under the new covenant, as the apostolic preaching (Acts 2:38f.), the practice of household baptism (Acts 16:15, 33) and Timothy's family tree all illustrate. Christian parents have every encouragement to believe that some, if not all, of their children will come to genuine faith in Jesus Christ as God uses and blesses their own faithful instruction, discipline, example and prayers (Eph. 6:1-4; Col. 3:20f.).

For this reason I remind you to fan into flame the gift of God, which is in you (verse 6). Because Paul is so certain of the sincerity of Timothy's faith, he is confident in urging him to rekindle God's gift to him. Although gifts of service cannot be completely separated from gifts of grace like faith or love, Paul is here referring to a service gift (charisma) such as teaching or leadership. The difficult circumstances of Timothy's missionary assignment, combined with his natural timidity, made this reminder by Paul necessary. The picture Paul uses is of a fire tending to die down and to die out, unless it is periodically prodded back into life. So Timothy had to stir himself up deliberately in the active service of Christ, as must all Christian leaders, through new acts of courage and leadership. Like the parts of the body, the gifts of the Spirit will atrophy unless constantly used and exercised (Matt. 25:24-29).

Paul reminds Timothy that this gift came **through the laying on of my hands**. This does not mean that Paul's hands magically conveyed the gift, rather the laying on of the hands of an apostle outwardly confirmed the gift of the Holy Spirit already given (Acts 6:3, 5f.; 1 Cor. 12:4, 11). The fact that Paul only mentions himself in connection with Timothy's setting apart for service, when other presbyters shared in the same act (1 Tim. 4:14), is due to the very personal nature of Second Timothy. On the principle that the primary offices of the church include the lesser, Paul was an elder as well as an apostle, and so joined with other elders in presbyterial acts of administration (1 Pet. 5:1).

For God did not give us a spirit of timidity (verse 7) is a follow-up to Paul's reminder in verse 6. Similar statements appear in Romans 8:15 and 1 Corinthians 2:12 where the reference is to the Holy Spirit, as here. Timidity is a chronic fear of people, suffering or responsibilities that paralyses the will from giving effective leadership, and it is not a sign of the Spirit's presence. **But** he did give us **a spirit of power, of love and of self-discipline.** The sure signs of the Spirit's presence are such attitudes and qualities as power, love and self-control. Power was promised with the Spirit's arrival (Acts 1:8), love is the primary fruit of the Spirit (Gal 5:.22), and self-discipline is the control of mind and emotions that the Spirit gives (1 Cor. 14:32f.). All three are necessary if the Lord's servant is to function effectively in public life.

Christian ministry must be conducted in conscious and continual dependence on the Holy Spirit. Only the Spirit can give power or inner strength, love or selfless devotion, self-discipline or a focused mind. Good advice and strong appeals are not enough to motivate people in Christian work, they must be given sound reasons for their motivation, as Paul does here. Their resources must be spiritual, and these can only come from outside themselves. Timid (and self-confident) Christians need to hear this message, and learn to turn felt weakness into real strength (2 Cor. 12:9; Phil. 4:13).

Study Questions

Verse 4: Do emotions have a legitimate place in the Christian's life, and if so what? (Mark 3:5; John 11:35; Acts 20:36ff.; 21:10-14; 1 Pet. 1:8).

Verse 5: What are the differences between a genuine and a false faith? (1 Tim. 1:5; Jas. 2:14-26; 1 John 2:22f.; 4:1-6).

Verse 7: What else can the Holy Spirit be expected to do for the Christian? (Mark 7:6-13; Rom. 8:10f., 12ff., 15f., 26f.; Gal. 5:16-26; Eph. 5:18-21; Tit. 1:15f.).

Suffering for the gospel (1:8-14)

So do not be ashamed to testify about our Lord reflects Paul's principal anxiety about Timothy because of his natural timidity. Paul was not ashamed of the gospel (Rom. 1:16) because of what it was and where it came from. But the temptation to be ashamed of the Christian faith is always present due to personal weakness or circumstantial factors. Jesus was aware of this danger when he warned against its damaging and enduring results (Mark 8:38).

Timothy is not to be ashamed of the gospel, **or ashamed of me his prisoner**. Paul was in prison and had been deserted by many of his former supporters (2 Tim. 1:15; 4:16). Timothy might also be tempted to forsake Paul in the interests of saving his own reputation. But Paul stood for the truth, and a genuine love of the truth will always extend to those who suffer for proclaiming it, no matter what their outward appearance or circumstances may be (2 Tim. 1:16). Paul helped Timothy to do this by calling himself 'his (that is, Christ's) prisoner'. Paul was suffering, not because he was a criminal suffering justly for his own crimes, but because he was a Christian being faithful to his heavenly Lord. What would in normal circumstances be his shame was in fact his glory.

But join with me in suffering for the gospel, by the power of God. Paul invites Timothy to share with him in the noble work of suffering for the gospel, the good news which in his time and ours is so often despised, rejected or ignored by the world. Paul did not mean that Timothy was to join him in his cell, but that in his own situation he would carry his quota of suffering for the advancement and transmission of the gospel. Between the world's way of thinking and that promoted by the gospel, there is a radical antithesis which only God's own loving action in Jesus Christ can reverse and overcome. Unless that happens, all who will live godly lives by being true to Jesus Christ in their service will suffer persecution (2 Tim. 3:12).

Suffering for the gospel is endurable only by the power of God. Only divine power can sustain the servant of the Lord under such a load (2 Cor. 12:9f.; Eph. 1:18ff.; Phil. 4:11ff.). This power comes from the secret working of the Spirit of Christ in those to whom he has given the gift of leadership (verse 7). It was in terms of this power that Paul defined the kingdom of God and measured the competency of those who claimed to represent it (1 Cor. 4:19f.).

The God of the gospel for which Timothy is invited to suffer is the one **who has saved us and called us to a holy life** (verse 9). The gospel makes known the purpose and action of God to bring about our salvation, a fact that more than compensates for all human suffering on its behalf. The gospel records the actual event of salvation ('he has saved us'), not the possibility or probability of salvation. God has acted decisively in a never to be repeated way that changes everything forever. Along with his saving act in Christ has come his personal call in the gospel. This call is effective and commits believers to a holy life, dedicated to godliness and good works (Heb. 3:1).

God's salvation and calling are **not because of anything we have done but because of his own purpose and grace**. Salvation owes nothing to human wisdom or goodness, it is due altogether to the wisdom and will of God. Paul makes the same point in Titus 3:5 in almost the same words. The total exclusion of any human achievement or input to the accomplishment of salvation is a fundamental principle that sets the Christian message apart from every other system. Every other theory of salvation is a form of self-help, a doctrine of human works and merit. The fallenness of human nature is such that people are blind to their own spiritual bankruptcy, and persist in believing in their own righteousness. Only the teaching of the Holy Spirit through the Scriptures can convince them that they will be saved, not because of anything that they have done, but because of God's own purpose and grace.

Salvation is God's 'own' purpose, a description that high-lights the utter freedom of his decision to save. In the forming of his purpose he was totally uninfluenced by anything in humans, it was all his own good pleasure (Eph. 1:9). His purpose is his determination to save by the means which he has appointed (verse 10). His purpose is gracious because it is for the total good of those who are totally undeserving of his favour and help. Paul makes the same point when he states that we are saved by grace, not by works (Rom. 9:16; Eph. 2:8f.). By excluding human works as a contributory factor in salvation, God's way of saving us also excludes human self-pride and boasting (Rom. 3:27f.). The glory goes to God alone (1 Cor. 1:31).

In fact **this grace was given us in Christ Jesus before the beginning of time.** This fact carries salvation back into the depths of God's own being, and reinforces the belief that it owes nothing to humans themselves. They are the recipients of salvation, but not its cause. The origins of salvation lie outside of time in the eternity of God himself. If grace was given in Christ Jesus be-fore time began (literally 'before times eternal', see the same phrase in Romans 16:25), then this must mean that Jesus Christ was forever chosen and appointed by God to be the carrier of salvation. When God chose us for salvation, he chose us in Christ before the foundation of the world (Eph. 1:4). Grace and salva-tion were 'given' or pledged in him, which is another way of saying that salvation was a certainty. The coming of Christ, the preaching of the gospel, faith and repentance are so many stages in the outworking of this eternal agreement between the Father and the Son about salvation.

This purpose and grace were formed before time was, **but it has now been revealed through the appearing of our Saviour, Christ Jesus** (verse 10). The eternal purpose of God could only become effective in time and space. The birth of Jesus Christ marked the moment when God's purpose to save penetrated into human history. The arrival of the baby Jesus was an epiphany ('appearing') or visit from God in which he personally became present as Immanuel (Matt. 1:23). The coming of Jesus revealed the heart of God and his firm purpose to save a people of his own (Tit. 2:14). All life and history since then stands under the 'now' of Christ's entry into the world and is illumined by the bright shining of the light of the saving purpose of God that he personifies. In his light we see light.

Jesus Christ is the one **who has destroyed death and has brought life and immortality to light through the gospel**. God's purpose of salvation leads to the destruction of death and a new gift of life and immortality. He achieves this stupendous result through Jesus Christ who died and rose again to bring it all about. Christ defeated death by dying as an innocent and free individual representing others (Heb. 2:14f.). Consequently, death could make no claims upon him, but was forced to quit the field.

In his resurrection Jesus confirmed and consolidated the victory of his death, by establishing a new world order, one that is distinguished by the rule of deathless life. By rising from the grave, Christ has banished the darkness of death and established forever a kingdom of light and life. 'Immortality' is more than endless existence (a Greek philosophical idea), it describes rather the hope of the Christian faith that because of Jesus Christ the world will never again be ravaged by the corrupting powers of sin and death (1 Cor. 15:53f.). This bright promise of life and immortality is now being proclaimed to all the world through the preaching of the gospel.

And of this gospel I was appointed a herald and an apostle and a teacher (verse 11). Paul had been commissioned by Jesus Christ in person when he confronted and called Paul on the Damascus Road (Acts 9:15; 1 Tim. 1:12). His commission was the threefold one of being Christ's herald, apostle and teacher (see also 1 Timothy 2:7). A herald, in ancient times, was a royal messenger who made public announcements in his king's name and with his royal authority.

As an apostle, Paul was appointed to the highest office in the

Christian church, one that gave him the right to disciple the nations as an itinerant evangelist or missionary and to establish churches anywhere. The apostle Paul could also act, speak and write (as he does in all his letters) in an error-free (infallible) way (1 Cor. 14:37). Because of their unique credentials and powers there are no successors to the apostles, but their task is carried on in a modified way by faithful missionaries, evangelists and Bible teachers around the world today.

As a teacher Paul was given the solemn responsibility of interpreting and transmitting the inspired body of doctrine that made up the apostolic tradition (that is, something that is delivered/handed on, as in 1 Corinthians 15:1-5). The local teaching elder is the one who inherits this task by accurately explaining and applying the instructions contained in the apostolic writings to the life situation of churches today (2 Tim. 2:2).

That is why I am suffering as I am (verse 12). Paul is in no doubt that his sufferings are due to his being a servant of the gospel of Christ. His experience of suffering is in fulfilment of what Jesus Christ promised him when he was called to his service (Acts 9:15f.). Although the gospel is good news for lost and sinful men and women, it also arouses the resentment and displeasure of the human heart. Opposition and sufferings follow, resulting in the alienation and rejection of the messengers of Christ. Like Paul, the faithful gospel servant will honestly be able to say that his sufferings are for Christ and not for his own fault.

Yet I am not ashamed. Paul had already (verse 8) told Timothy not to be ashamed of the gospel, now he explains why. It is **because I know whom I have believed.** Christianity consists in sure knowledge and personal trust. This certainty arises from the truth of God and the one in whom the Christian has placed his trust. The two are inseparable. Christianity is more than a creed which makes intellectual demands in the formulation of a worldview, it is essentially a relationship based on trust in the Son of God who has loved us and given himself for us (Gal. 2:20). A creed, however noble, could never have held Paul to the course

of suffering that he endured. It was only the abiding presence of
a divine Person that could constrain him to live no longer for
himself but for that Other, even to the point of death.

Paul could add – **and am convinced that he is able to guard
what I have entrusted to him for that day**. Some writers believe that Paul has the gospel in mind when he speaks of 'what I
have entrusted to him'. Paul, knowing that his death was imminent, had entrusted the gospel to Christ in the confidence that he
would preserve it in the world and would never allow it to die out.
Paul uses the identical word here that he uses for the gospel in
verse fourteen. It basically means a deposit, something entrusted
to another person for safe keeping.

On the other hand, it seems unlikely that Paul would entrust
the gospel to Christ, when Christ had already entrusted the gospel to Paul (Tit. 1:3). In addition, the tone of Paul's writing at this
point is intensely personal, he has just described his relationship
of ongoing trust in Jesus Christ. The traditional understanding
takes Paul to mean that he has entrusted himself, his whole life
and future, to Christ for safekeeping to the Day of eternity. At
the end of the letter the apostle expresses this very hope that the
Lord will preserve him through all his sufferings, through death
itself, and preserve him for his heavenly kingdom (2 Tim. 4:18).
This is still the most natural and satisfying reading of Paul's
statement in verse twelve. It is the language of Christian assurance ('I am persuaded') which he expresses in a similar tone
elsewhere (Rom. 8:38f.).

**What you have heard from me, keep as the pattern of sound
teaching, with faith and love in Christ Jesus** (verse 13). The
emphasis in the Greek is on *the pattern of sound words* which
Timothy has heard and received from Paul in his teaching. As
Paul faces the prospect of his own imminent death, his whole
anxiety is for the transmission of the gospel in the ongoing future.
The gospel consists of 'sound teaching' which alone can guarantee the spiritual and moral health of humankind. It is imperative
that Timothy, as Paul's most immediate successor, holds on to

the gospel. Timothy must preserve it not only for his own private use, but much more for the sake of the church of the future. Its survival is threatened by the numerous alternative systems of belief and lifestyle that surround it and compete against it.

With the same urgency, the apostolic message, which is contained in the writings of the New Testament, must be contended for and held fast by every servant of Christ in the modern world. The battle for the truth, and for the minds and hearts of men and women throughout the world, has intensified since Paul's day. Christian preachers and apologists must resist every pressure to compromise the gospel by denying its absolute sufficiency or its final authority. It alone is the power of God for salvation to everyone who believes in it (Rom. 1:16). When Christian leaders trim or withhold the gospel of the New Testament they are denying eternal salvation to their hearers. Instead they are to commit themselves to it as the only means under heaven by which people must be saved (Acts 4:12).

The gospel creates its own ethos, consisting in faith and love in Christ Jesus. Paul had discovered for himself that this was the moral environment of the gospel when God's grace so richly enveloped him (1 Tim. 1:14). He recognises that faith and love are the essential traits of the gospel everywhere. *Faith* brings people into a vital relationship with Jesus Christ, *love* is the new attitude of selfless giving that faith in Christ awakens. But both faith and love come with Jesus Christ who is the object of faith and the author of love. Truly Christ is all and in all (Col. 3:11).

Guard the good deposit that was entrusted to you. Paul repeats his plea for Timothy to do everything in his power to defend and propagate the gospel in the world. He must guard it from the admixture of man-made theories and humanistic philosophies which arise culturally in every generation and threaten the gospel. The gospel message is a 'good deposit', a sacred and beneficial gift of God that he has entrusted to faithful leaders like Timothy to be preserved and handed on. The best method of defence is offence in the guarding of the gospel. Where it is preserved in an introspective and selfish way it withers and dies, where it is proclaimed and shared freely it grows and blesses all those who work with it.

Guarding the gospel is a superhuman task, so **guard it with the help of the Holy Spirit who lives in you**. In considering the rigorous demands and awesome consequences of the ministry of the new covenant Paul cries out, Who is sufficient for these things? (2 Cor. 2:16). Only divine assistance, through the personal indwelling and continual empowering of the Holy Spirit, can give endurance and success in the daunting task of guarding the everlasting gospel. Thankfully, that divine help lies close at hand, for the Holy Spirit, who alone can effectively empower ministers for their work, dwells permanently in their hearts. Together with the faith that dwells there (verse 5), the servant of the Lord can draw at any time upon these God-given resources of power to accomplish the work.

Study- Questions

Verse 9: What does the New Testament teach about predestination in Christ? (Acts 13:48; Rom. 8:28ff.; 9:14-24; Eph. 1:3ff.; 2 Thess. 2:13f.; 1 Pet. 1:1f.).

Verse 10: What all did Christ accomplish through his death and resurrection? (Rom. 3:24ff.; 5:6-11; 6:6-11; 14:7ff.; 2 Cor. 5:14f., 18-21; Eph. 2:14-18; Heb. 2:14f.).

Verse 12: How can Christians get more assurance into their faith? (Luke 10:17-24; Acts 13:49-52; Rom. 5:1-11; 8:16f., 31-39; 15:13; 1 Pet. 1:3-9).

False and True Friends (1:15-18)

You know that everyone in the province of Asia has deserted me, including Phygelus and Hermogenes. Having admonished Timothy, Paul briefly reflects out loud on his own recent experiences. For undisclosed reasons Paul's former colleagues and supporters from the province of Asia had deserted him. His work there had been centred on Ephesus and marked a high point in his Gentile mission (Acts 19:1-20:38). But he had predicted that after his departure there would be division and defection within the Ephesian church (Acts 20:29f.). And so it had proved, in a defection that may have drawn away disciples from the other churches of Asia as the movement spread. Paul names two of the ringleaders whose actions had been particularly surprising and hurtful to Paul. The most faithful servants of Christ will meet with, and have to endure, the most painful experiences of personal disloyalty as they seek to honour Christ in their work (2 Tim. 4:10, 16).

May the Lord show mercy to the household of Onesiphorus (verse 16) who had proved to be an exception in the general defection from Paul. Because Paul wishes mercy for the household or family of Onesiphorus, rather than for the man himself (again in 2 Tim. 4:19), we may conclude that Onesiphorus had died since Paul's arrival in Rome. His prayer is therefore for those of his family who remain, on the basis of the unity of the Christian family in God's covenant promises (2 Tim. 1:5). Only the Lord can show or give mercy, it cannot be earned. Mercy in this case would mean that the blessings of the gospel would extend to each one of the members of the family of Onesiphorus.

'Onesiphorus', in Greek, means someone who brings profit to others (like the related name Onesimus). Paul recalls clearly how Onesiphorus had done that for him in two particular ways – **because he often refreshed me and was not ashamed of my chains.** He had often refreshed or revived Paul's spiritual condition by the enthusiasm and sincerity of his own loving faith in its practical expression of friendship and loyalty. Unlike many of the local Christians (2 Tim. 4:16), Onesiphorus had not been ashamed to associate with Paul by visiting him, although his outward circumstances were those of a criminal (2 Tim. 2:9).

For these two reasons Paul remembered Onesiphorus with affection and gratitude. Following the Christlike example of Onesiphorus, ordinary Christians may greatly encourage and re-fresh one another and their leaders in practical ways by visiting them and supporting them in personal sufferings and loneliness, and when facing death.

On the contrary, when he was in Rome, he searched hard for me until he found me (verse 17). Onesiphorus proved the strength of his friendship by taking pains to find Paul, when all that he knew was that the apostle was somewhere in a prison in Rome. Other Christians might have expressed sympathy for Paul, but only Onesiphorus took the trouble to go and visit him. Ac-tions that cost the individual time and trouble are the real proof of Christian love, after the supreme example of Jesus Christ (Phil. 2:5-8). Judged by this measure Onesiphorus was a truly Christ-like character.

May the Lord grant that he will find mercy from the Lord on that day! (verse 18) repeats Paul's desire expressed in verse sixteen, only he directs it now to Onesiphorus himself and links it with the day of Christ's return. Finding mercy in this context means that Onesiphorus will be graciously rewarded by the Lord for his acts of kindness to Paul. In visiting the apostle in prison Onesiphorus had ministered to Christ himself (Matt. 25:34-40). The Lord has promised to repay such acts of mercy with mercy in the day of judgement (Matt. 10:40ff.).

You know very well in how many ways he helped me in Ephesus. Going further back in memory Paul recalls the helpful ministry of Onesiphorus during his Ephesian ministry. Often, and in a variety of ways, he had served Paul there, as Timothy well knows. On this evidence Onesiphorus was a great-hearted Christian, whose shining example should stimulate all Chris-tians to engage in this kind of practical and caring ministry.

Study Questions

Verse 15: What causes people to decline in their religion? (Matt. 13:18-23; John 12:42f.; Acts 5:1-11; 2 Tim. 4:10; 2 Pet. 1:5-11; Rev. 2:4f.).

Verse 18: How can the Day of Christ bring mercy, and loss, to Christ's servants? (Luke 19:11-27; Rom. 14:10-13; 1 Cor. 3:10-15; 4:1-5; 2 Cor. 5:9f.; 2 John 7f.).

Verse 19: In what practical and personal ways can church members help and refresh their ministers? (Acts 12:5; 16:14f., 30-34; Phil. 4:10-19; 1 Thess. 3:6ff.; 5:25; Heb. 13:7, 17; 3 John 3f.).

2 TIMOTHY: CHAPTER 2

The chapter is in two parts. Firstly, Paul aims to encourage and fortify Timothy to be a faithful, suffering servant of Jesus Christ (2:1-13); secondly, he explains in many particulars what it means to be an exemplary worker for God and a true servant of the Lord (2:14-26).

Encouragements in Suffering and Serving (2:1-13)

After the digression about Onesiphorus Paul returns to advising Timothy. **You then, my son, be strong in the grace that is in Christ Jesus** (verse 1). The apostle builds his appeal on the close relationship of trust and affection between them (1 Cor. 4:17; 1 Tim. 1:2). Because of his natural timidity, Timothy needs to be exhorted and encouraged to stand fast and to be strong (1 Tim. 4:11f.). The source of this strength is not to be looked for in Timothy himself, but in Jesus Christ who strengthens all his servants for all their tasks (Phil. 4:13). An honest acceptance of our own weakness is the way to experience Christ's enabling power (2 Cor. 12:9f.).

And the things you have heard me say in the presence of many witnesses entrust to reliable men who will also be qualified to teach others (verse 2). Before everything else Timothy has the responsibility of transmitting the apostle's message to a new generation of Christian teachers. This is Paul's over-riding concern in writing this farewell letter. Along with numerous witnesses in the churches of Paul's mission field, Timothy has heard and become thoroughly acquainted with the contents of Paul's preaching. It is part of the faith once for all entrusted to the saints by the apostles and prophets of the new covenant era, and now deposited for permanent reference and availability in the inspired writings of the New Testament. No interpretation of the Christian faith is valid or saving unless it agrees in all essentials with the apostolic doctrine (2 Cor. 11:3f.; Gal. 1:8f.).

In order to safeguard and perpetuate the apostolic tradition, Timothy must be careful only to select men who are reliable and have a gift for teaching. It is not enough that candidates for the teaching office be eloquent, intelligent or socially acceptable. They must display those graces and gifts agreeable with their function as frontline witnesses. The church's teachers will show that they are Christ's gift to the saints (Eph. 4:11) when they teach the sound knowledge of the gospel and remain faithful to it all their lives. The true apostolic succession is a theological one: the continuity of saving doctrine in the teaching office of the church.

Endure hardship with us like a good soldier of Christ Jesus (verse 3). Here Paul introduces the first of a series of three popular pictures of the Christian ministry. The first is taken from military service and illustrates the principle of unqualified commitment. Paul reminds Timothy that the ministry, like soldiering, unavoidably involves hardship and sufferings. The character of the Christian teacher demands military (not militant) qualities such as endurance, loyalty and submission to authority.

No-one serving as a soldier gets involved in civilian affairs – he wants to please his commanding officer (verse 4). Paul's point is the single-mindedness demanded of the professional soldier. He must concentrate entirely on his personal orders, his one aim must be to please those who have trusted him to carry out orders. Nothing less is required from the Christian soldier-leader, whose single aim must be to please his heavenly commander Jesus Christ (2 Cor. 5:9f.). The Christian ministry demands a total concentration on being obedient and useful to Christ.

Similarly, if anyone competes as an athlete, he does not receive the victor's crown unless he competes according to the rules (verse 5). The second word-picture is taken from athletics, which had become a popular part of national and local life by Paul's time. There were established disciplines and rules that competitors had to abide by if they were ever to win the contests, disciplines that extended for months in advance. In just the same way, the Christian leader must gain control over his own passions and self-interests if he is to be faithful and fruitful in Christ's service, and not be disqualified on the grounds of his own moral indiscretions (1 Cor. 9:24-27).

The hardworking farmer should be the first to receive a share of the crops (verse 6). The third picture is taken from the world of farming where the farmer must work hard at land-care and planting if he is to enjoy a worthwhile harvest. The crop does not appear immediately, but only after months of sacrificial labour. In the same way, the Christian pastor must be prepared to spend himself in Christ's service over a long period of time before he sees the fruit of his labours in people being converted and Christians being built up (1 Cor. 15:58; 2 Cor. 12:14f.; Col. 1:28f.). The service of Christ is no place for easy-going or self-serving people.

Reflect on what I am saying, for the Lord will give you insight into all this (verse 7) contains an appeal and a promise. Reflecting means using the mind to understand God's truth. The mind matters in the living of the Christian faith, and is indispensable if Christians are to witness to their faith and defend it intelligently in the world. But Christian reason must always be subject to divine revelation if it is to communicate the true Word of God and not some human substitute. The place and use of the mind is a prominent part of New Testament Christianity (Rom. 12:1f.; Phil. 4:8f.; Col. 3:2), as is the promise that the Lord will increase the understanding of those who humbly seek him as their Teacher (Matt.7:7f.; Phil. 3:15; Col. 1:9f.).

Remember Jesus Christ (verse 8) is another line of thought Paul uses to encourage young Timothy to be strong and to bear up in the face of future suffering. Jesus Christ also suffered to bring about our salvation (1 Pet. 3:18). Yet he was **raised from the dead** when his righteous sufferings were openly vindicated and rewarded by God the Father. Timothy should take heart from the example of his Lord who, for the joy of heaven set before him, momentarily endured the cross but is now sitting down at the right hand of God (Heb. 12:2). Those who serve Christ must be prepared to follow him in suffering if they are to share with him in glory (John 12:26), but if they do suffer with Christ they can be assured of a triumphant outcome. This is the line of thinking Timothy must adopt.

Christ's resurrection marked the beginning of his rule as sovereign Lord and proved that he was **descended from David** as the promised Messiah (Rom. 1:3f.). The Davidic descent of Jesus is important because when the Lord made his covenant with David he promised that one of his descendents would ascend his throne and rule eternally and universally (2 Sam. 7:12-16; Psa. 89:19-37). Although Jesus was born the king of the Jews and died under the same title (Luke 1:30-33; 23:38), he did not begin to show his real power and glory until he was raised from the dead. This was because he had first to fulfil the role of suffering servant, giving himself as a ransom for the sin of God's people (Mark 10:45). In doing this he laid the moral and legal foundations of his kingdom of salvation. His real enthronement took place when, ascending into heaven, he sat down at the right hand of God (Psa. 110:1). The outpouring of the Holy Spirit at Pentecost was the sign that his rule had begun, and that his kingdom is heavenly not earthly (Acts 2:22-36).

This is my gospel does not mean that Paul claimed to have originated this gospel, a suggestion he vehemently denies elsewhere (Gal. 1:11f.). The words rather express his strong sense of responsibility for this gospel with regard to its propagation and progress in the world. Paul's gospel consists of a number of biblically-based propositions which centre around the historical figure of Jesus Christ, his royal descent, his saving death and resurrection. According to the apostle there is no other gospel than this, and any other that claims the name must be rejected (Gal. 1:8f.).

This is the gospel **for which I am suffering even to the point of being chained like a criminal** (verse 9). Because he believed in this gospel with all his heart, Paul was willing even to endure the shame and suffering of prison for its sake. His consolation comes in the second part of this verse. His reference to 'being chained like a criminal' supports the belief in a later imprisonment in Rome than that mentioned at the end of Acts. There he was only under house arrest and free to receive guests at any time (Acts 28:30f.). The charges against him now are so serious that he is in chains (literally), and he expresses no hope of being set free (compare Phil. 1:24; 2:24). In being treated like a criminal, Paul is sharing in the fellowship of Christ's sufferings (Phil. 3:10), who was treated in the same way for all God's people.

But God's word is not chained is Paul's strong consolation in the midst of his privations. The state authorities may silence Christ's messenger, but the Word of God cannot be silenced because it is the living and abiding Word of God (1 Pet. 1:23). This is the apostle's hope as he languishes in prison and faces almost certain death. All servants of Christ must come to terms sooner or later with the fact of their own mortality, and the fact that Christ's work in the world does not depend on any one individual, even an apostle. The work will continue because it depends on God who is always at work through his Word as the power of his salvation. The gospel not only finds its way into prison cells, but also penetrates into the far deeper dungeon of the human heart so as to throw it wide open and let God's light stream in.

Therefore I endure everything for the sake of the elect, that they too may obtain the salvation that is in Christ Jesus, with eternal glory (verse 10). This should be read as Paul's mission statement. He sets his sufferings in the gospel ministry inside the much larger framework of God's eternal choice of his people for salvation, which will eventually bring them eternal glory with Christ. This teaches us the need for a theology of mission and for theology in doing mission. Paul's sufferings help to bring God's eternal purpose to pass because they contribute to the spread of the gospel worldwide. At a deeper level Paul's self-denying sufferings bring forth life in others, because this pattern of self-dying love is actually the principle of Christ's own life-giving death at work in Paul (2 Cor. 4:7-12). This is the only way to genuine fruitfulness in Christian service. We must die with Christ in daily ministry if Christ is to live in us and in those we seek to serve in Jesus' name. Salvation is participation in the heavenly life and splendour of Jesus Christ himself.

Here is a trustworthy saying (verse 11) is the fourth of those community sayings of the churches which Paul quotes throughout the Pastorals (1 Tim. 1:15; 3:1; 4:9; Tit. 3:8). This one is a four-line extract from a hymn, the first two lines working around the theme of union with Christ, the second two working around the subject of denial. Each line is introduced by a conditional clause ('if'), followed by an answering one. Paul quotes it to give support from the church's own standards to his appeal to Timothy to stand fast in suffering.

If we died with him, we will also live with him; points to the Christian's spiritual union with Jesus Christ in his death and resurrection (Rom. 6:3-10). The Christian has become a new person (2 Cor. 5:17). He has died with Christ once for all to the ruling power of sin and self in his moral nature, and has risen once and for all with Christ to a new life in the practice of righteousness (2 Cor. 5:14f.). Dying with Christ guarantees living with him now and hereafter.

The hymn goes on, **if we endure, we will also reign with him** (verse 12). Enduring for Christ in suffering is an evidence of having died and risen with him, because it is the outworking of our faith in him. For this reason endurance is a cardinal Christian virtue (Matt. 24:13; 1 Tim. 6:11; 2 Tim. 2:10). Just as Jesus exchanged the cross of suffering for the crown of victory, so he has promised the crown of glory to all his suffering disciples (Luke 22:28ff.). Only fellow-sufferers will be fellow-conquerors (Rom. 8:16ff.; Rev. 2:10f.).

But **if we disown him, he will also disown us** turns the relationship around. What if someone rejects and denies Jesus Christ through outright unbelief or subsequent apostasy? Then Christ in the judgement will deal justly with such people by rejecting and denying them (Matt. 10:33; Mark 8:38). He will reward them according to their works. The New Testament denies that true believers can ever apostasise, though they may fall into sin and backslide (Matt. 26:69-75). It also teaches that people may claim to be believers in Christ, but deny this by their lives (Heb. 6:4ff.; 10:26-29; 12:14-17). This line of the hymn warns believers against the dreadful consequences of denying Christ outright, and in doing so provides them with one of the main incentives that prevents them from doing so.

The final lines of the hymn give the assurance that **if we are faithless, he will remain faithful, for he cannot disown himself** (verse 13). This could mean that the Lord will uphold his judicial threats against those who deny him, and that he will never be untrue to his own holiness and justice against those who defect from his side. But it can also mean that for the true believer united to Christ in the enduring bonds of the gospel covenant, the occasional or periodic lapse into sin does not negate the Saviour's commitment to them. Jesus is grieved by the failures of his people, but his love for them endures. By their more serious sins believers may lose the enjoyment of Christ's love, through wounding their conscience and grieving his Holy Spirit, but they can never lose their salvation (John 10:28f.; 1 Cor. 3:15). To the penitent disciple Christ promises his pardoning grace, and immediately works to restore the damage done to faith through sinning (Luke 22:31-34, 54-62; John 21:15-17). To do otherwise would be to deny himself as each Christian's faithful Friend and Brother. This is something that ethically he cannot do.

Study Questions

Verse 2: What is the explanation of Christian strength? (1 Cor. 16:13; Eph. 6:10; Phil. 4:13).

Verses 4 to 6: What illustrations from modern life can you think of which make the same points?.

Verse 7: What are the different methods the Lord uses to teach us? (2 Sam. 5:11f.; Prov. 20:5; John 14:26; Rom. 8:16; 2 Tim. 3:16f.; 1 John 2:20-27).

Verse 8: Why is it important to maintain the truth of the resurrection of Jesus Christ? (John 11:25f.; Rom. 4:25; 1 Cor. 15:12-22; Rev. 1:17f.).

Verse 9: What other qualities and functions does God's Word possess? (Psa. 19:7-11; Psa. 119:2; 2 Tim. 3:15ff.; Rev. 1:3).

Verse 13: What practical uses does God's faithfulness have for the believer? (Lam. 3:22-26; 1 Cor. 1:7ff.; 10:12f.; 2 Cor. 1:18ff,; 1 Thess. 5:23f.).

God's Worker (2:14-26)

Paul returns to the subject of Timothy's public ministry. **Keep reminding them of these things** (verse 14). No small part of the public teacher's work is that of reminding people what they may have already known but have forgotten through ageing, spiritual immaturity or backsliding (2 Pet. 1:12-15). If it is human to err, it is also human to forget. Repetition is an essential part of sound teaching method. 'These things' refers to the spiritual assurances and warnings enshrined in the lines of the trustworthy saying (verses 11-13).

Warn them before God against quarrelling about words; it is of no value, and only ruins those who listen. Paul will repeat this warning in verses 16 and 23. Timothy must solemnly forewarn those who are attracted by the impressive-sounding words of the false gospel teachers that their jargon only leads into conflict situations that eventually destroy people's faith. Words become an end in themselves, and they alienate parties. Technicalities get in the way of truth, and core issues like righteousness, self-control and the judgement to come are never addressed. These controversies are full of heat but no light, and lead to schism in the church and spiritual catastrophe (literally) for those who allow themselves to be sucked into them.

Do your best to present yourself to God as one approved, a workman who does not need to be ashamed and who correctly handles the word of truth (verse 15) is Paul's high ideal for the Lord's servant in public office. The pastor-teacher is like a workman seeking approval through the excellence of his work on the basis of maximum effort. Good workmanship does not just happen, it is the result of long hours, concentrated effort and high standards. If the Christian teacher aims to present himself and his work to God, then he will avoid the shame that will one day accompany all work that has been done for selfish reasons, with poor preparation or with the wrong materials (1 Cor. 3:12ff.). Correctly handling means 'cutting straight' and points to the personal uprightness with which the teacher must approach his task. Since the teacher is responsible for God's Word in public, this instruction also includes the idea of using the Scriptures rightly, believing them to be God's Word and aiming to interpret and apply them faithfully and fearlessly to real life situations for the lasting benefit of the hearers.

Avoid godless chatter because those who indulge in it will become more and more ungodly (verse 16). Again Paul warns Timothy against ruinous religious controversies. These are empty noises full of high-sounding terms but signifying nothing. The people who engage in this kind of blabbering ruin their own lives by becoming increasingly ungodly. Falsehood ruins morals. The only wise and safe response when confronted by religious novelty and speculation is to have nothing to do with it.

Their teaching will spread like gangrene (verse 17). False teaching that contradicts the gospel of truth has a similar effect to gangrenous cells that multiply and spread their poison through the whole body, destroying vital tissues and leading to death. So false theology, once admitted to the church, spreads throughout the Christian community producing division, spiritual decline and finally the death of the church.

In Ephesus two individuals stood out as ringleaders in the growth of the new ideas – **Among them are Hymenaeus and Philetus**. Hymenaeus had already been put out of the church for his rejection of Christian morality (1 Tim. 1:20), here he is putting false interpretations on the Christian doctrine of the resurrection (verse 18).

By their behaviour and teaching they show that they are men **who have wandered away from the truth** (verse 18). The same expression is used in 1 Timothy 1:6 and 6:21, and describes people who have literally 'missed the mark', or turned aside from the straight path of truth and righteousness. People may wilfully destroy themselves under the very sound of the Word of God.

In the present case **they say that the resurrection has already taken place**. These men were guilty of denying the fundamental doctrine of the resurrection (and by implication the significance or finality of Christ's death). They may have argued that the resurrection was spiritual not physical, or that Christ only rose in the spirit realm and not in the body, following the dualistic lines of pagan Greek thought. In either case the Christian hope of a material resurrection is seriously undermined, with equally serious consequences for Christian morality (1 Cor. 15:1-19). The spiritual resurrection of all believers in Christ which occurs in this life through faith-union with him (Rom. 6:8-11; Eph. 2:4f.) is but the first stage of a fuller resurrection state that the coming of Christ in glory will complete (Rom. 8:23; Phil. 3:20f.). The Christian's experience of resurrection follows the pattern of Christ's own resurrection, which was both spiritual and material (1 Cor. 15:20ff.). Salvation is complete conformity to Christ.

The destructive tendency of this heresy is clear – **and they destroy the faith of some**. Just as in Crete (Tit. 1:11), where whole church families were being corrupted by the persistent activities of the heretics, these false teachers are living off the local churches in a parasitic way, by drawing away adherents for their own rival movement. They were successful in overturning the professed faith of a number of church members. But falsehood in religion is never totally successful, as the next verse states.

**Nevertheless, God's solid foundation stands firm, sealed
with this inscription, 'The Lord knows those who are his,'
and, 'Everyone who confesses the name of the Lord must
turn away from wickedness'** (verse 19). Although it might appear that the new theologians had won the day, Paul builds his
hopes for the church and the gospel on the sovereignty of God.
In ancient times a seal was sometimes engraved on the foundation stone of an important building. The church is God's building
(1 Cor. 3:9ff., 16), and on its foundation stone are inscribed the
words 'The Lord knows those who are his' (the words of the
motto are taken directly from the Greek translation of Numbers
16:5). This motto guarantees the eternal security of those who
are true believers, because they have been loved, chosen and
are known by God in his sovereign purpose of mercy (John
10:27ff.; Rom. 8:28-39). Those members of the church who have
fallen away from the truth show that they were never part of
God's building or included in its foundation.

The second imaginary motto engraved on the church's foundation stone reads 'Everyone who confesses the name of the
Lord must turn away from wickedness'. This command, if
obeyed, will guarantee the integrity of the true church of God in
the world against the seductive teachings of false teachers. The
occasion in Numbers 16 was the rebellion of Korah, who arro-
gantly objected to what he saw as Moses' self-appointed leadership over the people. In the end he was destroyed along with his
supporters. In Timothy's situation Hymenaeus and Philetus are
re-enacting the history of Korah by resisting the gospel preachers and challenging their claims to truth. The end of these men
will be the same as it was for Korah and his supporters, while
God's people will continue to live godly lives in the truth.

Taken together, these two mottos provide a perfect blend of
teaching about the church of God in the world at any time. The
true church is built on God's secret choice of his people (Rom.
8:29), but those who are chosen in Christ strive for holiness, the

sure sign of their election (2 Pet. 1:10). The true church is founded on the sovereignty of God and the responsible action of believers. The one guarantees that it will always exist, the other guarantees that it will always persevere. Because this is the case, believers can be confident about the survival of the church throughout history, even when it is infiltrated by those who deny the truth on which it is founded. God's solid foundation will always stand firm.

In a large house there are articles not only of gold and silver, but also of wood and clay; some are for noble purposes and some for ignoble (verse 20). Paul holds onto the picture of a building, only now he goes inside the house to look at its contents. Some objects in the house are expensive, some are inexpensive; some are intended for useful purposes, some are for menial. The same range of value and usefulness is to be found in God's temple-house, the visible church. There are those who live ungodly lives and teach falsehoods, there are those who live godly lives and teach the truth. Not everyone who claims membership and holds office in the nominal church is truly valuable to the Master of the house, nor does everyone fulfil a useful purpose (Matt. 25:14-30). Individuals like Hymenaeus and Philetus appear along with Timothy and Onesiphorus.

If a man cleanses himself from the latter, he will be an instrument for noble purposes, made holy, useful to the Master and prepared to do any good work (verse 21). The onus for usefulness rests on the individual leader. He must cleanse himself from everything that hinders his progress or defiles his profession (Heb. 12:1f.). This self-cleansing operation is the precondition for being instrumental, holy, useful and prepared in the service of Christ. Paul's words are a promise of the assured results of cleansing oneself from sinful things ('if ... he will be').

- Becoming an instrument for noble purposes means being capable of doing great work for God.
- Holiness means being separated from all iniquity and being available for God.

• Being useful to the Master of the house means being effective in the Lord's service.

• Being prepared to do any good work means that a man is in a ready frame of mind to buy up every opportunity for doing good.

Flee the evil desires of youth (verse 22) is addressed to Timothy as a young man who knew for himself the strength and variety of youthful passions. These include such intensities as anger, impatience, impetuosity, rebellion, aggression, lust, vanity, self-centredness, self-will, obstinancy. Youth is the time when the natural passions are most strong, hence the need for a firm stand against them. Paradoxically the only safe way to control these passions is to run from them. This is not an act of cowardice but of wisdom that brings results (1 Cor. 10:6, 14), for once these passions are indulged they quickly take control of the bodily members and break out in sinful words and acts (Rom. 7:5).

But negative action is not enough, positive goals must also be set – **and pursue righteousness, faith, love and peace, along with those who call on the Lord out of a pure heart.** 'Pursue' means making an all-out effort to reach a goal, it requires resolution (Phil. 3:13ff.; 2 Pet. 1:5-11). Righteousness, faith, love and peace are all basic Christian virtues, and necessary ingredients in the character of the Christian leader. Righteousness is Christian righteousness, obedience to the will of God in daily living. It is born from faith, which is the foundational Christian stance of trust in God and his Word. Love and peace come out of faith and a reconciled relationship with God in Christ which produces loving and peaceful relationships all round.

If the battle against evil desires is to be pursued successfully, then individual believers must join with their brothers and sisters in the Christian community, where together they can work out and work at their common salvation. The urge to excessive privacy and individualism must be resisted, and fellowship with fellow-Christians on a regular basis must be established. But not any church gathering will do, only one where the members call on the Lord out of a pure heart. Corporate acts of prayer and praise must be the sincere expression of hearts that are cleansed and kept clean in the sprinkled blood of Jesus (Heb. 12:22ff.). Not all that goes under the name of Christian worship is either spiritual or up-building.

Don't have anything to do with foolish and stupid arguments, because you know they produce quarrels (verse 23). Yet again (1 Tim. 1:4; 4:7; 6:4; 2 Tim. 2:14, 16) Paul warns Timothy about the dangers of religious disputes that have nothing to do with the central truths of the gospel. They are the product of foolish and untrained minds (stupid or uneducated) and only give birth to ('produce') quarrels. There is nothing good to be said on behalf of these controversies, their end results are positive proof against them. The pastor-teacher who knows the true nature and effects of these arguments will have nothing to do with them, and will teach his people to respond in the same way.

And the Lord's servant must not quarrel; instead, he must be kind to everyone, able to teach, not resentful (verse 24). Conscious of being the Lord's servant and not his own, the Christian teacher must avoid all quarrelling of the kind produced by the sectarian groups (2 Tim. 2:14, 23). Avoiding quarrelling is quite consistent with contending earnestly for the truth (Jude 3). Rather he must be kind, responsive, and free from offence in his pastoral style. He must show kindness (or gentleness) like a nursing mother cherishing her children (1 Thess. 2:7). He must do this in a non-discriminatory way, treating everyone on an equal footing. He must be trained, ready and willing to take every opportunity to instruct others in the faith. He must keep himself free from all kinds of resentments due to being overlooked or badly treated.

Those who oppose him he must gently instruct, in the hope that God will grant them repentance leading them to a knowledge of the truth (verse 25). Being kind and patient is not the same as being indifferent about the truth. So in unavoidable conflict-situations he will do what he can to defuse the situation, and then gently lead his opponents from their prejudiced and er-ror-filled opinions through repentance to the truth. Repentance is a radical change of heart and mind that leads to a personal knowl-edge of the truth and affects the whole of a person's life. Indi-viduals are responsible for repenting, but only God can give it, when he works it in them (Acts 5:31).

The Lord's servant will only achieve this level of gentleness and forthrightness to the degree that he is controlled by love for his opponents and is seeking their real and lasting good. His secret prayer will continue to be that the Lord will work through his efforts to give them the needed repentance, causing them to know the truth for themselves in a life-transforming way.

His ultimate desire should be that they will come to know the truth **and that they will come to their senses and escape from the trap of the devil, who has taken them captive to do his will** (verse 26). In coming to know God's truth they will also come to know themselves as people rebelling against God, and resisting the Spirit of grace. When their eyes have been opened they will be free from Satan's power, and the traps which he sets for people in his wiles (1 Tim. 3:7). Until the Son of God sets people free, they are held fast by the devil in their sins, but once the Lord sets them free, then they become free indeed (John 8:21-24, 30-36; 1 John 5:19).

Study Questions

Verse 19: What other lessons are to be learned from the story of Korah's rebellion? (Num. 16; 2 Pet. 2:15; Jude 11).

Verse 22: What special counsels and helps does the Bible give to young people? (Psa. 25:64ff.; 119:9; Eccles. 12:1; 1 Tim. 4:12).

Verse 26: What does the Bible say about the devil, and how he can be overcome? (Job 1-2; John 8:44; 1 Pet. 5:8f.; Rev. 12:11).

2 TIMOTHY: CHAPTER 3

The chapter falls into two parts – predictions about the last days (3:1-9) and more instruction for Timothy as a man of God (3:10-17).

The Last Days (3:1-9)

But mark this: There will be terrible times in the last days (verse 1). Timothy should not be totally surprised by certain people rejecting the gospel and falling under the devil's spell (2:26). This is in line with what will take place in 'the last days', the period of time that coincides with the Christian era from Christ's first coming to his second. This is the period in which human beings will either find salvation through the word of the gospel or play out their ultimate rejection of God by disbelieving the gospel. Towards the end of the last days the rebellion and unbelief of humanity against God will increase in ways described now by Paul (see also 2 Thessalonians 2:1-12). By being aware of this, Timothy and all believers after him will be ready and not be unduly shaken by the outbreak of lawless behaviour when it comes. Yet these will be 'terrible' or dangerous times for all humankind, including God's people (Matt. 24:22ff.).

In describing these times Paul says that **people will be**

- **lovers of themselves**, instead of loving others,
- **lovers of money**, instead of loving higher things,
- **boastful,** of what they possess and think they know,
- **proud**, which makes them look down on others,
- **abusive**, rather than sympathetic,
- **disobedient to their parents**, instead of honouring them, as God commands,
- **ungrateful**, rather than naturally thankful,
- **unholy**, or wicked.

It is a horrendous list of evil and unnatural attitudes and reactions.

Paul goes on (verses 3-5). People will be

- **without love**, which is a natural human affection,
- **unforgiving**, because they are opposed to mercy,
- **slanderous**, insensitive to the reputation of others,
- **without self-control**, or any kind of moral self-discipline,
- **brutal**, unfeeling about the pain of others,
- **not lovers of the good**, because their natural affections are fixed on evil objects.
- **treacherous**, unable to be trusted,
- **rash**, rushing headlong into ill-considered plans,
- **conceited**, puffed up with their own imaginary importance,
- **lovers of pleasure rather than lovers of God,** because their hearts are set on the enjoyment of this world only,
- **having a form of godliness but denying its power**, since their religion is built on feeling rather than on faith.

These people are so far from the truth that Timothy should **have nothing to do with them**. The fact that Paul can advise Timothy not to deal with such people proves that the times that he is describing were not totally confined to the future, but were already appearing in his own day. The final outbreak of evil before Christ returns will be the final stage of the evolutionary spiral of evil that has been working itself out in human history from the beginning (John 8:44; 2 Thess. 2:7).

They are the kind who worm their way into homes and gain control over weak-willed women, who are loaded down with sins and are swayed by all kinds of evil desires (verse 6). These phoney religious teachers propagate their destructive heresies by exploiting certain kinds of women, as the serpent deceived Eve (1 Tim. 2:14). This is because their notions of spiritual reality are so far-fetched that only those who are psychologically or emotionally disturbed will give them a hearing and a following. These women present an easy prey because they are already burdened with an unresolved sense of sin and guilt, and are quickly overcome by their uncontrolled passions. By offering their services as spiritual guides and private mentors, these gurus gain access to the homes and hearts and wealth of such women. In the ancient world many women were isolated at home and relatively uneducated. This laid them open to the clever speeches of religious quacks who peddled a false gospel and played on their natural sensibilities and fears.

These women are **always learning but never able to acknowledge the truth** (verse 7). They are lacking in any real seriousness in their religious questions, being incapable of committing themselves to God's truth. They are only committed to novelty, without a genuine desire to change their lives by repenting of their sins.

Just as Jannes and Jambres opposed Moses, so also these men oppose the truth – men of depraved minds, who, as far as the faith is concerned, are rejected (verse 8). The names of these two men do not appear in the Old Testament record (Exod. 7:11f.; 8:6f.), but they were known in Jewish tradition and handed down in Jewish folklore and narratives. It is a common New Testament practice to find Old Testament precedents for the evils of the last days (1 Cor. 10:1-11). Like the leaders Timothy has to deal with, Jannes and Jambres actively and openly opposed the truth preached by Moses, the servant of God (Exod. 7:11). By their determined opposition they show themselves to be corrupt in mind about the truth and disqualified from believing it. Such is the wasting effect of error when it is received and loved in place of the truth, it finally prevents a person from ever believing the truth and finding salvation.

But they will not get very far because, as in the case of those men, their folly will be clear to everyone (verse 9). Jannes and Jambres also provide a message of encouragement because they failed in their bold plan to destroy Moses and the work of God. No more will latter-day antagonists against Christianity succeed in their arrogant boasting against the gospel. God, who is in control of all his enemies and critics, will bring it about that their foolishness and pride will be made plain to everyone. He can do this by allowing them to adopt more and more extreme points of view or by bringing public scandal or sudden judgements on them. God is not mocked, although he may bear long with those who oppose him.

Study Questions

Verse 1: Compare other New Testament passages that describe the last days and the lessons to be learned from them (Mark 13:5-37; 2 Thess. 2:1-12; 1 Tim. 4:1-5; 2 Pet. 2:1-3; 3:1-9).

Verses 2 and 4: What is the place of desires (love) in a sinful culture? (Rom. 1:24, 26f.; Eph. 2:1ff.; Jas. 1:14f.; 2 Pet. 1:4; 1 John 2:16).

Verse 7: What is involved in knowing the truth? (Luke 15:17ff.; John 8:31-36; 2 Tim. 2:25f.; Tit. 1:1f.; 2 Pet. 3:17f.).

More Personal Counsels (3:10-17)

In marked contrast to the men of the last times, Paul counsels Timothy, **You, however, know all about my teaching, my way of life, my purpose, faith, patience, love, endurance** (verse 10). The 'you' is emphatic (as in 3:14 and 4:5) because Paul wants to draw attention to Timothy's quite different status as a man of God (verse 17). He reminds Timothy of the long training he has had as Paul's confidant over many years, and in the many experiences they have shared. This is in keeping with Paul's first impressions about Timothy (Acts 16:1-3), that he had promise, and could become a Christian leader under Paul's personal tuition. As a result Timothy had been privileged to watch Paul in action – listening to his preaching, observing his lifestyle, studying his professional goals, and learning from his leadership qualities such as faith, love, patience, endurance. Paul had made himself a role model for his younger colleague and disciple, so that when his time for responsible leadership arrived he would know how to react and what to teach. Until the succession takes place with his death, the aged apostle will continue to tutor Timothy in the art of Christian leadership and oversight through this last letter and hopefully a final meeting. All this teaches us that the most formative lessons in leadership, and the most lasting impressions are received, not through books or seminars, but through the real life modelling of Christian truth and grace by older Christian leaders, as younger men observe and study their style and methods first-hand. The power of personal example and faithfulness is incalculable.

Paul adds, **persecutions, sufferings – what kinds of things happened to me in Antioch, Iconium and Lystra, the persecutions I endured** (verse 11). Sufferings and persecutions are no small part of the lot of Christian pastors, so Paul singles out the sufferings that he had endured in Timothy's own home area in the Roman province of Pisidia during his first missionary journey in that region (Acts 14:1, 5ff., 19f.). Suffering is Christ's school, in which he teaches his servants some of the deepest lessons of faith and life so that they can instruct and counsel those who are suffering (2 Cor. 1:3-11). How a Christian teacher handles and interprets suffering says a great deal about his own relationship to God and the quality of his work for Christ.

Paul was no armchair theologian, remote from the real struggles of life, but a missionary on the field of operations, leading from the frontline. He endured persistent and violent opposition to his message and to his person, as he himself records (2 Cor. 11:22-28). Although the sufferings Paul endured in Antioch, Iconium and Lystra took place during his first missionary journey, Timothy may well have observed them for himself at that time before he and Paul became acquainted, during the second missionary journey some time later (Acts 15:36; 16:1ff.).

Paul could also claim, **Yet the Lord rescued me from all of them,** not in the sense of remaining unscathed from pain, fear or physical injury, but in being remarkably upheld and rescued from dangerous situations and hostile crowds. Repeatedly Paul had managed to elude his enemies and to go on to do more work for Christ. He attributed all of this good fortune to the personal oversight of Christ his Lord who had intervened providentially for him again and again. Even in his present imprisonment in Rome Paul had been experiencing the same faithfulness of his Lord towards him (2 Tim. 4:17f.). These repeated experiences of divine deliverance had built up in Paul the confidence that the one who had called him to suffer in his service (Acts 9:15f.) would always stand by him to rescue him by his presence (Acts 18:9f.).

In fact, everyone who wants to live a godly life in Christ Jesus will be persecuted (verse 12) expresses Paul's general conclusion from his own sufferings over a lifetime. From one point of view his sufferings were exceptional, because he was given a special commission by the risen Lord to herald the gospel in regions that had known nothing of the softening influences of God's Word. Yet Paul saw also that his experience of persecution and suffering was typical of the way the Lord leads all his people. Righteous suffering is the mark of all Christ's disciples because it is the way the Master went. Those who want to rule with Christ in glory must suffer for him and with him on earth (Luke 9:23ff.; John 12:24ff.). Because a life of godliness lived out of loyalty to Jesus Christ as King runs directly counter to this world's ungodly aims and values, friction results which spills over into persecution of one degree of intensity or another (John 15:18-21).

This persecution takes place **while evil men and impostors will go from bad to worse, deceiving and being deceived** (verse 13). Just as people deteriorate in their physical health by bad habits, so people can degenerate in their spiritual and moral condition through indulging evil thoughts and behaviour. Once falsehood becomes an accepted way of life, people go from bad to worse, deteriorating rapidly into a terminal spiritual condition. Their moral world is one of mutual deception where people exploit one another, and are not really surprised to be exploited in return. All moral decency has gone, and cheating and lying have become addictive.

But as for you is emphatic (also 1 Timothy 6:11 and 2 Timothy 3:10; 4:5). Paul is contrasting Timothy sharply with the sorts of people he has just described. The motives and methods of a man of God are radically different from those of impostors. **Continue in what you have learned and have become convinced of** is Paul's advice to Timothy. For many years Timothy had been Paul's understudy. During that period he had learned the gospel as a disciple, and had become convinced of it for himself. Now that he is moving into the role of Paul's successor and coming under the sorts of pressures that he saw in Paul's life, he must not even contemplate forsaking the apostolic traditions. Instead he must adhere to them rigorously in the hope of saving both his hearers and himself (1 Tim. 4:16). Loyalty to the apostolic standards is the first law of authentic Christian leadership.

Timothy will be helped to do this **because you know those from whom you learned it**. He had enjoyed the benefits of many instructors over the years, ranging from his own mother and grandmother to the great apostle (2 Tim. 1:5). To receive instruction is one thing; to know, love and admire one's instructors is another. Timothy's learning experience fell into the second category. It was this intimate knowledge of his instructors that would be of such great benefit to Timothy now that he was about to stand alone, for he had seen the gospel reflected and vindicated in their lives under all the testing circumstances of life. The personal acquaintance of godly and admired teachers, whether in the home, church or academy, is a lifelong blessing, for it helps to inspire confidence in the Christian message, to set the highest standards and goals, and to encourage resolute loyalty to the Christian faith to the end of one's life.

Timothy is to remember those from whom he learned the gospel **and how from infancy** [he had] **known the holy Scriptures** (verse 15). Paul has already given his readers some infor-

mation about the home in which Timothy grew up (1:5); it was a
godly home in spite of the lack of spiritual input by his father
(Acts 16:1). Apparently his religious training had been left in the
hands of the women of the family, who had made him thoroughly familiar with the Old Testament Scriptures since his infancy. It is to this lifelong acquaintance with the written Word of
God that Paul now directs Timothy's memory. This Bible knowledge from childhood would give Timothy his main support and
be his primary resource as he faced the demanding task of supervising the churches after Paul's death. It is out of such training
that God's leaders come, a training that produces deep convic-
tions, stable character and sensitivity to spiritual things.

By calling the Scriptures 'holy' writings Paul assumes that
they are sacred, unlike any other literature, being the written
words of God's creative breath (verse 16). In this respect the
Scriptures are unique in their nature and function, compared with
which all other religious writings are only human compositions.
These sacred writings deliver up their secrets only to those who
acknowledge them to be holy by opening their minds and hearts
to their teaching, submitting to their authority and acting on their
precepts and promises. When biblical scholars or the reading
public elevate their own minds above the Scriptures under the
guise of impartiality or respectability, they actually deny the sanc-
tity of these writings and consequently miss their saving truth. It
is to those who ask, knock and seek for the truth in the holy
Scriptures that it will be given, opened and revealed.

These are the writings **which are able to make you wise for
salvation through faith in Christ Jesus**. Paul wanted to remind
Timothy of the scope and power of the sacred writings. They are
inherently able to communicate a wisdom that comes from God
and leads to salvation. Not only do the Scriptures teach a heavenly wisdom and the way of salvation, they also engender that
personal trust in and acquaintance with Jesus Christ that makes
salvation real to the individual. God's revelation of his covenant
throughout biblical history makes clear that the one way of sal-

vation was already being taught under the Old Testament. Yet the Old Testament pointed forward to the coming and kingdom of Jesus, the promised Christ. This is true of each of the major sections of the Old Testament – the Law books, the prophetic writings and the poetical books; they all find their focus of fulfilment in him (Luke 24:27, 44). That this is no perspective imposed on these writings by Christians is shown by the fact that the Old Testament writers themselves were conscious of addressing future generations about the coming salvation of Jesus Christ, his sufferings and subsequent glory (1 Pet. 1:10ff.).

From this we learn a number of important practical lessons about the holy Scriptures:

• Christians should read the Old Testament Scriptures as a Christian book which predicts and foreshadows Jesus Christ, his death and resurrection and spiritual kingdom.

• Salvation can only come to people as they personally trust in Jesus Christ as he is presented to them in the pages of the Scriptures, including the Old Testament (Acts 8:26-35).

• the Scriptures themselves are the most powerful evangelistic tool available to Christians in doing evangelism since they are the primary and God-breathed witness to the person and work of Jesus Christ.

All Scripture is God-breathed (verse 16) is Paul's way of explaining the power the Scripture has to give the wisdom of salvation to its readers who come to trust in Jesus Christ. Its power to make wise and save lies in its nature as God-breathed writing. But what does Paul mean by this term? It means 'out-breathed' by God, and refers to the holy writings as finished productions. It is true that for this to happen the human authors must have been inspired when they wrote, in the sense of being enlightened and controlled by the Spirit of God (2 Pet. 1:21). But Paul is here describing the holy Scriptures, not the writers. What they wrote, the original parchments and codices, is what was breathed by God in the sense of a creative, originating act (similar to the origins of humanity (Gen. 2:7), the creations of the universe (Psa. 33:6), and the giving of the Spirit by Jesus (John 20:22). 'Out-breathed' (expiration) is therefore a better translation than 'in-breathed' (inspiration) because it indicates more clearly that the sacred writings themselves are what was created by God. This means that in getting back to the original text of the Scriptures, by comparing and arranging the available biblical manuscripts, and through accurate modern language versions, modern readers are put in possession of the very Word of God.

When Paul says 'all Scripture' or the whole (of) Scripture, he includes the whole canon of Old Testament writings, which by the time he wrote was more or less fixed by the Jews, who had excluded those fanciful writings that the circumcision groups on Crete (Tit. 1:14) and the speculative teachers in Ephesus (1 Tim. 1:4) were anxious to study and use. The translation 'every Scripture' is less likely in the context of this passage where Paul has just referred to the holy writings as a body of literature with which Timothy has been familiar since childhood (verse 5). But even if the rendering 'every Scripture' is allowed, it would only confirm the same belief in the God-breathed and, therefore, totally reliable nature of Scripture, by considering the parts rather than the whole. Either way Scripture possesses and reveals the very same quality of God-breathedness, whether one examines the whole of Scripture or any one section of it.

One translation that is inadmissible is 'every inspired Scripture is also profitable', because this introduces the idea that some parts of the Scriptures may not be inspired by God, a suggestion that robs Scripture of its unity, as well as denying the basis of Paul's claim for its profitability. Such a translation owes more to philosophical presuppositions and theological prejudice than to objective study of the Greek text. The combination of two adjectives ('God-breathed' and 'profitable') predicated with the one verb 'to be' makes this translation grammatically irregular (for a perfect parallel construction see 1 Timothy 4:4). Inspiration, or better *expiration*, was never a selective process or a stop-start experience so far as the biblical authors and their writings are concerned. If that is not the case, we could never know which parts of the Bible are God-breathed and which are not. Such a mixed production would also reflect badly on the God of truth. The Bible does not support anywhere the idea of limited or selective inspiration. The entirety of Scripture, in part and as a whole, is God-breathed and is trustworthy and profitable as a result.

Biblical inspiration is a mystery because it combines what is humanly sinful and fallible with what is divinely infallible and sinless. The Scriptures, as the finished product of this process, display a remarkable diversity of styles, interests and literary form. All this suggests that the act of God in breathing out his Word, in the thirty-nine writings of the Old Testament, and by analogy the twenty-seven writings of the New Testament, took place in such a way as to allow genuine freedom to the individuality and personality of the human writers, while guiding these same writers into all truth and preserving their writings from every kind of error.

Holy Scripture is God-breathed **and is useful for teaching, rebuking, correcting and training in righteousness**. The one follows from the other since all God's creative works are useful to human beings. Scripture is God's *paideia* (the classical Greek ideal of education), his appointed means for human instruction and discipline. Scripture has a definite utilitarian purpose which Paul now sets out under four distinct but related functions. Properly understood and handled, Scripture impacts on the full extent of human need, and works like a remedial medicine bringing progressively enlightenment, self-knowledge, moral correction and wholeness.

• Scripture is useful for teaching about God, his creation, human nature created and fallen, and the way of salvation in Jesus Christ.

• Scripture is useful for rebuking us about our sinful selves, for exposing particular sins and faults, along with all those dishonest reasonings that we use to rationalise our wrongdoing.

• Scripture is useful for correcting our lives by pointing out the right way to live, and by presenting supportive arguments and promises with which to implement the necessary changes.

• Scripture is useful for training us in righteousness by empowering us to recognise and choose what is good and to reject what is evil, so that we begin to live in ways that are pleasing to God and useful to others.

Contrary to the claims of post-modern culture, the Creator God has put into our hands a complete guide to the meaning of life and the living of it. The Scriptures show us that we can have certainty about the ultimate issues of life. The God of the Scriptures never meant us to live without knowing, so he has given us his God-breathed Word which the men and women of the third millennium, like those of the first and second, can access and read to find the way of salvation through believing in Jesus Christ as he is represented in its pages.

The whole Scripture has been God-breathed **so that the man of God may be thoroughly equipped for every good work** (verse 17). The man of God in the Old Testament was the prophetic messenger (2 Chron. 25:7, 9). In the New Testament this expression refers in the first place to the Christian leader who teaches God's Word and acts with authority (1 Tim. 6:11). But the servant of the Lord will never be complete until and unless he reads himself constantly into the text of Scripture and responds to the voice of God speaking there. Timothy (and the modern Christian leader) will find there all the knowledge, encouragement and resources he needs for effective leadership. They will train him to be practically useful in doing good as every opportunity arises. The leader will only display his personal obedience to the Scriptures when he exemplifies in his own life the good works that the Scriptures themselves everywhere enjoin and inspire (1 Tim. 4:12). The real test of knowledge of the Scriptures is our productivity level in doing good works.

Study Questions

Verse 15: Discuss the different ways in which different parts of the Old Testament point to Jesus Christ and to salvation through faith in him (Matt. 12:39-42; Luke 22:37; 1 Cor. 5:6-8; 9:1-15; 10:1-11).

Verse 16: What answer would you give to those who distinguish the Bible from the Word of God? (Matt. 4:1-11; John 10:34f.; 2 Pet. 1:19-21; Rev. 22:18f.).

Verse 17: If the Scriptures make Christians wise and complete, is there any need for them to study the physical, human and social sciences?

2 TIMOTHY: CHAPTER 4

In the final chapter of this most personal of letters, Paul makes a final appeal to Timothy to adhere to the truth (4:1-5), he reviews his own life and work (4:6-8), and lastly makes comments on a number of individuals by name, with which are mingled remarks about his experiences in court (4:9-22).

A Final Charge (4:1-5)

In the presence of God and Christ Jesus is Paul's way of bringing weight and solemnity to his final words to Timothy before his own departure out of this world (verses 6ff.). The overwhelming sense of God's unseen presence, along with that of Jesus Christ, inspired Paul to speak in this way, as it has always done for servants of God (1 Kings 17:1; 18:15). An abiding and deepening sense of the heavenly world is the most powerful stimulant for producing sincerity, urgency and integrity in the work of Christ in the midst of sufferings.

In particular Jesus Christ is the one **who will judge the living and the dead**, an article of faith constantly repeated in the apostolic preaching (Acts 10:42; 17:31; Rom. 14:9-11; 1 Pet. 4:5) and which goes back to Jesus himself (Matt. 7:21ff.; 16:27; 25:31f.). The fact that Jesus Christ will be the personal Judge of all those who have died, as well as those who will be alive at his coming, is positive proof of his divine majesty. This judgement will include all believers, whose life and work for Christ will be assessed and rewarded in that day (Rev. 11:18). This is a powerful incentive to faithfulness and sincerity in the service of Christ (2 Cor. 5:10; Jas. 3:1).

Paul reasons from Christ's judgement **and in view of his appearing and his kingdom**. His appearing will usher in the judgement, and the judgement will establish and advance his kingdom. Paul here appeals to that unique complex of events that will bring about the end of this age and lead into the age of eternity. Christ's appearing will be a public disclosure of his person, literally an epiphany (Tit. 2:13), a moment when the full glory of God will be revealed and fill the whole of creation. So Christ will appear in the midst of his own created universe, to right its wrongs and to set up his eternal kingdom of right, all to the glory of God the Father (Phil. 2:9ff.). The love and grace of God that began to be revealed in Christ's first epiphany, under the veil of Christ's weakness and sin-bearing form (Tit. 2:11; 3:4), will reach its culmination in open splendour through the final epiphany of the Man born to be King.

These future, climactic and awesome events set an eschatological framework or endtime viewpoint for all Christians to work from in their service here and now. So Paul adds **I give you this charge:** in the form of five plain mandates which sum up, in an easy-to-be-remembered way, the principal activities and goals that are meant to shape all pastoral leadership. When Paul says 'I give you this charge' he is using a technical term which can be used for putting people under oath before God and points to the seriousness of the matter under discussion (Acts 20:23f.; 1 Tim. 5:21; 2 Tim. 2:14).

• **Preach the Word** is Paul's first mandate. Timothy, like every Christian preacher, is a herald (this is what the word signifies) of the King, and his message is the word of the King – the gospel. The word of the gospel covers all the themes of Scripture and their applications to life in the world. This is the principal task of the teaching elder (1 Cor. 9:16; 1 Tim. 4: 11, 13, 16; 5:17) compared with which, every other activity is secondary (Acts 6:1-4). Paul had consistently followed this priority in his own ministry (Acts 20:17-21, 24-27). Through such preaching Christ builds his church, by bringing sinful men and women to faith in him and by adding to the faith of those who are already joined to him (Acts 2:47; 5:14; 20:32).

• **Be prepared in season and out of season** is the second mandate and follows as an extension to it. The servant of Christ must always stand by for opportunities to preach the Word night and day (Acts 20:31). These opportunities may come in both favourable and unfavourable circumstances, they may be looked for, or they may occur at random. But the preacher-pastor must be ready to recognise them when they fall across his path and to seize the moment (Eph. 5:15f.). This imperative implies a frame of mind very far from those who want to make the pastoral ministry a nine to five job, or to set off-limits to their congregation.

• **Correct** is a necessary but most delicate part of the preacher's task. It means confronting and exposing the faults of others even with boldness (1 Tim. 5:20; Tit. 1:13). Only by such faithful preaching can the hearers gain the real benefits of the Word, as it sinks into their hearts, wins a favourable verdict in their conscience, and brings about real changes in their behaviour.

• **Rebuke** means warning solemnly and censuring those who persist in wilful error or in wrongdoing. It involves using that authority which the Lord gives to those whom he appoints to the work of shepherding his people (2 Cor. 13:10).

• **Encourage** – preaching the Word involves both the law and the gospel, the one to reprove and rebuke (1 Tim. 1:8-11), the other to encourage. Christian preaching must be a mixture of both if it is to have its intended effects in changing human lives and making them fruitful in good works. Encouragement is a vital part of evangelical preaching because it gives strong reasons for hope and personal effort. This kind of strengthening is the final goal the preacher must always aim for if his hearers are not to become disheartened.

The primary work of preaching the Word of God must be conducted **with great patience and careful instruction** if it is to be at all successful. The Lord's servant must be patient with people because they are slow to learn and grow, and because they present him with an endless catalogue of needs (2 Tim. 2:24ff.). The church is rarely reformed overnight, rather it succumbs to the patient toil, faithful witness and prayerful efforts of the man of faith. He must dependently wait for God to work through his efforts, instead of forcing people to listen to him and do as he says, in the false belief that his own energies and commitment will carry the day. Careful instruction is literally 'all teaching', which indicates that the whole counsel of God in the special revelation of Scripture must be used to meet the varied needs of people. This is the wisdom and practical value of systematic Bible-teaching ministry.

The task of preaching the Word of Christ is all the more urgent because **the time will come when men will not put up with sound doctrine** (verse 3). Paul has already made predictions of this kind (2 Thess. 2:1-12; 1 Tim. 4:1-3; 2 Tim. 3:1-5). Although the Christian message has met with a mixed response from the beginning, Paul here predicts a time that had not yet arrived when people will react to the gospel with unusual impatience. For them it will not be heard as good news but treated with intolerance and exchanged cheaply for hopeless substitutes. They will reject the redemptively healing powers ('sound teaching', 1 Tim. 1:10; 6:3; 2 Tim. 1:13; Tit. 1:13; 2:8) contained in the gospel, preferring the quack remedies held out by self-appointed teachers in the realm of the spiritual. Symptoms of this spiritual sickness have been evident in most ages of the church.

Instead, to suit their own desires, they will gather around them a great number of teachers to say what their itching ears want to hear. Instead of beginning with God's Word and submitting themselves humbly to its light and truth to straiten out their thinking and the way they live, they reverse the process by starting with their own corrupt passions and unexamined prejudices against the truth, then seek out teachers to confirm them in their errors and sins. They applaud and pay for what they want to hear, whatever leaves them comfortable in a totally secular and hedonistic lifestyle. The objective authority of the Word is deceptively replaced by the subjective autonomy of their passing

whims. They only want to hear what is trivial, titillating and speculative, the latest and most daring in the realm of religious innova-
tion.

This is the mindset of a great deal of modern religious faith,
theology and writing: the unrestricted exploration of religious psy-
cho-space, the syncretistic marrying of Christianity with eastern
mysticism, and the reconstruction of historic faith along psychological and sociological lines. The end-product is theosophy, a
mishmash of theology and philosophy, realising itself in myriad
forms of post-Christian spirituality. The possibilities and openings for new insights are endless, but in the process the saving
truth of the gospel of Christ has been bartered away for the trin-
kets of new age mythologies.

**They will turn their ears away from the truth and turn
aside to myths** (verse 4). A craving for theological novelty creates a distaste for the truth, the new ousts the old for the simple
reason that it is older and therefore suspect or pre-scientific. The
minds of these disciples of change are closed to the truth but
wide open to the sensational speculations invented by their chosen teachers (1 Tim. 1:6; 5:15). Myths are stories concocted from
sacred sources like the Bible, but without any regard to the original historical context or the rules of sound interpretation (1 Tim.
1:4; Tit 1:14). Though these advocates of religious novelty lump
biblical Christianity together with ancient mythology, the New
Testament writers are very clear that their form of Christianity is
fundamentally historical, and qualitatively different from all kinds
of religious myths, ancient or modern (2 Pet. 1:16ff.).

But you (verse 5) is an emphatic appeal to Timothy (as in 1
Timothy 6:11 and 2 Timothy 3:14) because he must uphold the
independent authority of the Word of Christ. To do this **keep
your head in all situations**, which means not allowing himself
to panic but to maintain a rational approach to the problems by
retaining self-control. There is the need to **endure hardship**
because faithful preaching and ministry will always encounter
opposition, even outright hostility (2 Tim. 1:8; 2:3, 10; 3:12).

Timothy must **do the work of an evangelist**, which could be a technical reference to the office of this name (Acts 21:8; Eph. 4:11). There is little information about the New Testament evangelist except that he must have received a roving commission to proclaim the gospel message. The call to Timothy to do the work of an evangelist could simply mean that he must be careful to preach the gospel in all his teaching work. There is no hard and fast distinction between teaching the Word and preaching the gospel. All teaching should be evangelistic and all evangelism should be didactic.

In a word Timothy must **discharge all the duties of** [his] **ministry**. He must aim at an all-round ministry centred on the Word of God, holding nothing back that is helpful, teaching publicly and from house to house, testifying to all races repentance toward God and faith in the Lord Jesus Christ, not shunning to declare the whole counsel of God. In all this he must serve the Lord with all humility, in the midst of tears and trials, showing by example how the gospel works.

Study Questions

Verse 1: What does the New Testament say about the final judgement and how should it influence the way we live here and now? (Matt. 25:31-46; Rom. 2:5-11; 1 Cor. 4:1-5; 2 Cor. 5:7-11; 2 Pet. 3:10-14).

Verse 4: Can you recognise parallels between these myths and some of the false teachings popular today? Give actual examples.

Paul's Farewell (2 Timothy 4:6-8)

Having sounded his final alarm to Timothy about carrying on the work of the gospel ministry, Paul now reflects out loud on his own condition and future. These are very moving words for they are the testimony of a great servant of God facing imminent death.

They provide a lens for viewing the rest of the letter. **For I am already being poured out like a drink offering, and the time for my departure has come** (verse 6). Paul is already conscious of the approach of death. Although he had faced death on many occasions, and the Lord had delivered him from them all (2 Cor. 1:8-10; 2 Tim. 4:18), this time he senses that there will be no turning back. But in this prospect the apostle is not at all defeatist.

He likens his death to a drink offering which is being poured out on the ground as a libation to the gods, in his case the one God and Father of the Lord Jesus Christ. Such offerings were made in Israel as acts of consecration to the Lord, the God of the covenant (Num. 15:6-10; 28:7). So Paul sees the ending of his life as such an event, in which his life is gathered together in the inner momentum and logic of its obedience, and given over to God in a final act of voluntary submission and self-giving. During his first imprisonment in Rome, Paul had faced the same possibility of being offered as a sacrifice in Christ's service (Phil. 2:17), but this had been averted as he expected (Phil. 1:19). Now several years on, he is facing the same prospect but this time believes that he will not escape.

Yet Paul is not crushed by this prospect, nor is he stoically indifferent. He speaks about his death in triumphalist tones as the time of his 'departure'. In doing so he expresses a radiant faith that overcomes death, even death in the violent form of martyrdom (Paul was beheaded). Death and dying for the Christian is truly a departure, not the close of a journey but the setting out on a new stage of it. The Christian departs to be with Christ in heaven, which is so much better than even the best of spiritual conditions here (Phil. 1:23). So 'departure' is more than a euphemism for the harsh reality of death and burial, it is the moment and the method of the Christian's liberation into the expansive and joyful presence of his Lord that takes the believer to his heavenly home. The Christian departs in death, just as a ship looses its moorings and sets sail into the open sea, or as a soldier strikes camp and sets out on a new day's march.

The Christian's death never happens by chance, for Paul declares his confidence in the 'time' of his departure. This is a nuanced New Testament word which indicates a moment planned and brought about by God in his eternal purpose, even although it might have been fixed by Caesar's judicial bureaucracy. The time and circumstances of the Christian's death are appointed by God, and the believer can rest comfortably in this knowledge, as Paul does here. The Christian's times are in the Lord's hands both in living and in dying.

The approach of death naturally concentrates the mind and quickens memory as one's life passes by in vivid review. As Paul engages in such reverie he can honestly say that he has performed Christ's service with a high degree of faithfulness. **I have fought the good fight, I have finished the race, I have kept the faith** (verse 7). It is through Christ's grace that Paul makes these claims, not in any spirit of self-congratulation (1 Cor. 15:9f.).

• **I have fought the good fight**. The life of the Christian from beginning to end is an intense contest against the world, the flesh, and the devil. In this contest the divinely-supplied armour of God is necessary if the Christian is to survive to the end (2 Cor. 10:3ff.; Eph. 6:10-18). The fight is good because the war is just and the cause is noble – the glory of God, the triumph of Christ, the salvation of men and women, and the vindication of righteousness in the earth. The Christian may therefore engage in it heartily with all his powers. Even as he wrote, Paul was confronting the enemy for the last time, for he was laying final hold of eternal life.

• **I have finished the race**. Paul continues with a sporting image, likening the Christian's life of faith to a race, a marathon perhaps, because it is run over a long distance and calls for endurance. Now that he has reached the last hurdle of death, Paul can claim that he has run his race to the end, and

that he looks forward with expectation to receive the crown
which was awarded to successful competitors (verse 8). But
Paul's successful completion of his earthly race of faith has
been achieved by means of strict self-discipline, faithfulness
to his appointed ministry and the careful cultivation of conformity to Christ (Acts 20:24; 1 Cor. 9:24-27; 11:1; Phil.
3:13f.).

• **I have kept the faith**. He had also kept the faith in the sense
of defending and proclaiming without shame the full gospel
of Jesus Christ from the day the Lord called him (2 Tim. 1:8-
12). The risen Lord had appeared to him in person for this
very purpose (Acts 26:15-18; Gal. 1:11f.). He had faithfully
proclaimed the whole counsel of God in Christ (Acts 20:27).
As Paul faced Caesar's tribunal for the first time in this second imprisonment in Rome, so that the seriousness of the
charges against him could be investigated, he had continued
to witness openly to the faith entrusted to him so that the
Gentiles and their rulers might hear the gospel (2 Tim. 4:16f.).

Paul's dying testament is a fitting tribute to what can be accomplished in a human life that is fully given over to God. It is
also a solemn call to all Christians so to live that when death
comes they may have few regrets and be able, like Paul, to witness to the triumphs of God's grace in the life they have lived.

Paul has looked back, now he looks forward. **Now there is in
store for me the crown of righteousness, which the Lord, the
righteous Judge, will award to me on that day** (verse 8) –
Paul's immediate prospect is bright because he anticipates the
reward of the heavenly inheritance which Christ in person will
award to him. He speaks of this as a victory crown, continuing
the athletic picture from verse seven. The classical Greek crown
was a wreath of laurel leaves woven together and placed on the
head of the winner. Christ's crown of thorns was a cruel mock-
ery of this celebration. Paul's crown, and every Christian's, will

be a wreath of righteousness, illustrating the final victory of salvation, eternal life itself (1 Cor. 9:25; Jas. 1:12; Rev. 2:10).

Paul describes that victory wreath as already in store in heaven and waiting him (1 Pet. 1:4), a statement that reflects the tension in the Christian's experience of salvation between what he now already possesses and what he does not yet possess. Salvation comes to the Christian by instalments: first at conversion when Christ makes the believer his own, then progressively throughout their earthly life as the Christian grows in grace and knowledge, next at death when he appears before Christ in glory, and finally at the resurrection when his conformity to Christ is complete.

Paul looks to the final act of the drama of salvation when Christ comes for universal judgement. He is the righteous or just Judge who will render to everyone, including Christians, what their works and lives deserve. As believers in Christ Christians have already been justified with God, and are secure in their relationship with God. Because of Christ their works will be rewarded and they will be given a place among the redeemed people of God in heaven as their rightful inheritance forever (Col. 3:24). The works of believers do not in themselves merit any reward since they are tainted by sin, but in his grace Christ will graciously and righteously reward whatever they have done or suffered for him (Matt. 25:31-42; 1 Cor. 3:7-17; Rev. 11:17f.).

Paul is not just thinking of himself, for Christ will award the prize **not only to me, but also to all who have longed for his appearing**. Christ is impartial in his judgement and will treat all his people alike. To each of them he will award the crown of victory. Christ's people are known, among other things, by their loving longing for their Lord's return in public glory (Phil. 3:20; 1 Thess. 1:9f.; 2 Thess. 4:13-18; Tit. 2:13; Heb. 9:28). They are those who have loved and continue to (literally) love his epiphany, they have always longed for it and hastened it (2 Pet. 3:12). The final prayer of the true church of Jesus Christ in Scripture is, 'Even so, come, Lord Jesus!' (Rev. 22:20).

Study Questions

Verse 6: What is the point of likening the Christian life to a sacrificial offering? (Rom. 12:1f.; 1 Cor. 5:7f.; Heb. 13:15f.; Jas. 1:18).

How else does the Bible picture the believer's death? (Luke 16:22, 25; Phil. 1:21ff.; 1 Thess. 4:13f.; Rev. 14:13).

Verse 8: Why should Christians long for Christ's appearing? (Matt. 13:41ff.; John 14:1ff.; 1 Pet. 1:8).

Men and Movements (4:9-18)

Do your best to come to me quickly (verse 9) is a request that conveys a sense of the urgency Paul feels as he lives from day to day, not knowing just how long he may still have to live. He longs to see Timothy one more time before he dies (2 Tim. 1:4), but if that is to happen then Timothy must move quickly. By the time it took for this letter to reach Timothy, and for him to make arrangements for his own travel to Paul, he would have been still weeks or even months away from Rome, measured by ancient postal and travel times.

Paul gives another reason for his longing to see Timothy again: **for Demas, because he loved this world, has deserted me and has gone to Thessalonica** (verse 10). Paul's ministry was sprinkled with disappointments over individuals and groups of former friends (1:15; Phil. 1:14-18). Demas is the latest example of such disloyalty. He is mentioned by Paul as one of his fellow-workers (Philem. 24) along with Luke, Paul's beloved doctor (Col. 4:14). His 'loving this present age' we conjecture meant that Demas preferred the personal and material rewards to be found at Thessalonica, such as popularity and comforts, to the more rigorous demands and the popular stigma of working with Paul. The love of this world had, to a large extent, replaced the love of Christ's appearing (verse 8).

The case of Demas is a tragic one that teaches important lessons to all Christian ministers:

• The defection of former colleagues is a painful experience that Christian leaders who are faithful to Christ will experience at more than one point in their career. Jesus did (John 13:18), so did Paul (Phil. 1:14-18), and so will all those who choose to follow the apostolic style of leadership in their churches today.

• The danger of worldliness is ever-present for Christian ministers, who can begin well but compromise later like Demas, with negative results for their public ministry. The good fight of faith needs to be fought right to the end and renewed every day (2 Tim. 4:6f.); the Christian leader must not rely on yesterday's grace and achievements.

Crescens has gone to Galatia, and Titus to Dalmatia. The movements and motives of these men must be carefully separated from those of Demas. They were engaged in the service of the gospel for the best reasons. Crescens is mentioned only here in Paul's writings, but there is a persistent report in early Christian writings of him going to Gaul. Galatia may therefore refer not to Asia Minor (Turkey), but to Gaul (France), and point to further expansion of the gospel in Europe.

Titus is a well-known and highly trusted co-worker of Paul (see Tit. 1:4). Dalmatia (Yugoslavia) had been visited by Paul (Rom. 15:19) as the limit of his missionary travel and work. Since Paul had earlier asked Titus to meet him in Nicopolis, a city in that region (Tit .3:12), it may well be that Titus had decided to do more work there instead of coming to visit Paul in Rome across the Adriatic.

Only Luke is with me (verse 11) communicates something of the loneliness Paul was experiencing in Rome, but he had learned in all his circumstances to be strengthened by Christ and to be content (Phil. 4:11ff.). Luke was Paul's longtime friend, travelling companion, fellow-worker and private doctor (Acts 16:8-15; Col. 4:14; Philem. 24). He may also have been Paul's secretary and scribe in writing the Pastoral letters (see Introduction).

Get Mark and bring him with you, because he is helpful to me in my ministry. Mark was the surname of John, the cousin of Barnabas (Acts 12:25; Col. 4:10). He had accompanied Paul on his first missionary journey but had lost his favour when he withdrew from the work (Acts 13:13; 15:36-39). By the time of Paul's first imprisonment in Rome he is with Paul again, apparently reconciled (Col. 4:10; Philem. 24). Now Paul commends him for his usefulness in ministering either to himself privately or in the apostle's wider mission. Like Onesimus, and all true believers, Mark had been made useful (helpful) by Christ. This is also a tribute to the reconciling power of the gospel in human relationships over a period of time.

I sent Tychicus to Ephesus (verse 12). Tychicus was another longtime friend of Paul. He accompanied him as one of the Gentile delegates on his mission of mercy to Jerusalem (Acts 20:4), and is commended in Paul's letters to the churches at Ephesus (Eph. 6:21f.) and Colosse (Col. 4:7-9). Now Paul has sent/is sending (both translations are possible in the Greek) him back to Ephesus where Timothy may have been at the time of writing, in which case Tychicus would have been the bearer of this letter to him.

When you come, bring the cloak that I left with Carpus at Troas, and my scrolls, especially the parchments (verse 13). This is a personal piece of evidence which defenders of the Pauline authorship of the Pastoral letters rightly appeal to as strongly supporting their case. A forger would have been unlikely to think up such a personal request. The cloak, a heavy outer garment worn against the elements, was remembered with longing by Paul in his cold and lonely prison, especially with winter coming on (verse 21). About Carpus we know nothing beyond this single reference. The leaving of these items at Troas may have been due to Paul's arrest there, and the speed with which he was escorted away.

The 'scrolls' would have been made of papyrus for writing purposes. 'Parchments' is a Latin-based word (*membrana*) used to describe codices which were used as notebooks for personal records and writing. Much as every reader of this letter would love to know what was written on these scrolls and parchments, there is now no way of knowing, the secret having died with Paul. What is instructive is Paul's commitment to reading, writing and productive activity right up to the end of his life, even in prison. Many worthy ministers of Christ have followed him in this.

Alexander the metalworker did me a great deal of harm (verse 14). This may be the same individual as Paul had excommunicated from the church at Ephesus (1 Tim. 1:20). If so, then this might explain his personal animosity and opposition to Paul, now that their paths had crossed again. Alexander has also been identified with the individual of the same name who was put forward by the Jews during the mob scene in Acts 19:33, but he appears to have been an unwilling spokesman, not possessed of the steely character of Paul's accuser here.

Since Paul goes on to speak about his trial appearances in Rome, it may be that this Alexander had something to do with Paul's arrest or the prosecution against him. Whatever the explanation, we learn from this how severely the Lord allowed his servant Paul to be tested and accused at the hands of evil opponents, even to the very end of his life.

The Lord will repay him for what he has done. This is a calm assertion of faith, based upon the often repeated principle of God's justice in judgement (Psa. 62:12; Rom. 2:6-11). It is uttered without vindictiveness, since Paul entrusted himself for justice to his faithful heavenly Judge, in accordance with the Scriptures and following the example of his Saviour (Prov. 20:22; Rom. 12:19; 1 Pet. 2:21ff.). The Lord's persecuted servant can rest assured in the knowledge of God's moral sovereignty: that one day all personal wrongs will be righted by a perfectly just Creator (1 Pet. 4:19).

Since Paul believes that Timothy will encounter Alexander in the future he forewarns him. **You too should be on your guard against him, because he strongly opposed our message** (verse 15). Alexander was no ordinary unbeliever, but an outspoken and determined antagonist. Particularly in situations of outright opposition and danger, the servant of Christ must clothe himself with God's spiritual armour (Eph. 6:10-18), and not be naive, but be constantly on the alert through prayerful dependence on God (Matt. 10:16).

At my first defence, no-one came to my support, but everyone deserted me (verse 16). This is a reference to Paul's preliminary appearance before the emperor, in which his case was investigated and the accused and witnesses were heard. Sadly for reasons that Paul does not even hint at, no-one from the Roman church community came forward in his support, so that the apostle was left alone to make his own defence.

In a gesture of Christlike generosity (Luke 23:34), he wishes his disloyal friends no ill-will by saying, **May it not be held against them**. While it is true that all believers in Christ have been justified now from all their offences, it is also true that their attitudes, choices, words and actions as believers are being judged now, and will be judged by Christ the Lord in the day he comes (Rom. 14; 2 Cor. 5:10; 1 Pet. 4:17). This is a solemn prospect that should inspire them to live by a good conscience by aiming to please their Lord in everything.

The disloyalty of Paul's friends highlighted all the more the faithfulness of his heavenly Lord. His treatment of Paul was far more generous than that of his people. **But the Lord stood at my side and gave me strength, so that through me the message might be fully proclaimed and all the Gentiles might hear it** (verse 17). Paul was Christ's ambassador to the end, placing the opportunity to proclaim the saving message above every consideration of personal safety or comfort. His original mandate had been to proclaim Christ among the Gentiles and from this Paul had never resigned (Acts 26:15-18; Gal. 1:15f.). Indeed he had turned his first appearance before the emperor and a cross-section of imperial society into an opportunity to complete his missionary mandate to evangelise the nations of the world.

At the same time Paul had experienced the supportive presence of Christ through the Spirit, and received from this the courage and confidence to proclaim the message of Christ without fear or shame. Christ had promised that he would stand by Paul in this way and deliver him from his enemies (Acts 26:17). So it had often turned out in the past (Acts 18:9f.), and now again at the end of Paul's earthly service.

The faithful servant of Christ may rest assured that Christ will strengthen him in proportion to his own weakness (2 Cor. 12:9f.). Christ's spiritual presence and support had meant everything to Paul, and had carried him through his most recent trial. The same pattern of fellowship and empowering from above can be expected by those who follow Paul in his courageous faithfulness in the service of Christ and the gospel. Those who honour him, he honours and keeps (Matt. 10:32f.; Phil. 4:13, 19; 2 Tim. 2:11f.).

And I was delivered from the lion's mouth should not be taken literally, for Roman citizens could not be thrown to the lions in the Roman amphitheatre. He uses the same vivid expression in 1 Corinthians 15:32 as a way of describing extreme danger at the hands of unbelievers. The next verse confirms the metaphorical understanding of Paul's language. This experience leads Paul to make a concluding confession of faith and doxology about the faithfulness of the Lord.

The Lord will rescue me from every evil attack and will bring me safely to his heavenly kingdom. To him be glory for ever and ever. Amen (verse 18). Buoyed by this recent deliverance, Paul breaks out into an expression of heartfelt confidence in the Lord's trustworthiness for the future. Although Paul

knew that he faced almost certain death and that he would not
get out of prison alive, he understood that he was in Christ's
hands and that God would preserve him *from* the destroying power
of death and *for* his heavenly kingdom (verse 8). All Christ's
true servants are similarly indestructible until their work is done,
being kept by God's power for their heavenly inheritance (1 Pet.
1:3-5). The thought of Christ's faithfulness draws a spontaneous
doxology from the apostle, which he seals with a concluding amen
(let it be so).

Study Questions

Verse 9: What inducements and temptations cause Christian leaders to compromise their sincere commitment to Christ? (Gal. 2:11-
16; Phil. 1:15f.; 2:19ff.; 1 Tim. 3:3, 6).

Verse 15: Is being on one's guard against people a Christian virtue? (Matt. 10:16; John 2:23ff.; Rom. 15:30f.; Tit. 1:10-13).

Verse 16: Does the Lord hold the faults of his people against
them? (Psa. 51:5-13; 1 Cor. 3: 10-15; 2 John 7f.).

Greetings (4:19-22)
**Greet Prisca and Aquila and the household of Onesipho-
rus**. Paul's final words are for friends. He first met the Jewish
Christian couple, Aquila and Priscilla, in Corinth, where he stayed
with them because they were fellow-tentmakers (Acts 18:2f.).
Originally from Rome, they had been expatriated eastwards due
to the emperor's edict against the Jews. They travelled with Paul
to Ephesus, where they remained after his departure and instructed Apollos in a more accurate understanding of the gospel
(Acts 18:18f., 24ff.). They were still there when Paul wrote to
the Corinthians (1 Cor. 16:19). Then when Paul wrote his letter
to the church in Rome they were back there, the first to be greeted

by him at the close of his letter where he commends them highly (Rom. 16:3f.). Prisca (Priscilla is a variant) is sometimes named first, either because she owned their business or because she was of more noble birth than her husband.

Onesiphorus has already been mentioned in this letter (1:16ff.). The way in which Paul sends greetings to his household on both occasions rather suggests that Onesiphorus himself may have been dead. His household was remembered because of the high esteem in which he was held. The New Testament thinks in terms of families, as well as individuals, as part of its covenant teaching about salvation (Acts 16:31ff.; 18:8; 1 Cor. 1:16).

Erastus stayed in Corinth, and I left Trophimus sick in Miletus (verse 20). Paul may be referring to his final journey to Rome, when these two fellow-workers accompanied him as far as Corinth and Miletus respectively. Erastus could be either the city treasurer of Corinth (Rom. 16:23), which might tie in with his decision to go no further than that city, or the Erastus who accompanied Timothy into Macedonia on Paul's third missionary journey (Acts 19:22).

Trophimus, an Ephesian, was one of the Gentile delegates who travelled with Paul on his mission of mercy to the Christians in Jerusalem (Acts 20:4; 21:29). The fact that the apostle left him sick at Miletus shows either that the gifts of miraculous healing were departing from the church, or that they were not available on call. Sickness and suffering can usually accomplish more in the lives of believers than immediate, miraculous healing, as Paul himself testifies (2 Cor. 12:7-10).

Do your best to get here before winter (verse 21) is Paul's last request to Timothy, and the most personal reason for writing this letter. Paul was now virtually alone, and winter conditions around the Mediterranean closed off many of the shipping lanes that led to Rome. Paul derived a special pleasure and profit from Timothy's presence (Phil. 2:19-22), and longed to see him in one last act of fellowship. He could foresee that his end was relatively near.

Eubulus greets you, and so do Pudens, Linus, Claudia and all the brothers. This is the only mention of these four Christians in Paul's letters, and so they may not have been close acquaintances of his. They are all Latin names, with the exception of Eubulus. This would confirm the Roman origin of the letter. The church father Irenaeus (*Against Heresies,* III.3.3) identifies this Linus as the man who became bishop of the church in Rome in the second half of the first century, about the time of Paul's martyrdom. The inclusion of a woman among Paul's acquaintances and supporters (Claudia) is typical of his other correspondence (Rom. 16:1-15; Phil. 4:2f.; Philem. 2).

Because of Paul's remarks in verse 16 we should conclude that not all the local Christians were in a position to aid him in court. In any case he still speaks of them as brothers in Christ, just as in verse 16 he wished them well in spite of their momentary disloyalty to him. Clearly Paul's own heart was free from bitterness as he faced death.

The Lord be with your spirit (verse 22) is Paul's closing prayer for Timothy. The 'your' is singular and so must refer to Timothy alone. By this prayer Paul requests that Timothy will know the personal communion of the Lord Jesus Christ through the indwelling of Christ's Spirit in him (Eph. 3:16f).

Grace be with you are the last recorded words of the apostle Paul. They are addressed to the church because the 'you' is now plural, and are typical of his final greetings in letters (Rom. 16:20; 1 Cor. 16:23; Tit. 3:15). How fitting that the great apostle of the gospel of the grace of God (Acts 20:24, 32) should end his mortal life still speaking on this theme.

Study Question

Verse 20: What uses does sickness have? (Isa. 38:1ff.; 2 Cor. 12:7-10; Phil. 2:25-30; Jas. 5:13ff.).

Titus

INTRODUCTION

In its layout and contents Titus reminds the reader more of 1 Timothy than of 2 Timothy. 1 Timothy and Titus are alike in their concern about some of the same church issues – the qualifications of elders (1:5-9), how to deal with false teachers and their ideas (1:10-16), advice on the right handling of different groups within the congregation (2:1-15; 3:9ff.), and the place of good works in the church's public witness (3:1f.; 3:14).

Distinctives

But Titus has its own distinctives too, which make it stand out, not only among the Pastoral Letters, but within the New Testament as a whole. It contains one of the finest summaries of the Trinitarian gospel message anywhere in the New Testament (3:4-7). Nor does this passage stand by itself, for there is an earlier evangelical passage of comparable quality (2:11-14). These two passages alone make this letter worth studying as a representative theological document from the apostolic era of Christianity. The fact that Titus is one of the shorter writings of the New Testament (certainly the shortest of the Pastorals) makes these confessional sections all the more noteworthy.

Main Message

The main message of Titus can be summed up as *adorning the gospel of God our Saviour in all things* (2:10). While Titus shares the concern of 1 Timothy for sound teaching in the churches, it lays even greater stress on the need for godly living on the part of Christians. This explains the unusual number of references to good works in this letter (1:16; 2:7,14; 3:1,8,14). These are never held up legalistically as opening the way to salvation, rather they are seen as the natural outworking of a faith already in possession. These good works are required of believers from all sectors of the church and society: they are the badge of Christians living in the world.

Not only do good works help to identify Christians from their pagan neighbours, they also help to silence the unjust criticisms of their neighbours against Christianity. The exemplary lives of Christians will often speak louder than their words, and will promote goodwill and openness of mind towards the faith. Good works are an important tool for winning a hearing for the gospel, they also give visible proof of the moral power of the gospel to change human lives and social relationships.

Place and Time of Writing

The fact that Paul asks Titus to visit him at Nicopolis (3:12), a small town situated on the west coast of the mainland of Greece, across the Adriatic Sea from Italy, has been taken by some scholars to mean that Paul himself was mentally facing westwards towards Rome and a planned expedition to Spain beyond that (Rom. 15:23-28). If this is so, then this incidental reference could suggest that Titus was written on the eve of Paul's mission to the western empire. In this case it would tie this little gem of a letter to momentous events in the life of Paul and the western church. But otherwise Paul himself gives no clue as to his whereabouts when writing this letter.

Destination

The letter to Titus is about the church on the island of Crete, where Paul had previously worked (1:5). Crete lies south of the Aegean Sea, towards the middle of the Mediterranean Sea. It is elongated in shape and runs east-west for a distance of about one hundred and fifty-six miles, and varies in breadth from about seven to thirty-five miles.

The history of the church there is uncertain. Cretans were present on the day of Pentecost in Jerusalem (Acts 2:11). If any of them were converted then they would have planted the church in Crete on their return. Paul landed on the island during his tempestuous sea journey to Rome as a prisoner (Acts 27:7-13, 21), without doing any evangelistic work there or meeting with the local Christians.

Historically Crete had experienced a period of high culture during the middle of the second millennium BC. After this it was in decline, with local feuds springing up between rival cities. In 67 BC the island was captured and settled by the Romans. By the time Paul wrote his letter, Cretans were known universally for their self-indulgence and dishonesty (1:12). This information helps us to understand some of the local difficulties that Titus faced in re-organising the churches there.

Modern Message

Because good works are rooted in and grow out of the gospel received into the heart, this letter to Titus shows us in a very simple way the unity of sound teaching and godly living or, as people might say today, of theology and ethics. This is a valid and valuable point, because in the modern context there are those who want to teach ethics without first grounding it in the apostolic doctrine. Without this grounding, ethics will lack depth and moral direction. Equally there are those who want to study theology and make it relevant to the modern and post-modern worlds, but their zest for theology is hardly matched by a zeal for morality and godliness.

Paul in his letter to Titus, with a few brush strokes, fills in the contents of the gospel for us, while at the same time we hear his insistent call for godliness and good works that make the gospel become visible in human lives. Titus informs us that the gospel is for living and confessing.

TITUS: CHAPTER 1

The first chapter of Titus consists of an extended introduction (1:1-4), followed by a detailed qualifications chart for local elders (1:5-9) who need to be appointed because of the activism of heretical teachers in the vicinity (1:10-16).

Introduction (1:1-4)

The introduction to the letter to Titus is much more developed than those to Timothy, and recalls the more elaborate openings of the letters to Romans (1:1-7) and Galatians (1:1-5). As in those letters, the longer introduction to Titus highlights some of the main themes of the letter, and so expresses Paul's main concerns in writing it. Such themes as faith, knowledge of the truth, godliness and the hope of eternal life stand out on the religious side, while God's truth and promise, the gospel and Jesus Christ stand out on the historical side.

The undisputed author of the letter is **Paul** who styles himself simply **a servant of God and an apostle of Jesus Christ** (verse 1). Paul's first allegiance was not to himself, nor even the church, but to God, who had chosen and called him in grace to his service. Paul was an appointed apostle in the service of Jesus Christ, which was the most responsible function in Christ's church (1 Cor. 12:28; Eph. 4:11). As a result of his call to faith in Jesus Christ Paul, out of boundless gratitude, saw himself as forever bound to God's service in his spirit and body (Rom. 1:9; 2 Cor. 5:14f.; Gal. 2:20). The love of Christ constrained him in his Christian service (2 Cor. 5:13ff.).

Paul's servant relationship to God is stated along with but before his relationship to Jesus Christ, because he saw that he owed his standing in grace primarily to the eternal goodness of God the Father (Rom. 8:28ff.; 1 Cor. 1:9). Being an apostle of Jesus Christ grew out of his prior relationship to God the Father. But he was an apostle of Jesus Christ because *he* is the church's Lord from whom, and through whom, all gifts for church service have been conferred on chosen individuals (Eph. 4:7-11). Being

Christ's apostle means that Paul speaks and writes with the full
authority of Jesus Christ himself in the service of his church (Eph.
3:1-7). The spiritual reader will receive his writings as the commandments of the Lord (1 Cor. 14:37).

Paul realised that he had been appointed an apostle **for the
faith of God's elect**. God's chosen people are those whom he set
apart for himself in love through Jesus Christ before time was,
and who have come to personal faith in Christ in fulfilment of
that eternal purpose. His eternal choice precedes the preaching
of faith to them in the gospel, at the same time it carries the
secret promise of faith to them in Christ (Acts 13:48; Rom. 8:29f.;
1 Cor. 1:26-31). Through the gospel and the secret energy of the
Holy Spirit, God graciously opens the hearts of his people and
persuades them to embrace freely Jesus Christ. Paul's apostleship was a secondary means appointed by God to bring the gospel to bear on human lives.

God's predestination of his people is sometimes confused with
philosophical determinism (what will be will be). But in the
preached message of the gospel the Lord respects the free agency
of humans by presenting his truth to their affections, minds and
wills. Free agency is not the same as free will, for sin has robbed
humans of free will in spiritual matters, yet without destroying
their total responsibility. God's sovereign election, properly understood, is the most powerful incentive to active evangelism.

In the same way his apostleship was intended to bring about
the knowledge of the truth that leads to godliness. Knowledge
of the truth is a recurring phrase in the Pastorals (1 Tim. 2:4; 2
Tim. 2:25). It stands for a saving, personal acceptance of the
truth of God's Word in the gospel. Knowledge, in this context,
points to the place of the understanding in the acceptance of the
Christian faith, but at the same time it involves a wholehearted
commitment to God as Saviour in Jesus Christ. Knowledge of
this kind is existential, a lived experience of God's presence and
power in a person's life.

Godliness – a constant ideal in the Pastorals (1 Tim. 2:2; 3:16;

4:7f.; 6:3, 5f., 11; 2 Tim. 3:5) – is really Godlikeness, a moral likeness to the revealed character of God, in his qualities such as holiness, justice, goodness and truth. It is the natural result of coming to a saving knowledge of God, and at the same time it is the sure proof that God's truth has been sincerely received into the heart. The connection between truth and godliness needed to be accentuated in the immoral atmosphere of Crete, where some people claimed to know God but lived ungodly lives (verse 16). It is only the truth of God's Word that can produce true godliness, or that has the moral resources to transform society into a godly commonwealth.

The foundation of this faith and knowledge is now described as **a faith and knowledge resting on the hope of eternal life** (verse 2). Faith and knowledge bring the Christian into the realm of salvation, but they do not immediately bring the complete experience and enjoyment of salvation. The Christian is saved in the hope of sharing in God's glory when Jesus Christ comes back (Rom. 5:2; 8:24f.). Jesus Christ is our hope (1 Tim. 1:1) because the Christian hope is grounded in his saving life, death and resurrection. It is also true that the Christian hopes to see Christ and to be with him forever. Paul defines the Christian hope as eternal life, a most common Pauline description in the Pastorals of the hope of heaven (1 Tim. 1:16; 6:12; Tit. 3:7).

This eternal life is something which **God, who does not lie, promised before the beginning of time**. The hope of eternal life rests on the truthful character of God and his eternal promise (1 Tim. 1:1). Its fulfilment is therefore a test of the moral character of God. Since God cannot lie, the hope of the promise of eternal life is absolutely secure. God is truth (Rom. 3:4) and so his words are truth (Psa. 12:6; John 17:17). 'Before the beginning of time' is literally 'before times eternal', and highlights the fact that our salvation originates in God alone, without any consideration of what we are or what we may do (see 2 Timothy 1:9f., where Paul uses the same expression). From all eternity God planned his covenant purpose and made his covenant promises.

There is a difference between the eternal promise of life and the actual fulfilment of that promise in the time-scape of history. So Paul adds, **and at his appointed season he brought his word to light through the preaching** (verse 3). 'His appointed season' is literally 'in its own times' (Paul uses the same phrase in 1 Timothy 2:6) and points to the moment in history which God judged to be right for the fulfilment of his promise. This was the time when he sent his Son into the world to redeem and adopt his people (Mark 1:14f.; Rom. 5:6; Gal. 4:4f.). The promise of eternal life was historically fulfilled by Christ's personal coming, but since then it has been disseminated throughout the world by the public preaching of the Christian message.

Paul's preaching of the Christian message was both a stewardship and a duty because it was **entrusted to** [him] **by the command of God our Saviour**. On God our Saviour see 1 Timothy 1:1. Being Christ's ambassador to the nations involved both privilege and responsibility. Proclaiming the word of Christ was a special trust for which Paul would have to give an account one day (1 Cor. 4:1; 1 Thess. 2:4; 1 Tim. 1:12). It was also a command to preach, which he dared not disobey (1 Cor. 9:16f.; 1 Tim. 1:1; 2 Tim. 1:1). In a similar way Paul encouraged Timothy to regard the ministry of God's Word as a sacred trust and an obligation which must never be compromised (1 Tim. 6:20; 2 Tim. 1:14; 2:2).

The letter is written **to Titus, my true son in our common faith** (verse 4). This is the same expression of endearment used by Paul to Timothy (1 Tim. 1:2) and proves that although Titus is less prominent than Timothy in Paul's letters (in Acts he is never mentioned at all), Paul regarded him and treated him with the same fatherly affection. The father-son relationship was a spiritual one, the result of sharing in the common faith of God's people. This is the one faith that unites all God's people everywhere, across generational, ethnic and gender gaps.

Titus was a Greek who had accompanied Paul to Jerusalem in support of Paul's defence of a gospel of grace without works of the law (Gal. 3:1-5). He was Paul's partner and fellow-worker

(2 Cor. 8:23) who frequently comforted the apostle by the news he brought from the churches (2 Cor. 7:6f., 13ff.). Paul recognised the successful work Titus performed around the churches, even the most troublesome (2 Cor. 8:1-6, 16f.). No wonder that Paul had chosen Titus for the demanding task of putting the churches of Crete in order! Unlike Timothy, who needed regular doses of encouragement from Paul, Titus only needed to be told what to do and he would do it.

The greeting consists of **grace and peace from God the Father and Christ Jesus our Saviour**. Grace and peace are the beginning and end of Christian life. Grace is the unmerited and continued kindness of God, which enshrines the Christian message of salvation in Jesus Christ alone, without any addition of human works. Peace is the outcome of grace, as grace is the source of peace. Peace stands for the settled and right relationship with God that Jesus Christ brings about through his obedience and blood. Grace and peace mean new relationships with God as Father and Jesus Christ as Saviour. God becomes our Father through Jesus, and Jesus becomes our Saviour in accordance with the will of the Father (verse 3; Gal. 1:3f.). That salvation is the shared gift of God the Father and Jesus Christ the Son is a common theme of the Pastorals (1 Tim. 1:1; 2:3; 4:10), the letter to Titus being no exception (Tit. 2:10, 13; 3:4, 6).

Study Questions

Verse 1: What is the faith of God's elect? (1 Cor. 1:27-31; 1 Pet. 1:2; 2 Pet. 1:5-7, 10f.; 1 John 5:13, 18-20).

Verse 2: Why is it important that God cannot lie? (Psa. 12:6; 119:160; John 8:44-47; Rom. 15:8; 2 Cor. 1:19f.).

Verse 4: What does it mean in daily living for God to be our Father? (Matt. 6:6, 9-13; Rom. 8:15f.; 2 Cor. 6:17-7:1; 1 Pet. 1:17).

Overseers (1:5-9)

After the unusually long introductory greeting, Paul comes straight (as in First Timothy 1:3) to the local church situation in Crete. **The reason I left you in Crete was that you might straighten out what was left unfinished** (verse 5). This implies that Paul himself had been in Crete with Titus, beginning a work that now needed to be completed. The work had reached a certain stage of development, but was lacking in some respects. Paul had left Titus to complete the business (literally 'the things that are left over').

Above all it was imperative for Titus to remain **and appoint elders in every town, as I commanded you**. From the beginning of his missionary work Paul had appointed elders or overseers, following the Old Testament model of the elders of the people, in every newly-formed congregation, men suitably gifted and chosen by the people themselves (Acts 14:23). Titus was personally authorised by Paul to appoint such men, no doubt in accordance with the choice of the people, by laying his hands on them and setting them apart officially for their work (1 Tim. 4:14; 2 Tim. 1:6). This was necessary because of the critical shortage of such leaders in the churches. It is not clear why elders had never been appointed, since this was standard procedure in Paul's mission field. 'In every town' could mean that one council of elders supervised several congregations in one city, or that in every city there was only one congregation and one council of elders. For the biblical background of eldership see comments on 1 Timothy 3:1.

An elder must be blameless (verse 6), that is, free from offensive traits that would invite criticism or ridicule of the church or the gospel by outsiders. The elder must mirror the best fruits of the gospel in his life, both as an example to the membership and as a public defence against outside critics. This stipulation is so necessary in the Pauline understanding of eldership that he repeats it in verse seven, and it is mentioned in his other list in 1 Timothy 3:2. The personal qualities that follow, twelve in all, give some idea of what being blameless means. It does not mean sinlessness, but it does define a life and character that are on the side of virtue and opposed to vice. Qualities to do with home life come first because they reveal leadership potential and whether he has the necessary gifts for pastoral oversight.

He must be **the husband of but one wife**, which refers to his known marital faithfulness and that he is not guilty of having affairs with other women, or of polygamy. See 1 Timothy 3:2. Sexual purity is as essential now as then in those who bear the name of a holy God.

In addition, he must be **a man whose children believe and are not open to the charge of being wild and disobedient**. This specification points to the fact that the elder should ideally be a married, family man, the quality of whose faith can be seen in his children. They ought not to be prodigals, open to the charge of reckless behaviour or an ungodly lifestyle. They should be believers, following the faith of their father(s). The failure of a man to produce believing children does not suggest that he is capable of exemplary leadership, discipline and the ability to pass on the faith to others. If a man cannot succeed in the more inti-mate circle of the family, he will not succeed with the more strin-gent relationships of the household of God (1 Sam. 2:12-36; 1 Tim. 3:4f.).

Since an overseer is entrusted with God's work, he must be blameless (verse 7) is self-evident and repeats the special quality of verse six. All-round godliness is an absolute must in Paul's ideal overseer. This is because the overseer is a steward (1 Cor. 4:1), entrusted with God's Word and work, in the interests of God's glory and the good of God's people. Paul substitutes the word 'overseer' for that of 'elder', clear proof that the two are one, since he is still speaking about the same office (see Acts 20:17, 28 and 1 Peter 5:1f.). Being an overseer means that he has the special responsibility of watching over the whole congrega-tion, with a view to defending and guiding it (Acts 20:28-31).

Paul gives five negatives for measuring the overseer with:

• **not overbearing,** since this will crush the people;

• **not quick-tempered**, since this destroys good relationships;

• **not given to much wine**, because this displays an absence of spirituality (Eph. 5:18);

• **not violent**, because this is an outright denial of the Christian way of peace (Matt. 5:9, Rom. 12:18);

• **not pursuing dishonest gain**, since this would undermine his position of trust.

Some positives follow (verse 8):

• **he must be hospitable,** one who literally 'loves the stranger'. The overseer must model the social fruits of the gospel by opening his heart and his home to visitors from other churches and places (Rom. 12:13; 1 Tim. 3:2);

• **one who loves what is good**, a broad indication of his moral character, shown today by his preference for good people, good books and good works;

• **who is self-controlled**, or serious-minded, in view of his solemn responsibilities before God (1 Tim. 3:2; Heb. 13:17);

• **upright,** or just in all his decisions, and impartial in his treatment of those under his care and discipline;

• **holy**, in being devoted to God and the things of God, in his Christian service (1 Thess. 2:10);

• **disciplined**, as someone who is in control of his passions, words and actions, because he is under the control of the Holy Spirit (Gal. 5:22f.).

He must hold firmly to the trustworthy message as it has been taught (verse 9) is a reminder of the doctrinal responsibilities of the overseer, as a steward of the truths of the Christian faith. He must make sure that he adheres to its teachings exactly as he has been taught and in accordance with the teaching of Christ's church in history. In order to do this he must himself be firmly grounded in the Word of God, making it his own by faith and life. 'The trustworthy message as it has been taught' refers to the faith once for all delivered to the saints (Jude 3), the sacred deposit of teaching given first by the Lord, and then confirmed and finalised by his apostles and prophets in the New Testament Scriptures (Rom. 6:17; Eph. 2:20; 3:2-5; Heb. 2:3f.; 2 Pet. 3:15f.; 1 John 1:5). This provides the objective standard of the overseer's doctrinal commitment.

This demand is **so that he can encourage others by sound doctrine**. The overseer is a pastor, appointed to build up others in the faith. Unless he himself is committed to the apostolic teachings, he cannot engage in any ministries of pastoral encouragement, using the moral and spiritual healing powers of the gospel and applying them to the various moral and spiritual ailments of men and women.

The overseer is also an apologist, a defender of the faith. By his firm grasp of the trustworthy message he should be able to strengthen the saints **and refute those who oppose it**. He must be able to present the Christian faith in a reasoned way, in answer to the objections that people bring against it. But he must do this with gentleness in the fear of Christ the Lord (2 Tim. 2:24ff.; 1 Pet. 3:15). To achieve this goal he must be well-versed in the tenets of the Christian faith and their grounds in biblical revelation.

Study Questions

Verse 5: Why is it important to appoint elders in every local church? (Acts 20:28; 1 Tim. 4:11f.; Heb. 13:17).

Verses 6 and 7: What does it mean to be blameless? (1 Cor. 10:32f.; Phil. 1:9ff.; 1 Pet. 2:20ff.).

Verse 9: Should all the elders be able to preach and teach, or is this the province of only one elder? (Rom. 12:6-8; 1 Cor. 12:28; Eph. 4:11; 1 Tim. 3:2; 5:17).

Subversive Talkers (1:10-16)

For there are many rebellious people (verse 10) explains Paul's urgency in wanting Titus to appoint elders in every church in Crete. 'Rebellious' means disorderly, defiant of the God-given authority of apostles like Paul and their message of submission and obedience to the lordship of Christ. Some church members in Thessalonica were charged with the same offence because they refused to live in accordance with the sacred teachings (traditions) of the apostles which originated with Jesus (2 Thess. 3:6-14). These same doctrinal standards remain in the church today, carrying the same final authority of the Lord.

They are also **mere talkers**, enjoying the sound of their own voices, and the appearance of authority that their public pronouncements appear to give, but in reality lacking anything of value to say (1 Tim. 1:6f.) and without good works (verse 16). They are idle talkers **and deceivers**, deceiving themselves first of all into seeing themselves as people of importance, but also deceiving all those foolish enough to listen to them and follow them. The power of error lies wholly in its ability to deceive.

The apostle picks out **especially those of the circumcision group**. The movement contained a mixed membership of Gentiles and Jews, though the latter ('the circumcision group') predominated, and were more successful at getting a hearing and causing a threat to the church. Sizable Jewish communities existed on Crete at this period, their long and enlightened history giving them a head start in religious proselytising. Jewish prophets and occultists were active throughout the empire (Acts 13:6f.; 19:13f.), and Jewish writings and traditions were a favourite and fertile source for syncretistic groups in the first century (Col. 2:16ff.; 1 Tim. 1:3f., 7).

Paul's forthright instruction to Titus is that **they must be silenced** (verse 11), which in the Greek means placing something over the mouth of an animal to muzzle it. So Titus must take immediate action to terminate the propaganda of these self-appointed teachers of error (1 Tim. 1:3f.). When the gospel is undermined, those who are propagating erroneous views within the church are not to be negotiated with or pandered to for the sake of a false peace, but are to be confronted firmly with their destructive heresies, and are to be admonished or put out of the church.

The reason for Paul's strong language is **because they are ruining whole households by teaching things they ought not to teach**. The word for 'ruining' literally means overturning, as when Jesus upset the tables in the temple courts (John 2:15). In 2 Timothy 2:18 it is used again of people being overthrown in their faith. Such is the effect that conjectural teachings can have, relying, as they do, on human speculation instead of biblical revelation. The aim of breakaway groups is always to win over families, in the hope that they will form the nucleus of a new movement and give it some strength. In the purpose of God the family is meant to be the bastion of his truth, forming the fundamental unit of his church (Gen. 17:7; Acts 16:1, 30-34; 1 Tim. 3:4f., 12).

'Teaching things they ought not to' means that they were giving out error under the guise of truth, twisting the more obscure parts of Scripture to deceive the ignorant and unstable, and so bringing about their own destruction.

The methods and beliefs of these groups were wrong because their personal motives were wrong to begin with. They were teaching wrongly **and that for the sake of dishonest gain**. Like the self-appointed teachers in Ephesus (1 Tim. 6:5), these Cretan apostates had seen religion as an opportunity to make money. Centuries before, the Greek sophists had begun this practice of charging high fees for private consultations or for public lectures addressing philosophical questions. These Cretans were adopting this style by setting themselves up in public life as spiritual gurus, inviting the anxious, unstable and gullible to pay money to find answers, peace and security. They were making themselves rich by shamefully exploiting others, and all under the guise of the Christian religion.

Even one of their own prophets has said 'Cretans are always liars, evil brutes, lazy gluttons' (verse 12). The activ-

ity and character of these local pundits should not surprise Titus
since the degenerate qualities of the Cretans was well-known
and documented in their own literature. Paul quotes a line from
the poetry of Epimenides, a Cretan popularly regarded as a prophet
and a miracle-worker from the sixth century BC. Its description
of the Cretans as self-indulgent and dishonest was proverbial in
the ancient world. There was even a verb concocted 'to Cretize/
Cretanize', which meant to cheat and to lie! All peoples have
national characteristics which can be a significant factor in the
growth or hindrance of the gospel in a locality. Those who engage in local evangelism and pastoral oversight need to analyse
and offset these factors.

This testimony is true (verse 13). Paul denies that this is a
stereotype, for he had found the description all too true in his
work among the Cretans. But he is far from content to leave it a
matter of private observation, so he encourages Titus to take
drastic action. **Therefore, rebuke them sharply**. Some situations call for patience and prayerful waiting on God; others call
for immediate confrontation and sharp rebuke. The wise and
faithful pastor will discern these times when strong leadership is
called for as the only remedy, and give it (Tit. 2:15).

This use of pastoral authority is never pleasant, nor is it to be
used lightly (2 Cor. 13:2, 11), but **so that they will be sound in
the faith.** 'Sound' is a medical word and points to the spiritual
health of people. Disciplinary action in the church is like spiritual
surgery – radical where necessary. It should always aim at the
recovery of the spiritual health of those who have erred from the
truth. 'The faith' stands for the objective body of truths to which
believers in Jesus Christ commit themselves and corresponds to
the parallel expression 'the truth' throughout the Pastorals (1
Tim. 2:4; 3:15; 2 Tim. 2:15, 18, 25; 3:7f.; 4:4).

Paul's aim is that these individuals will be sound in the faith
**and will pay no attention to Jewish myths or to the com-
mands of those who reject the truth** (verse 14). Paul has
already noted the Jewish make-up of these troublesome groups

(verse 10). He underlines the fundamental antithesis between the mythologies and commandments of men and the truth of God. Between the two there can be no compromise. The one is the product of man's darkened reason and lacks any final authority, the other is the very truth of God and binds people absolutely. People wander into error when they reject the truth. In God's truth lies all the wisdom that the human mind ever needs to know or wants to know.

According to Paul **to the pure, all things are pure** (verse 15). This is a moral principle which strikes at the heart of the issues raised by the self-styled teachers. They promised purity of heart and purity before God through rituals of their own invention, rituals that were given the aura of respectability through being connected with Jewish traditions and regulations. Paul's point is that purity is a moral property which arises in the heart through believing in Jesus Christ (Acts 15:8f.), not something that people can achieve through religious rites. Purity comes from the inside not from the outside, as Jesus taught (Mark 7:18f.).

Once a person is made pure through a heavenly rebirth (John 3:3, 5), everything in practice becomes pure to the believer in Christ. The Christian can enjoy the good things of God's creation – food, sexuality, knowledge, music, beauty, the body – with a good conscience and use these things to the glory of God. This does not mean that the Christian can now indulge in morally unclean activities such as fornication, claiming that in Christ everything is made clean. Paul rebukes the Corinthians for this very mistake of using Christian liberty as an excuse for indulging in immorality (1 Cor. 6:12-20). The Christian is not his own, and must use his freedom in Christ by pleasing God in what he enjoys.

The reverse of the maxim reads, **but to those who are corrupted and do not believe, nothing is pure**. Because the nostrums of the false teachers could never change the hearts of their devotees, the problem of purity remained unsolved and unsolvable. Purificatory ceremonies of a religious kind can never lead to purity of heart before God, or a pure conscience in the moral issues of living, since this is the priceless gift of God through believing in Jesus Christ within the fellowship of his church (Heb. 10:19-22). Until this inner change takes place the Cretan unbelievers remain unclean before God, and so do their ceremonies. A rotten tree makes for rotten fruit (Matt. 7:15-19).

Paul reinforces the inner nature and source of the problem when he asserts that **in fact, both their minds and consciences are corrupted**. The problem of the breakaway teachers is both a spiritual and a moral one which they have failed to recognise. The inner person of the heart is corrupted, from which centre stems all their false hopes and claims. Fallen men and women are inwardly thoroughly corrupt, and cannot produce anything that is morally pure (Rom. 8:6ff.). Because of sin the moral powers no longer function in true knowledge and holiness (cf. Ephesians 4:23f.). This is a condition that Paul notes elsewhere in the Pastorals (1 Tim. 4:2; 6:5; 2 Tim. 3:8). In the case of such people religion becomes a subtle substitute for genuine spirituality (Col. 2:23), and moral regression takes place amidst a medley of religious rites.

They claim to know God (verse 16) on the basis of a new revelation and a revised method of interpreting the Scriptures. As a result they lay claim to a knowledge of God that is more advanced when compared with what Christian teaching offers. They thus dispense with the apostolic preachers and set up their own centres of religious learning, where those with ears that itch for novelties can join them (2 Tim. 4:3f.). Knowing God is the very heart of salvation (John 17:3; Gal. 4:9; Phil. 3:8ff.), a life lived in a fellowship of love with God on the sure basis of his Word (2 Cor. 13:14). Knowledge of God is what humans lost through the Fall and what is restored through Christ (1 John 5:20).

The Cretan defectors claimed to know God **but by their actions they deny him**. The proof of their claim to a knowledge of God lay in the practical and moral realm, and by this test they failed miserably, because their behaviour was unsavoury and degenerate. The fruits of salvation are the sign of salvation (Gal. 5:22f.), otherwise people's claim to faith lacks the sure proof of works (Jas. 2:14-26).

Paul's final opinion is that **they are detestable, disobedient and unfit for doing anything good**, which stands in outright contradiction to the standards and goals of the gospel of God's saving grace (2 Tim. 3:15ff.; Tit. 2:11-14). Such people are abhorrent to God (Luke 16:15), insubordinate towards God-given authority (Jude 8), and reprobate with respect to the kingdom of God (2 Tim. 3:8).

Study Questions

Verse 12: How far do local, cultural and national traits help or hinder people's response to the gospel? (John 4:19-26; Acts 17:11, 19ff.; 23:6-10; 1 Thess. 2:14ff.).

Verse 14: When should Christians obey the commandments of men, and when not? (Matt. 22:21; Acts 4:18 with 5:29; Col. 2:8; Heb. 13:17; 1 Pet. 2:13-16).

Verse 16: What is the relation of a profession and its practice according to the New Testament? (Matt. 7:15-23; 25:31-46; Gal. 5:6; Jas. 2:14-26; 1 John 3:16-19).

TITUS: CHAPTER 2

This chapter illustrates well the way in which godly living (ethics) and sound teaching (theology) are seen to be interdependent. Paul first outlines the practical priorities of Christian living for the different groups within the church (2:1-10), then he describes the teaching of salvation that underlies these priorities in the first of two memorable passages dealing with this subject (2:11-15). The way in which he integrates teaching and practice makes for a very compact section of the letter.

Adorning the gospel (2:1-10)

You must teach what is in accord with sound doctrine (verse 1). These words introduce what follows. Once again in the Pastorals Paul is concerned about the wholesome teaching of the gospel (1 Tim. 1:10; Tit. 1:9), this time in the work of Titus (the 'you' is emphatic) as a teaching elder. Since the pure teaching of the gospel is the way to spiritual and moral health and strength in the body of Christ, it is imperative that Titus should give it first place. There can be no godliness without it; theology and ethics are one. 'What is in accord with sound doctrine' indicates that the gospel forms a coherent body of truths that can and should be stated and used as the measure of all Christian preaching. Paul now instructs Titus how to do this *situationally*, as each age, gender and social group requires.

First, Titus is to **teach the older men to be temperate, worthy of respect, self-controlled** (verse 2). These are three social qualities which also provide an example of moral and spiritual maturity. Temperate means restraining one's natural desires and presenting a balanced Christian life; being worthy of respect is the result of cultivating the dignity of the Christian believer as a child of God; and being self-controlled is the opposite of being agitated and excitable. These same specifications are demanded from elders, deacons and women workers (1 Tim. 3:2, 8, 11), but they are also appropriate in older men to whom the congregation ought to be able to look for a living example of mature Christian character.

To these outward qualities are added three inward ones – **and sound in faith, in love and in endurance**. These three Christian virtues often appear together in Paul's writings (1 Thess. 1:3; 1 Tim. 6:11; 2 Tim. 3:10) as a basic set of Christian qualities. *Faith*, which here must stand for the trust of the believer rather than the message of truth in which he believes, is the primary grace because it unites us to Jesus Christ from whom all blessings flow. *Love* is the immediate flowering of faith in the world of the believer's social relationships (Gal. 5:6). It is the faith of the heart made visible and useful in caring attitudes, words and acts. *Endurance* is another effect of faith, the ability of the believer to keep going under stress by holding fast to the promises of God. It produces strong character (Rom. 5:3f.).

These are all qualities that a pastor has the right to expect well developed in older Christian men. Such men give stability and strength to a congregation simply by being present in it.

Likewise, teach the older women to be reverent in the way they live (verse 3) means that the older women have their responsibilities too for the spiritual welfare of the congregation, and that they must not leave it all to their male counterparts. 'Reverent' can mean either that the older women must conduct themselves in a reverent way before God and the congregation, or that they must conduct themselves in such a way as to become revered themselves by the congregation. The first really includes the second. Along with the previous verse, this one underlines the teaching that the older believers of both sexes should be an invaluable resource, a stabilising influence and a living example of the mature fruits of the gospel for the younger generation of the congregation.

At the same time there are dangers and vices to be avoided by the older women. They are **not to be slanderers or addicted to much wine**. Old age and retirement do not come alone, they bring subtle opportunities for older women to engage in destructive talk about other members of the congregation, or to escape into the fantasy world of alcohol dependency.

They are not to fall into either of these practices, **but to teach what is good**. Since Paul excludes women from the teaching office of the church (1 Tim. 2:11f.), the teaching by the older women under consideration here must be of another order. It takes place in the course of those friendships and contacts that occur informally in the daily life of the congregational family. But it is definitely a teaching ministry, and one that the older women are to undertake deliberately and responsibly, in the interests of the younger women (verse 4). This ministry of women to women opens up numerous possibilities in terms of the format, content and medium of this type of teaching in the modern context. This teaching could take the form of home visitation, Bible study groups, social outings, one-to-one friendships, book readings and more. The one proviso is that what is taught should be good, that is, thoroughly Christian and practically helpful.

Then they can train the younger women to love their husbands and children (verse 4). This verse and the next amounts to Paul's directions to the younger women. But he offers the directions through the medium of the older women. The text assumes that the younger women are married and have husbands and children, the ideal Christian scenario not always met with in the modern world because of secular feminist propaganda or popular morality. Training the younger women means more than simply urging them, it suggests an advisory and mentoring role for the older women in the art of Christian homemaking.

The primary responsibility of the younger woman is to her husband and children, in that order. In each case the accent falls on love, which more than any other quality makes for a stable and happy home. The older women can only exercise this supportive kind of ministry to the younger women if they themselves have successfully married and raised a family in an atmosphere of love. By this means, the ideals of Christian womanhood and homemaking are passed down from one generation of Christian women to the next.

In the modern world where the family, marriage and womanhood are so much undermined, often by women themselves, Paul's defence of the nuclear Christian family is of paramount importance to the Christian community. More than ever before, the experienced counsel of older godly women, offered with sensitivity to the younger wives and mothers, is needed to support the institution of the family, and to help establish it on Christian principles. At the same time younger Christian women should be open to the advice of older women they admire and trust, willing to seek advice and to take it in the interests of their family well-being.

In addition, they can train the younger women **to be self-controlled and pure** (verse 5), which means respectively to be prudent and sexually faithful. In a very real way Christian wives and mothers are the guardians of Christian morals and culture.

They are **to be busy at home, to be kind.** Literally they are to be home-workers and good, two domestic qualities that indicate the total involvement of the younger women in the life of their homes (1 Tim. 5:14). Homemaking is full-time work and demands a quality of character that is morally strong and resourceful.

They are to be busy at home **and to be subject to their husbands**. Subjection is a key New Testament concept that applies in a variety of contexts, such as the church in relation to Christ (Eph. 5:24), the Christian citizen in relation to the state (Rom. 13:1; Tit. 3:1; 1 Pet. 2:13), and Christian slaves in relation to their masters (Tit. 2:9; 1 Pet. 2:18). Being subject to their husbands means that Christian wives recognise that there is an inner structure of law and order in the world of human relationships that God, as Creator, has sanctioned and blessed for the good of everyone, and that within the family circle the highest authority is vested in the husband and father. Being subject is basically a religious attitude that is fitting in the Lord (Col. 3:18) and pleasing to him.

Sin is a principle of rebellion against God's appointed order with its legitimate, inbuilt authorities. Satan began the great apostasy when he refused to submit to the place and function that God had appointed for him (Jude 6). Ever since, he has been teaching human beings how to do the same, by rejecting those authorities that God has appointed in the family, church and state. Christian wives, in being subject to their husbands, are actually hastening the day when all things will be in subjection to God, when all rebellious rule will be put down and when God will be all in all (1 Cor. 15:24-28). Their submissive behaviour gives promise of that time, and is a firstfruits of it.

On an everyday level, being subject to their husbands does not mean that:

° wives must be subject to the unreasonable demands of their husbands;
° they must be subject to the abuse of male authority in physical or psychological ways;
° they should have no say in the running of the home or in the decision-making process.

In a crisis of conscience wives must obey God rather than men (Acts 5:29). The wife has marital rights equal to those of her husband (1 Cor. 7:3f.), they are heirs together of the grace of life in Christ (1 Pet. 3:7). The home is the domain of the wife where she exercises her own form of authority and rule (1 Tim. 5:14, 'homerulers', 'managers'). Modern feminism urges women to break free from their homemaking ties and their subjection to men, but the Christian gospel strengthens the ties of women to home and husband, in keeping with the natural order of creation (Gen. 2:18-25).

So that no one will malign the word of God reveals an apologetic purpose on Paul's part which is not uncommon in the New Testament (1 Tim. 6:1; Tit. 2:9f.; 1 Pet. 3:15f.; 4:15f.). The respectful attitudes and responsive behaviour of Christian wives will help to silence public criticism of Christianity as being a possible threat to society. The wives will show by the spirit and pattern of their lives within the home that the evidence points in the opposite direction, that Christianity makes for the best social order, through building good relationships between husbands and wives, and their children. The orderly example of the younger wives can even become a positive tool in God's hands for the conversion of unbelieving husbands (1 Pet. 3:1f.). All this provides the strongest incentive for young wives to work at being subject to their husbands and to the Word of God.

'The word of God' does not refer here directly to the written Scriptures, although they are indirectly in view. The word of God is the preached message of salvation through faith in Jesus Christ which sums up the central message of the Scriptures. This is its usual referent in Acts (4:31; 8:14; 12:24), the Pastorals (2 Tim. 4:2) and the rest of the New Testament (1 Pet. 1:23ff.). Parallel terms are 'the truth', 'the faith', 'sound doctrine', 'the teaching'. These two forms of the Word of God (Scripture and preaching) are inseparable, though distinct. Because the written Word of the Scriptures is alone inspired by God (2 Tim. 3:16), it gives authority, content and focus to the preaching of the word of the gospel.

Similarly, encourage the young men to be self-controlled (verse 6) is Paul's advice to Titus about the last group of persons to be singled out within the congregation. It is a general word that certainly includes the control of the strong desires of young male sexuality, but also takes in the natural impatience with established authority that is so characteristic of young men everywhere. Contrary to every notion that there is a crisis experience in the Christian life that brings an end to frustration and struggle, the New Testament is thoroughly realistic and insistent in its demands for constant self-discipline, watchfulness and co-operation in living the Christian life (1 Cor. 9:24-27; Eph. 6:10-13; Phil. 2:12f.; 3:13f.).

If Titus's teaching is to carry weight then he must **in everything set them an example by doing what is good** (verse 7). The leader must lead by example and incarnate his own principles (1 Cor. 11:1; 2 Thess. 3:8f.; 1 Tim. 4:12), otherwise he is no better than a hypocrite (Matt. 23:2f.). In setting an example he is modelling the gospel by giving it a human face, a living pattern that others can relate to and follow. The example of good works is basic Christianity on the practical and moral side, and is much insisted on in the Pastorals (1 Tim. 2:10; 5:10; 6:18; 2 Tim. 2:21; 3:17; Tit. 2:14; 3:1,8,14). In a time of moral collapse and widespread selfishness and greed, the good works of Christians, especially their leaders, should stand out as a clear witness to that higher, divine life that is open to all (Matt. 5:16; 1 Pet. 2:11f.).

But Titus's teaching is just as important as his life, so **in your teaching show integrity, seriousness**. This pair of qualities has to do with the style and motives of the man behind the teaching. *Integrity* is sincerity, the utter refusal to be corrupted by worldly interests such as popularity or ecclesiastical preferment. *Seriousness* is the opposite of light-heartedness, because the matters the Christian message deals with are weighty, and they carry eternal consequences for the men and women who hear them. Both these qualities are marks of the true servant of Christ, indispensable to one who has been entrusted with the Word of God, since the way in which a man teaches will confirm or detract from what he teaches.

But the content of Titus's teaching is just as important as the spirit in which he preaches. So he must show integrity, seriousness **and soundness of speech that cannot be condemned** (verse 8). Sound speech is teaching that conforms with the apostolic preaching and is rooted in the written Word. Because of this it will do good to those who hear it (2 Thess. 2:15; 1 Tim. 1:10f.; 4:6, 16; 6:3f.; 2 Tim. 1:13; Tit. 1:9). Christian preaching should be free from offence, in being an intelligent, accurate and gracious presentation of the Word of God. Those who come to scoff may then remain to pray.

Paul's larger concern now comes to light: **so that those who oppose you may be ashamed because they have nothing bad to say about us**. It is not enough that Christian preaching should avoid unfair criticism, it should actually put pressure on the critics themselves by causing them to experience shame for their uninformed views. This aim of overcoming evil with good is frequently proposed in the New Testament (Rom. 12:21; 1 Pet. 2:12, 15; 3:16). The best advocacy for Christianity ('us' stands for the whole Christian community) should be the quality of the lives of its leaders, the spirit of their service and the content of their message. Unfortunately, the public discrediting of the church at large by a few of its leaders is a body-blow from which the church can only recover with the utmost effort and with divine help.

Teach slaves to be subject to their masters in everything (verse 9) reminds us that the Christian church from the beginning has catered for the lowest classes as well as for different races and genders. Just like the other groups the slaves needed instruction in how to live in a Christian way in the face of unjust treatment and poverty (Eph. 6:5-8; Col. 3:22-25). Peter showed the slaves that Jesus, in the physical and verbal abuse that was meted out to him, shared in their world, and left them an ennobling example that would set them spiritually free (1 Pet. 2:18-25).

By teaching the slaves to be subject to their masters, Paul was neither approving slavery as an institution, nor showing himself indifferent to the sufferings of the slaves. Rather he was being realistic about their condition, believing in the longer-term prospects for lasting emancipation that the gospel would bring, through its ability to overturn the entrenched attitudes of the human heart and to amend the ways in which men and women treat one another. And so it proved, for where armed uprisings of slaves, such as that of Spartacus, failed to achieve freedom and only ended in a mass crucifixion of his followers, the gospel of Christ triumphed through its inherent powers of moral and spiritual revolution and rebirth. See 1 Timothy 6:1f.

Being subject to their owners means that slaves are **to try to please them, not to talk back to them, and not to steal from them**. Paul manages to combine here a positive attitude to work with a twofold warning against bad work ethics. Behind the call to try to please their masters lies the Christian doctrine of work and its intrinsic worth, however menial its form may take (Gen. 2:15; Eph. 4:28). Talking back and stealing were common practices among slaves, but Christian slaves are expected to show a higher standard of behaviour, one befitting the gospel of Christ. In the modern company office and workplace, the same standards apply. Christian workers and employees should avoid the unethical but widespread practice of backchatting the employer and stealing from company equipment. By their mental attitudes and work practices they should aim to be approved by and pleasing to their employer.

But to show that they can be fully trusted (verse 10) is the ultimate aim of Christian slaves in all that they do. Trustworthiness must be consistent, since it only takes one serious breach of trust to destroy the effects of a good past record that has been long in the making. In a world where cheating on others and the pursuit of self-interest were the accepted ways of doing business, the exceptional behaviour of the Christians would stand out above the common run. In the modern world of business, dishonesty and unreliability are again the accepted norm. In this working environment Christians are called to be the salt of the earth and the light of the world (Matt. 5:13f.).

Paul demands this level of trustworthiness **so that in every way they will make the teaching about God our Saviour attractive**. This can be taken as the main focus of Titus (see Introduction). The reputation of the gospel, involving the very name of God as Saviour, is in the hands of those who represent him in public life. The quality of their lives and the services they render will tell for or against the truth. The trustworthiness of Christians commends the message and the God they profess. Even Christians in the most lowly forms of service have the opportunity to promote the common cause, and to glorify their God and Saviour by their personal attitudes and morals and the quality of their work. By living in this way Christian employees and workers will oblige unbelievers around them to come face to face with the inherent beauty of the gospel and with the God of salvation.

Study Questions

Verses 1-10: What other groups, within a typical congregation, can you think of, and how should they be addressed? (Eph. 5:22ff., 25ff.; 6:1ff.; 1 Thess. 5:14; 1 Tim. 5:3ff.; 6:17ff.).

Verse 4: How does Paul's insistence on the homemaking responsibilities of the Christian woman compare with the image of the modern career woman? (Prov. 31:10-31; 1 Cor. 7:35; Eph. 5:22-24; 1 Tim. 5:14).

Verse 9: Is it always right for Christians to try to please other people? (Gen. 3:17; Jos. 24:15; Mark 12:13-17; Acts 5:29; 1 Pet. 4:12-15).

The Saving Grace of God (2:11-15)

The practical and ethical prescriptions of the first part of this chapter are now shown to be deeply rooted in the distinctive beliefs of the gospel as it is summed up in this second part ('For'). **For the grace that brings salvation has appeared to all men** (verse 11). The last time Paul mentioned grace was in the greeting (1:4) and he will mention it again in the ending (3:15). In between, in a comparable context (3:4-7), he will include it again in relation to the believer's justification in Christ. Grace is God's special love that achieves salvation and reveals him as the three-personned God. Paul makes a threefold affirmation about this grace:

• It has appeared, or become visible in history. This appearing is like the dawning of a new day for the world, the birth of a new age. The Creator God intervened personally in the life of his creation (John 1:10). Paul has in mind the event of the birth of Jesus, when God was incarnated (put on human flesh or nature, John 1:14) and began to live among us in the revelation of his glory;

• It has appeared to all men everywhere. The message of God's saving grace is meant for the whole world and every type of human being in the world. The immediate proof of this is found in the way in which Paul has just been addressing all kinds of people about the gospel ethic – young and old, men and women, and slaves (1 Tim. 2:1-7). Christianity is truly a world religion;

• It brings salvation, that is, personal and final deliverance from all evil in this world and the next. Salvation was the very purpose of Christ's coming and self-giving (verses 12, 14), it was actually achieved by him and it is now offered to people everywhere.

The gospel has a pedagogical and remedial purpose for **it teaches us to say 'No' to ungodliness and worldly passions** (verse 12). The gospel is God's answer to the moral and spiritual ills of humanity because it actually empowers its disciples to renounce their godless way of life and to cut off those evil passions that formerly controlled them. In order to succeed where other systems fail, the gospel begins with the root cause of ungodly behaviour, it begins with the heart (Mark 7:20ff.). Ungodliness is the condition of being without God, and living as though he did not exist. In practice it translates into worldly passions which are cravings for the objects, pleasures and rewards of this evil age. These passions consist of the sinful desires of our fallen nature, the lusts of the eyes for sensual objects, and the pride of worldly living (1 John 2:16).

The gospel is more than good advice or a set of ethical ideals, which are powerless against ungodliness and worldly passions. The gospel succeeds over its competitors in the reformation of morals because it puts real moral steel into the hearts of Christian believers, and motivates them to live a godly life of goodwill towards their neighbours and of self-control over their own passions. The secret of this power is explained in verse fourteen when Paul discusses the death of Christ.

Yet the gospel is more than a set of prohibitions; it commands believers **to live self-controlled, upright and godly lives in this present age**. Nothing could be more positive than the high and holy mandates of the Christian faith. Three qualities are listed here:

- *self-controlled* stands for the mastery of the sinful self, which is the origin of all the evil that is in the world. This is often referred to in the Pastorals (in Titus alone 1:8; 2:2, 4, 5, 6);

- *upright* stands for practical conformity to the moral demands of God's law;

- *godly* refers to the person who fears and serves God above all else, whose life is controlled by reverence for God;

All these three qualities are essential to Christian character and are the direct products of the gospel of the saving grace of God.

The greatest challenge of the gospel is its demand for self-control, uprightness and godliness 'in this present age'. This age is a fallen one, in which Satan has gained control over the minds of people through the ruling power of darkness (2 Cor. 4:3f.; Eph. 6:12). For this reason it is evil (Gal. 1:4), and Satan is the god of it. The gospel makes its greatest play by calling believers to live their self-controlled, upright and godly lives within this very age of evil, in the presence of moral and spiritual darkness. Christians are not to drop out of the world but to illumine it (John 17:14f.; 1 Cor. 5:9f.). The best news of the gospel is that what it demands it gives to those who submit to it. This is the meaning of grace.

All this takes place **while we wait for the blessed hope – the glorious appearing of our great God and Saviour, Jesus Christ** (verse 13). Christian morality is driven by Christian eschatology, the confident expectation of the visible coming in glory of Jesus Christ at the close of this age. Believers are saved in this hope (Rom. 8:24f.), because the final events of the history of salvation have still to be played out when Jesus comes again. So believers wait for the hope of righteousness (Gal. 5:5; Col. 1:4f.). Their hope is blessed because it will bring in their perfect blessedness in the enjoyment of the presence of their Lord forever.

Christ's coming in glory will actually be his *re*-appearing (Paul uses the same word here as in verse eleven for Christ's first coming), for it is the same Jesus who rose to heaven at his ascension (Acts 1:9ff.) who will descend from heaven at his return (1 Thess. 4:16ff.). That promised coming is the continuing focus of the Christian's faith and hope, whether in the meantime he departs through death to be with Christ (the experience of most believers), or lives to see the actual event of Christ's return.

The Lord's coming will be a 'glorious appearing' because the full extent of his personal glory as God and Saviour will be revealed on that day for the very first time. The glory of Christ, that is hidden from creation now, will then become universal knowledge, so that every knee will bow to him and every living thing proclaim him Lord (Phil. 2:9ff.). It will be as God and Saviour that Jesus Christ will be revealed in that day. He is God no less than Saviour, a Saviour because he is God. Paul is consistent in his ascription of deity to Jesus (Rom. 9:5; Phil. 2:5f.; Col. 1:19; 2:9), as are the other writers of the New Testament (John 1:1ff.; Heb. 1:3; 1 John 5:20; Rev. 5:6). The glorious appearing of Jesus will only confirm believers in what they already know. Christians have always sung hymns and said prayers to Christ as God.

As our God and Saviour, Jesus is the one **who gave himself for us to redeem us** (verse 14). Paul's interpretation of the saving work of Christ builds on the sacrificial imagery from the worship of Israel in the Old Testament, where animals were presented by priests to God in place of sinful worshippers (Exod. 29:38-46; Lev. 4; 16; 17:11). Instead of the sacrificial blood of animals, Jesus offered himself to God as the one true and final sacrifice to take away human sin (Heb. 9:11-14). He was God's lamb of sacrifice (John 1:29), a lamb without spot or blemish (1 Pet. 1:18f.). In being the perfect God and a sinless man, Jesus' self-giving sacrifice was more than acceptable to God the Father. To him it was the sweet-smelling aroma of a perfect sacrifice and offering that gave him delight (Eph. 5:2). In so acting, Jesus gave himself 'for us', as our priestly representative before God and as our perfect sacrifice substituted in our place.

Redeeming is another Old Testament picture, one that conveys the idea of liberation. The Lord redeemed Israel from the slavery of Egypt, when he intervened for her in the Exodus event (Exod. 3:7-10; 6:5-8; Deut. 7:7f.). He set his people free to know and serve him. In a similar way, though on an infinite scale of reckoning, God acted, in the momentous event of Jesus' death, to liberate his people throughout the ages. Calvary is the climactic event of his work of human redemption, and the one true source of enduring human liberty. As such, Christ's death was a form of ransom, the price paid as the costly condition of our liberty (Mark 10:45). Jesus' self-offering was so effective and final that he will never have to repeat the transaction (Rom. 6:10; Heb. 9:24-28).

Christ came to redeem us **from all wickedness and to purify for himself a people**. Christ's saving work had a single goal – redemption, but redemption has a double aspect. One aspect is that Jesus died to free us from all wickedness. Wickedness is lawlessness (1 John 3:4), not just in the social sense of criminal behaviour, but in the far more profound sense of breaking God's law, the moral law that is written on our human hearts (Rom. 2:14f.). We break this law in all our sinful thoughts, desires, words and actions. Christ's redeeming death breaks the power of cancelled sin, that is, it cancels our liability to the eternal death penalty and it terminates the controlling power of sin within us. The redeeming death of Christ is complete ('all wickedness').

The other aspect of the redeeming work of Christ is his purpose to purify a people for himself. The background here comes from the Old Testament, when the Lord through Moses set the people of Israel apart for a covenantal relationship with himself as his special people. What he did through the rescue operation of the Exodus historically, he confirmed later legally through the sprinkling of the blood of the covenant in a special ceremony of consecration (Exod. 24:4-8). In an infinitely greater way Christ's death on the cross was both the rescue operation of redemption which set his people forever free, and the moment when the everlasting covenant of grace and free promise between God and his people was sealed with his own life-blood (Heb. 13:20).

God's redeemed people are **a people that are his very own, eager to do what is good**. This is the language of intimacy and love, recalling the terms in which the Lord addressed Israel as his covenant people, chosen and called to be his own (Exod. 19:4f.). These terms are now transferred to the Christian church, which stands in the same relationship to God through Jesus Christ (1 Pet. 2:9). God's redemptive covenant is one, made first with Israel as the church in its minority, and now with the body of Christ as the church in its majority (Gal. 3:19-4:7).

Christians are intended to be devotees of good works, totally committed to them as their chosen way of life. These good works only exist where people are believers in Jesus Christ, they cannot exist before this since only Jesus Christ can make our works good. Even the good works of believers in Christ do not contribute anything to their salvation, since they are always infected with the sin that remains in Christians. Only the works of Jesus Christ are inherently and perfectly good, which is why believers trust in them alone for salvation. Good works are the inevitable outcome of faith in Jesus Christ and so are the visible evidence of saving faith in the heart (Gal. 5:5f.; Jas. 2:14-26; 2 Pet. 1:5-11).

By saying **these, then are the things you should teach** (verse 15), Paul closes the whole section from verse one with three action words of command (teach, encourage, rebuke). The things that Titus should teach consist of the practical responsibilities of the groups within the congregation (verses 2-10), along with the redemptive truths about the saving work of Jesus Christ that lie behind them (verses 11-14). Titus, like any other pastor, must be a teacher of God's truth, by faithfully and perseveringly explaining its contents and duties. But he must also **encourage and rebuke with all authority**, by insisting on the truth of his message as an authorised messenger of Jesus Christ. By encouraging and rebuking, Titus will be applying and enforcing the message in the lives of his hearers so as to promote an honest response to its demands.

Finally Paul says **do not let anyone despise you,** advice that echoes his words to Timothy though for rather different reasons (1 Tim. 4:12). If the church pastor is to be heard and heeded by his people, then he must not only insist on the trustworthiness of his message, but he must also show himself to be worthy of respect by the quality of his life and leadership.

Study Questions

Verse 12: What is meant by Christians being in the world, but not of the world? What practical steps can be taken to achieve this goal? (Rom. 12:1f.; Heb. 10:19-25; Jas. 1:21-27; Jude 20-23).

Verse 14: What other metaphors does Scripture use to represent the saving work of Jesus Christ? (Rom. 3:24ff.; 5:10f.; 6:5-10; 2 Cor. 5:18-21; Col. 2:11-15; Heb. 2:14f.; 1 John 2:2; 4:10).

Verse 15: What is the nature of church authority? (John 20:21ff.; 1 Cor. 5:3ff.; 9:16f.; 2 Cor. 13:10; Eph. 4:7-11; Rev. 3:7f.).

TITUS: CHAPTER 3

The third chapter of Titus falls into four short sections – counsels to the whole congregation (3:1-2), a description of the dark side of human nature which provides the background to a rich presentation of the saving gospel (3:3-7), final instructions to Titus about supervising the congregation (3:8-11), and Paul's closing requests, plans and greetings (3:12-15).

Being Good Citizens (3:1-2)

Remind the people to be subject to rulers and authorities, to be obedient (verse 1) is a frequent New Testament demand (e.g. Rom. 13:1-7; 1 Pet. 2:13f.), based on the assumption that all legitimate authority (political, civil, police, military) ultimately comes from God, the supreme Ruler, as part of his providential order. For this reason Paul recommends prayers for all kinds for civil rulers (1 Tim. 2:1f.). Being subject to civil rulers is therefore a form of obedience to God through his earthly representatives, and should be a matter of conscience for Christians. When these authorities exceed their powers by making totalitarian or ungodly claims on citizens, then Christians must obey God rather than men, even if that brings penalties (Acts 5:29).

Titus must 'remind the people' about these things because the Cretans by nature were unruly. But Christians generally need to be reminded of truths and duties which they already know, because they tend to forget, especially as they grow older. This is one important function of the Scriptures, to stir believers up by reminding them (2 Pet. 1:12-15).

They are also **to be ready to do whatever is good**, which in the framework of civil life must include good deeds of a community nature, such as being good neighbours and being willing to do community service. Christians ought to make the best citizens because they are on principle law-abiding and should be public-spirited. That can only happen as they are conscientiously obedient to the truths and principles of the Word of God such as Paul has already outlined (Tit. 2). Being a good citizen should be a natural continuation of being a good Christian. Like their Lord, believers are to go about doing good to everyone, especially those who belong to the household of faith (Gal. 6:9f.). If they are to achieve this in practice, then they must always be mentally prepared ('ready') to spring into action.

This means that they are **to slander no-one** (verse 2), literally 'to blaspheme' no-one. Belittling others is a form of blasphemy because it is a verbal attack on another human being who is a bearer of the divine image (Jas. 3:8f.). Sadly, slander is not uncommon among Christians themselves, with the result that the unity and peace of the body of Christ is broken, local churches are divided, the spiritual growth of individuals is arrested and the bright claims of the Christian faith are publicly contradicted.

Christians are rather **to be peaceable and considerate**, two qualities that exist in sharp contrast to the sorts of attitudes that men and women often show to one another (verse 3). The habitual presence of these two characteristics is visible evidence of the transforming grace of God in human lives and characters (verses 4-7). Being *peaceable* means avoiding conflicts wherever possible, cultivating peaceful and friendly relations as a matter of policy and always being open to reconciliation. Being *considerate* means being gentle, courteous and patient towards others by not reacting against them.

And believers are **to show true humility towards all men**. The word for humility is 'meekness', which is the strong grace of self-restraint when confronted by criticism or unfair treatment. It is exemplified by Moses (Num. 12:3) and shown supremely by Jesus (1 Pet. 2:23). Christians are to follow the example of their Lord with the help of the Holy Spirit (Gal. 5:22f.; Jas. 3:17). Such meekness must become visible ('to show') in the attitudes, words, actions and reactions of Christians if their lives are to have an influence for Christ and the gospel.

This humility is to be shown to people of all kinds ('all men'), since the Christian believes that everyone is created by God and worthy of respect. Especially in an abusive and volatile society

like Crete, the Christian grace of humility/meekness would stand
out and invite questions about the Christian's Lord. In the modern world, which has become no less hostile a place to live in
than the ancient, the quiet and controlled responses of Christians
can be a powerful co-ordinate witness to the truth of salvation.

Study Questions

Verse 1: Develop the New Testament ethic of subordination and
discuss its modern equivalent (Luke 2:51; Rom. 13:1; 1 Cor.
14:33f.; 15:27f.; Eph. 1:22; 5:22; 1 Pet. 2:13f., 18; 3:1f., 5f.; 5:5).

Verse 2: Study biblical references to meekness and humility, and
discuss the lessons they teach (Num. 12; Matt. 11:28ff.; Rom.
12:3, 16; 2 Cor. 10:1; Phil. 2:3ff.; 1 Pet. 5:5).

The God Who Saves (3:3-7)
As an incentive to Christian living, Paul reminds his hearers of
their sordid past way of living, for **at one time we too were
foolish, disobedient, deceived and enslaved by all kinds of
passions and pleasures** (verse 3). Paul includes himself ('we
too') since he does not believe that Jews are essentially better
than Gentiles: both are under sin's control and blight (Eph. 2:1-3).
He lists seven dark characteristics of those who are living without God. They are:

• **foolish** or *ignorant* of the true purpose of life, because they
do not know God (Gal. 4:8);
• **disobedient** because they repress the natural light of revelation and the witness of conscience within them (Rom. 1:18ff.;
2:14f.);
• **deceived** by their own false reasonings and the seductive
voice of temptations;

- **enslaved** to various passions, because they do not control their own destiny but are at the beck and call of sinful desires and illicit pleasures.

When Paul continues **we lived in malice and envy, being hated and hating one another**, he paints an even darker and more damning picture of their former life of unbelief and diso-bedience. After the sins of dissipation he names some of the sins of the human heart that are so prevalent and produce such a bitter and destructive harvest in people's lives and relationships. We lived in:

- **malice and envy**, nurturing aggressive attitudes to others that were fed by personal jealousies and ambitions;
- **being hated** by others for the same reasons because they too are exploiting others for their own ends;
- **hating one another** as a way of life that knows nothing of the reconciling and pacifying grace of God.

Along with Romans 1:18-32; 3:9-18; Ephesians 2:1-3 and 4:17-19, this passage stands out as one of the most penetrating de-scriptions in the New Testament of the human condition in the depths of its sinfulness and misery. Overall the root of the prob-lem lies within humans themselves in their uncontrolled desires and anti-social attitudes (Mark 7:20-23).

But when the kindness and love of God our Saviour ap-peared (verse 4) can only refer to the first coming of Jesus Christ in the flesh. Christ's coming into the world was inspired and modulated by the lovingkindness of God as Saviour, which took historical and human form in Jesus himself. Not only above the cross, but over the manger we see the letters 'God is love'. When everything on the human plane was pitch-dark and hope-less, the God of love burst into the darkness of this world in the person of his earth-born Son, in a definitive moment of divine epiphany (2 Tim. 1:10). His advent was like the dawning of a bright new day (Luke 1:77-79), the beginning of a truly new age. God's kindness is his generous and gentle mercy, his love is his philanthropy (literally), a genuine concern for humankind. Since philanthropy was publicly prized and praised by imperial rulers, its inclusion here may be meant to highlight the special and altogether superior type of philanthropy that lies at the heart of the Christian religion. Unlike the gods of the pagan cults, the God of Christianity is a God who really cares about men and women.

He saved us, not because of righteous things we had done, but because of his mercy (verse 5). No words could express more succinctly the totally undeserved nature of salvation, since God is the one who gives salvation to us on the basis of his mercy alone, and we are the ones who receive it in spite of our being destitute of God-pleasing lives. This is salvation by grace alone (Eph. 2:8f.), in which God receives all the praise and glory, and believing sinners are prevented from any boasting or pride (Rom. 3:27f.). The natural instinct of unbelievers is to seek the reason for God's love or the ground of their acceptance within themselves (works of righteousness that we have done). This means that the first casualty of the gospel, correctly understood, will always be a person's sinful pride and self-righteousness. Salvation is under consideration here, not as the existential moment of first believing in Christ, but in its historical aspect when Jesus was born and appeared in the world. That was when God began to save us.

He saved us through the washing of rebirth and renewal by the Holy Spirit. This carries the story of human salvation forward in time into the existential realm of the believer's own life by introducing the person of the Holy Spirit. He is the one who applies God's saving mercy in Christ directly to the Christian, in the mysterious event of spiritual rebirth that we call regeneration (John 3:3). This is a washing of the heart or moral nature of the individual which leaves them holy and pure within (see Ezekiel 36:25ff., where the imagery of water is taken from, as in John 3:5), a fit residence for the indwelling Spirit.

Other groups in the Graeco-Roman world offered salvation through the promise of washing and rebirth. Prominent among these were the mystery cults, so-called because they claimed to know the secrets or mysteries of the gods. Knowledge of these mysteries, combined with the washing rituals and cultic vigils of these groups, were said to bestow salvation and the mystical powers of eternal life. What these religious centres offered in appearance, Christianity gives in reality, since only the Holy Spirit can change the human heart in its moral bias and powers. For this reason Christianity could well be called the one true mystery religion (1 Cor. 2:7f.; Eph. 3:3ff.; Col. 2:2f.). While the mystery religions, and their modern successors, believed in a number of different ways of salvation, the Christian religion claims that there is salvation in no other than Jesus Christ (Acts 4:12).

Does the mention of washing have Christian baptism in mind? Some writers think so, but the New Testament does not teach that Christian rituals, in themselves, bring about what they represent (1 Pet. 3:21). Certainly Paul connects the spiritual reality closely with symbolical acts in his teaching about the sacraments of the church (Rom. 4:11; 6:3f.; 1 Cor. 11:27; Col. 2:11f.). However, the language of the Old Testament prophets, which lies behind the picture-language of washing, is clearly used in a metaphorical sense when it speaks about a spiritual rebirth through the gift of God's Spirit (Ezek. 36:24-27). This strongly suggests that Paul is speaking in the same non-literal way when he refers to the washing of regeneration, following the similar teaching of Jesus (John 3:5).

Not only does the Holy Spirit wash God's people once for all in the new birth, he also continually renews them inwardly (the word for 'renewal' indicates an ongoing activity rather than one that has stopped). This is because the new birth does not make the believer sinless, it makes him holy. While it is true that the Christian is responsible for living the life of obedience, godliness in practice has its rise in the secret and sovereign working of the Holy Spirit in the heart. The Spirit needs to be constantly renewing the thoughts, purifying the affections and inclining the will of the Christian towards holy and heavenly things. This does not mean that Christians must wait for a conscious feeling of the renewing work of the Spirit within them before they obey God's will. Yet believers must proceed in their obedience in the expectation and dependence that the Spirit will continuously assist them in the course of their obedience.

The Holy Spirit also has a history for he is the one who was **poured out on us generously through Jesus Christ our Saviour** (verse 6). The outpouring of the Holy Spirit looks back to the day of Pentecost (Acts 2), when for the first time the Spirit was given in such generous measures by God the Father in fulfilment of his Old Testament promises (Joel 2:28; Acts 2:17f., 33). The gift of the Spirit was 'through Jesus Christ our Saviour', because the perfect obedience and completed service of Jesus Christ on earth was the condition of the promise of the Spirit's coming. Although the Holy Spirit was active under the old covenant (Num. 11:16-30; 1 Sam. 16:13f.; Psa. 51:11; Isa. 63:10ff.; Hag. 2:5; Zech. 7:12), his influences were restrained by the fact that Jesus the Messiah had not yet come into the world to suffer, die and be glorified (John 7:38f.). The Spirit's work is the same under both Testaments, but differs in degree. The day of Pentecost following Christ's enthronement, therefore, marks a really new stage in the Spirit's activities in the church and in the world.

The initial outpouring of the Spirit at Pentecost did not and does not rule out later outpourings of the same Spirit; such outpourings will have the same effects in awakening and converting sinners out of the world and in awakening and building up believers. Though all Christians share in this outpoured Spirit at conversion (Rom. 5:5; 1 Cor. 12:13; Eph. 1:13f.), the degree to which they enjoy the fullness of the Spirit may vary greatly from one believer to another, and from one period and part of the church to another. Christians in every age and place may legitimately pray for fresh outpourings of the Spirit of Christ in answer to the special needs of their time.

All this was **so that, having been justified by his grace, we might become heirs having the hope of eternal life** (verse 7). Being justified is a once-for-all act of God, in which he declares the person trusting in Jesus Christ alone for salvation to be acquitted of all wrong and accepted into his favour as though perfectly righteous the way Jesus is (Rom. 3:24ff.; 8:33f.; Phil. 3:8f.). This verdict of justification (for it is a law-court decision made in the supreme court of heaven) forms the fixed foundation of the believer's relationship to God as Judge. It comes about through 'his grace', which could refer to the grace and goodwill of God the Father which lies back of the sacrifice of Jesus (Eph. 2:8f.), or to the gracious obedience and suffering on our behalf of Jesus himself (Rom. 5:17f.). Either way it affirms the gift nature of justification.

At the very same time as this righteous acquittal and acceptance (justification) takes place, the believer in Jesus becomes a child of God with a right of inheritance (Eph. 1:13f.; 1 Pet. 1:3ff.). This is the gift of adoption into the family of God as sons and daughters, and is the highest privilege the Christian can receive in this world or the next (Rom. 8:15ff.; Gal. 4:4-7; Eph. 1:3-6). The indwelling Holy Spirit is both the foretaste and the guarantee of the Christian's heavenly inheritance (2 Cor. 1:21f.). This inheritance is a future hope, though it is awaited with strong expectations in this life (Rom. 8:24f.; 1 Pet. 1:3ff.). It consists in eternal life, the life of the age to come, and so the believer looks forward to the time when the limitations and weaknesses of the Christian's present bodily existence will be done away with, and he will be swallowed up by life in the full splendour of the resurrection glory (2 Cor. 5:4f.).

In these verses (4-7) Paul provides a compact digest of the gospel. It centres on the three persons of God and their respective roles in the total drama of salvation. The kindly love and mercy of God the Father, irrespective of our sinful deeds, lies behind the events of Jesus' earthly coming and the Spirit's generous outpouring. Through the grace of Jesus' voluntary life and death we have been justified from all our wrongs and received into the number of God's own children. The Holy Spirit, whom the Father sends through the Son from Pentecost onwards, regenerates God's people and renews them throughout their earthly lives, until at last they enter into their glorious inheritance in heaven. Without oversimplifying we can say that God (the Father) designs salvation, Jesus Christ (the Son) enacts salvation, and the Holy Spirit applies salvation. Salvation is therefore eternal, historical and experiential. It is the one grand plan, work and gift of the triune God. This paragraph invites a close comparison with Ephesians 1:3-14 which shows the same theological infrastructure.

Study Questions

Verse 3: Study other passages describing the sinful condition and way of life of unbelievers, and discuss their relevance today (Mark 7:20-23; Rom. 3:10-18; Eph. 2:1-3; 4:17ff.; 1 Pet. 4:3; Rev. 9:20f.; 22:15).

Verse 4: What makes the love of God so marvellous? (Deut. 7:6ff.; John 3:16f.; Rom. 5:5-8; 8:35-38; Eph. 1:3-6; 2:4-9; 1 John 3:1f.; 4:7-11; Rev. 1:5f.).

Verses 5 and 6: What is the connection, if any, between the outpouring of the Spirit at Pentecost and the regeneration of individual believers? (Ezek. 36:27; 37:14; 39:29; John 1:33; 3:5; 7:38f.; Acts 4:31; Rom. 5:5; 1 Cor. 12:13).

Verse 7: How are people justified by grace? (Gen. 15:1-6; Psa. 32:1f.; Rom. 3:23-28; 4:13-25; 5:8f., 15-21; Eph. 2:8ff.; Phil. 3:3-9).

Necessary Disciplines (3:8-11)

The previous paragraph is the fourth of the faithful sayings which Paul introduces with the formula (1 Tim. 1:15; 3:1; 4:9; 2 Tim. 2:11) **this is a trustworthy saying**. Paul has been making use of common Christian teaching to write as he does. Whether these verses (4-7) should be taken verbatim or as Paul's paraphrase of the trustworthy saying is not clear. But he knew that the Cretan Christians would recognise the source and the theological sentiments it expresses. A trustworthy saying of this kind could have formed the basis for catechetical instruction in the early churches, and would be a biblical warrant for the composition and use of church catechisms today for the instruction of church members and covenant children in the knowledge and practice of the Christian faith.

And I want you to stress these things refers to the truths about salvation set out in verses four to seven above. 'To stress' means to speak out confidently about something, to insist on it.

Paul's purpose in this is a thoroughly practical one: **so that those who have trusted in God may be careful to devote themselves to doing what is good**. The gospel of grace naturally promotes good works, but believers must be careful not to allow the grace of God to become a blind for sinful living, a temptation to which they are always exposed (Gal. 5:13; 1 Pet. 2:15f.). The gospel achieves this because it regenerates human nature and puts in motion a set of motives and desires that lead to good works. Unsound teaching, on the other hand, always ruins public morals because it lacks the moral dynamic to fulfil the moral imperative. Devotion to good works is a recurrent theme of the Pastorals which insist on good works in every social setting (1 Tim. 2:10; 5:10; 6:18; 2 Tim. 2:21; 3:17; Tit. 3:1, 14). Being 'careful to devote themselves to doing what is good' is essentially a mental attitude in which good works are a fixed goal of daily living. Christians are those 'who have trusted in God', a construction in the Greek that indicates that trusting in God is never once for all but a lifelong spiritual response.

These things are excellent and profitable for everyone

is a commendation of those Christian truths (verses 4-7) that lead into a lifetime of usefulness in neighbourly service. Correctly understood, Christian doctrine is never remote from the real world of everyday living; on the contrary it provides the only convincing reasons and incentives to practical and moral behaviour. The godliness of the gospel alone is useful (1 Tim. 4:8), as are the Scriptures in practical ways (2 Tim. 3:16). Judged by the practical test – Does it work? – the Christian faith scores highly. Those who entrust themselves to it discover a world of unexpected delights satisfying to the mind, nourishing to the heart and leading into an even brighter future.

But avoid foolish controversies and genealogies and arguments and quarrels about the law, because these are unprofitable and useless (verse 9). The alternative to the profitable teachings of the gospel are the public controversies stirred up around peripheral and obscure parts of the Old Testament, such as its genealogies and laws (see 1 Timothy 1:4; 6:4; and 2 Timothy 2:23). The heat and divisions produced by these sorts of discussions are a sure indication that they do not proceed from the true spirit of the Scriptures, and are to be avoided. This means walking around them (literally), and not giving them the appearance of legitimacy by even spending time in discussing them. Judged by the practical test (verse 8), these controversies fail miserably, because they are mindless, divisive and useless.

Warn a divisive person once, and then warn him a second time (verse 10). 'A divisive person' is here called a heretical person, not because they deny any of the essentials of the Christian faith as in the modern sense of the word, but because they separate off from the main body of believers, perhaps drawing others away with them into a faction (Acts 20:30; 1 Cor. 11:18f.). A divisive person is a schismatic, who for no valid reason breaks away from the fellowship of God's people (Heb. 10:24f.). Such behaviour is a work of the flesh (Gal. 5:20) and shows an unspiritual condition, even although the individual concerned may defend it on religious grounds.

Because such a person threatens the unity and well-being of the congregation, they must be warned officially by the church leaders. There should be at least two warnings, which are meant to show both the church's resolution and its patience.

After that, have nothing to do with him. If this series of warnings fails then a new approach must be followed. The offender must be shunned, separated from, in return for their own schismatic behaviour. This is a form of congregational discipline which the apostle recommends elsewhere (Rom. 16:17; 1 Cor. 5:11; 2 Thess. 3:14). It is intended to produce a sense of shame and lead to repentance. Because the issues at stake here are not about the fundamentals of the faith or Christian morals (as in 1 Corinthians 5:1-5 and 1 Timothy 1:18f.), the discipline to be applied falls short of excommunication. It must be decided by all the circumstances of the case and follow the steps laid down by Jesus (Matt. 18:15ff.).

You may be sure that such a man is warped and sinful; he is self-condemned (verse 11). Such people are not innocent, rather they are self-willed and culpable, knowing within themselves that their disruptive course of action is wrong. Unfortunately such individuals normally persist in their error and harden in their attitudes because they lack the spiritual maturity to talk through their difficulties amicably and to confront their own faults. They leave behind them a line of broken friendships and churches.

Study Questions

Verse 8: Why and how can we trust in God? (Psa. 125:1f.; John 14:1; 2 Tim. 1:12; Heb. 11; 1 Pet. 1:8f., 20f.; 1 John 5:4f.).

List some of the advantages of good works (Matt. 5:16; 25:31-46; Tit. 2:7f.; Jas. 2:14-18; 1 Pet. 2:11f.; 2 Pet. 1:5-10).

Verse 10: What causes divisions within the church, and can they ever be justified? (1 Cor. 1:10-13; 1 Cor. 11:17-34; 2 Cor. 11:3f., 13ff.; Phil. 1:14-18; 2 Thess. 3:14f.; 2 Pet. 2; Jude 5-19).

Final Counsels (3:12-15)

Paul closes his letter with a number of personal requests and remarks. **As soon as I send Artemas or Tychicus to you, do your best to come to me at Nicopolis, because I have decided to winter there** (verse 12). This is the kind of statement that discredits theories of non-Pauline authorship because these comments are so incidentally true to life. In view of 2 Timothy 4:12 we must conclude that Paul did dispatch Artemas (this is the only mention of him in Paul's correspondence) to assist Titus, or to take over from him (2 Tim. 4:10) on Crete. Tychicus was from Asia (Acts 20:4), which is why Paul made him the bearer of his letters to the Ephesians and to the Colossians (Col. 4:7ff.) during his first imprisonment in Rome (Eph. 6:21).

Nicopolis means 'city of victory' and was built by Augustus on the site of his camp before his decisive victory over Mark Antony at the battle of Actium in AD 31. Paul's decision to winter there was due to the fact that all sea-lanes closed down during the winter months, making further travel by that means impossible. The mission of Titus there when Paul was back in prison in Rome (2 Tim. 4:10) may be due to Paul's evangelising work at his time of writing.

Do everything you can to help Zenas the lawyer and Apollos on their way and see that they have everything they need (verse 13). Nothing more is known about Zenas apart from what Paul tells us here, that he belonged to the legal profession and was travelling with Apollos, the eloquent preacher, on some undisclosed mission through Crete. Although the first Christians were mostly from the lower classes (1 Cor. 1:26), some were from the upper, more educated and influential echelons of society (Acts 16:14; Rom. 16:23; Phil. 4:22). Although it is not clear whether these two men were carrying Paul's letter to Titus, it was his normal habit to request provisions for those who travelled on his behalf (Rom. 16:1f.; 1 Cor. 16:10f.). Hospitality was strongly recommended and widely practised among the early Christians (Acts 16:15; 27:3; Rom. 12:13; 3 John 5-8). In countries in the modern world where Christians are a minority, the opening of the homes of believers to one another, and especially to visiting Christians from other parts of the world, is an important means of keeping in contact and strengthening one another.

In this way the Cretan Christians can put their faith into action and become fruitful for the kingdom of God. **Our people must learn to devote themselves to doing what is good** (verse 14). 'Our people' distinguishes the real church group from the partisans who were creating distractions and divisions. Learning to be devoted to good works is a matter of practice, looking out for and seizing every opportunity to act in Christ's name for the good of others and the church. Paul has already told the members of the church 'to devote themselves' to doing good (verse 8), his repetition here being a clear indication that he is determined not to allow the Cretans to fall back into their natural tendency to laziness (Tit. 1:12). Faith without the good works that God has commanded and commended is no faith, only a delusion (Jas. 2:14-26). Christians should be known and recognisable by their devotion to good works.

Attention to good works is **in order that they may provide for daily necessities and not live unproductive lives**. The idea of an unfruitful Christian is a contradiction in terms, although the New Testament does conceive of the possibility (2 Pet. 1:8f.). Under normal circumstances faith will always be expressing itself through love (Gal. 5:6; Jas. 2:15f.). Christian faith is nothing if it is not practical, the practice of love in action being the ultimate test of Christian knowledge (1 Cor. 8:1ff.). Practising good works means meeting the pressing needs ('daily necessities') of those around us. Coming at the end of his letter, the demand for good works clearly voices Paul's overall goal for the churches in Crete, and his real estimate of their spiritual development.

Finally comes the exchange of greetings. **Everyone with me sends you greetings** (verse 15). Who these associates were, Paul does not say, but even this anonymous communication of greetings expresses the warmth of interpersonal relationships within the apostolic churches. The early Christians did love one another and have left us a noble example to follow. **Greet those who love us in the faith** distinguishes true brothers and sisters in Christ from counterfeit Christians. Genuine believers are motivated by love for other believers on the basis of their common faith (here taken as equivalent to the gospel).

Grace be with you all is Paul's final word. The 'you' is plural (as in 1 Timothy 6:21 and 2 Timothy 4:22), intimating that the letter, though formally to Titus, was intended to be read aloud to the whole church gathered for worship. This aids understanding of the contents of the letter.

Study Questions

Verse 14: In what practical ways can Christians today learn to maintain good works? (Acts 9:36, 39; 16:33f.; 2 Tim. 1:16f.; Heb. 13:1f.).

Verse 15: What is it about the faith that makes it productive of love? (1 Tim. 1:3ff.; 1 John 5:1; 2 John 1f.).